Holocaust Education

Related Titles

Teaching and Studying the Holocaust
Samuel Totten and Stephen Feinberg, Editors
ISBN 0-205-18495-2

Teaching Holocaust Literature
Samuel Totten, Editor
ISBN 0-205-27402-1

For more information or to purchase a book, please call 1-800-278-3525.

Holocaust Education

Issues and Approaches

Samuel Totten

University of Arkansas, Fayetteville

Allyn and Bacon

Boston ▪ London ▪ Toronto ▪ Sydney ▪ Tokyo ▪ Singapore

This book is dedicated to a few of the many special individuals who have significantly influenced my work in the field of Holocaust education: Harry James Cargas, Michael Berenbaum, Stephen Feinberg, Henry Friedlander, William S. Parsons, Sybil Milton, and Elie Wiesel.

Series editor: *Traci Mueller*
Editorial assistant: *Bridget Keane*
Manufacturing buyer: *Suzanne Lareau*
Executive marketing manager: *Stephen Smith*
Cover designer: *Suzanne Harbison*
Production coordinator: *Pat Torelli Publishing Services*
Editorial-production service: *Stratford Publishing Services, Inc.*
Electronic composition: *Stratford Publishing Services, Inc.*

Copyright © 2002 by Allyn & Bacon
A Pearson Education Company
75 Arlington Street
Boston, MA 02116

Internet: www.ablongman.com

Chapter One is also published in the work *Teaching and Studying the Holocaust,* edited by Samuel Totten and Stephen Feinberg, copyright © 2001 by Allyn and Bacon. Excerpts from the United States Holocaust Memorial Museum's *Guidelines for Teaching the Holocaust* used with permission; this material provided courtesy of the United States Holocaust Memorial Museum, Washington, D.C.

Library of Congress Cataloging-in-Publication Data

Totten, Samuel.
    Holocaust education ; issues and approaches / Samuel Totten.
        p.   cm.
    ISBN 0-205-30929-1
        1. Holocaust, Jewish (1939–1945)—Study and teaching.   I. Title.

    D804.33 .T68 2002
    940.53'18'071—dc21   2001046034

Printed in the United States of America

10 9 8 7 6 5 4 3 2 1   05 04 03 02 01

CONTENTS

INTRODUCTION

Holocaust Education: Issues and Approaches is the third book in a series of Holocaust education–related texts developed for publication by Allyn and Bacon Publishers. Along with *Teaching and Studying the Holocaust* (coedited by Samuel Totten and Stephen Feinberg) and *Teaching Holocaust Literature* (edited by Samuel Totten), *Holocaust Education: Issues and Approaches* examines a wide array of curricular and instructional issues germane to Holocaust education. While *Teaching and Studying the Holocaust* includes essays on such eclectic topics and issues as the significance of developing strong rationales for teaching about the Holocaust and ways to incorporate such components as primary documents, first-person accounts, literature, art, music, and technology into lessons and units in a historically accurate and pedagogically sound manner, *Teaching Holocaust Literature,* as its title implies, is comprised of rationales and units of study vis-à-vis novels, short stories, plays, and poetry. *Holocaust Education: Issues and Approaches* is unique in that it addresses a host of issues that the other two books either do not address or only touch upon. Among these issues are: various ways to initiate and conclude lessons/units on the Holocaust in a thought-provoking manner; critical issues germane to teaching the history in a historically accurate and pedagogically sound manner (e.g., ways to assist students to "get at" the why(s) behind the whats, wheres, whens, and hows of the Holocaust); essential topics that merit serious consideration when preparing to teach this history; common misconceptions and inaccuracies that plague the teaching and study of the Holocaust; and the need to "complicate"—in the best sense of the word—students' thinking about complex issues regarding the Holocaust. It concludes with a chapter that challenges teachers to seriously consider, once they have concluded a study of the Holocaust, broadening their students' understanding of the world today by developing and implementing lessons that address major human rights infractions and/or more contemporary acts of genocide.

The development of all three of these books has been informed by two basic considerations: the critical need to teach this history first, in a historically accurate way, and second, in a pedagogically sound manner. Concomitantly, it is informed by Stanford University's Elliot Eisner's (1979) perspicacious insight regarding the "null curriculum":

> It is my thesis that what schools do not teach may be as important as what they do teach. I argue this position because ignorance is not simply a void; it has important effects on the kinds of options one is able to consider; the alternatives one can examine, and the perspectives with which one can view a situation or problem. (p. 83)

Eisner's thesis, I believe, is germane to various aspects of Holocaust education. First, although more teachers than ever now teach their students about some aspect of the Holocaust, it is still true that a vast number of history, social studies, government, and English teachers do not teach their students about it (Sabol, 1995). As for those teachers who do "touch" on this history, many either avoid or ignore the need to teach their students about the "why" behind the whats, wheres, hows, and whens of the Holocaust. A possible reason is that "getting at" the "whys" involves the examination of numerous and complex issues (e.g., the influence of traditional Christian antisemitism on Nazi thinking; the key differences between traditional Christian antisemitism, political antisemitism, and the impact of such concepts on the Nazis' virulent and deadly form of racial antisemitism; social Darwinism; extreme nationalism; totalitarianism; and industrialism), some of which teachers are either not conversant with or believe their students would find baffling. Exacerbating the situation is the fact that some of these issues—such as the influence of traditional Christian antisemitism on the Nazis' philosophy— are controversial in the eyes of many, and teachers are often wont to avoid controversial issues. However, to attempt to teach this history without addressing such critical issues results in students learning that a great human disaster occurred during the years of the Holocaust, but being bereft of an understanding as to what caused it or how it could have been avoided.

On a different note, teachers who teach this history in a traditional fashion— that is, exclusively via a didactic, frontal approach (e.g., lectures)—and do not provide ample opportunity for student discussion, also contribute, in their own way, to the "null curriculum." This is true because such an approach frequently denies students an opportunity to wrestle with this history by positing their own questions and/or discussing their fellow students' insights—all of which is needed in order to gain as deep an understanding as possible of the motives and actions of the perpetrators and others.

Finally, teachers who do not assist their students to understand and appreciate the fact that there are no simple answers to the profound questions raised by the Holocaust, and, thus, teach about it in a way where all of the "answers" are neatly wrapped in a package of lectures, also contribute to a null curriculum.

Throughout the course of my work on these three books, I have been influenced by the important insights of Grant Wiggins, especially his concept of "essential questions." "Essential questions" are "provocative and multilayered questions that reveal the richness and complexities of a subject" (Wiggins and McTighe, 1998, p. 28), those that "get at matters of deep and enduring understanding" (Wiggins and McTighe, 1998, p. 28). The concept of essential questions has prodded me to constantly attempt to focus on the most significant issues vis-à-vis this history *and* the most efficacious ways to teach about them.

I have also been influenced by a question that Herbert Spencer (1860) raised close to 150 years ago, "What Knowledge is of Most Worth?" It is not a question that can be answered easily, not if one wishes to avoid a facile response. Indeed, it is a question that prods me *to continually wrestle* with various facts, ideas, concepts, and theories as I attempt to come to a deeper understanding of various issues related to the Holocaust and to develop guidelines, teaching strategies, and learning activities vis-à-vis the Holocaust.

It is my hope that the ideas, approaches, and suggestions included in this book will assist teachers and curriculum developers to plan and implement highly effective lessons and units of study. Again, this means that such lessons and units should be as historically accurate and pedagogically sound as possible. Ultimately, it is my ardent hope that such lessons and units will prove to be thought-provoking and meaningful for the students who study this history.

It is worth noting that some information, particularly the historical trends that combined to make the Holocaust possible, as well as key topics teachers need to consider when teaching this history, is addressed in more than one chapter. I have taken the prerogative to be repetitive in this manner, for I perceive this book to be more of a reference work than one to be read during the course of a single sitting. In that light, I perceive the redundancy as a positive component. Indeed, the inclusion of the same information in various chapters avoids the need to reference other chapters, and, more importantly, it avoids the need for readers to skim other chapters to locate information germane to a discussion in the chapter they are reading.

Furthermore, some rather lengthy quotes are included throughout the book. Again, there is a rationale for this. First, in certain cases, it was impossible to convey the full thrust of an author's discussion, let alone the exact nuance of an argument, without including extensive quotes. Second, many pedagogical essays on the Holocaust are bereft of the insights and/or the arguments of historians, and since the focus of so many chapters in this book deals with the critical need for teachers and students to become familiar with the work of key historians, it seemed appropriate to include their thoughts and words throughout the book. Third, since a major emphasis of this book addresses the need for teachers to be historically accurate in their teaching of this history, it, again, seemed important to include key points regarding some of the more complex and/or controversial issues germane to the Holocaust.

As I complete this third volume, it is appropriate at this time for me to thank a few of the many fine colleagues, friends, and acquaintances who have informed my thinking about the Holocaust and how to teach about it. Before doing so, it should go without saying that I am also indebted to many fine scholars whose works I've pored over. It would be unwieldy to name them all, but a few of the more significant are Michael Berenbaum, Christopher Browning, Lucy Dawidowicz, Henry Friedlander, Israel Gutman, Raul Hilberg, Deborah Lipstadt, Michael Marrus, Donald Niewyk, Sybil Milton, and Leni Yahil. I would also like to thank the following reviewers for their helpful comments on the manuscript: Helena Waddy, SUNY Geneseo, and William G. Wraga, University of Georgia, Athens.

I have been extremely blessed to correspond, meet, converse, and work with a host of sterling scholars and educators. I've also had the honor of meeting, speaking and, sometimes, working with an impressive group of survivors. Their passion has continued to fuel my passion. They have done so by contributing to my drive to continue to probe into the darkness of the Holocaust—something that is not easy to do—for the purpose of educating current and future generations about it, *and* to work toward the amelioration of human rights wrongs, including contemporary genocidal actions. In doing so, each has constantly challenged my thinking and provided me with new insights and provocative questions to wrestle with and to ponder. Among these individuals are: Michael Berenbaum, Harry James Cargas, Israel W. Charny, Stephen Feinberg, William Fernekes, Maxine Greene, Franklin Littell, Sybil Milton, William S. Parsons, Karen Shawn, and Elie Wiesel.

REFERENCES

Eisner, Elliot (1979). *The Educational Imagination: On the Design and Evaluation of School Programs.* New York: Macmillan.

Sabol, Marcia (1995). "Status of Holocaust Education in the United States." Washington, DC: United States Holocaust Memorial Museum. Unpublished paper.

Spencer, Herbert (1860). "What Knowledge is of Most Worth?" In Herbert Spencer's *Education: Intellectual, Moral and Physical.* New York: A.L. Burt.

Totten, Samuel (Ed.). (2001). *Teaching Holocaust Literature.* Boston: Allyn & Bacon.

Totten, Samuel, and Feinberg, Stephen (Eds.). (2001). *Teaching and Studying the Holocaust.* Boston: Allyn & Bacon.

Wiggins, Grant, and McTighe, Jay (1998). *Understanding by Design.* Alexandria, VA: Association of Supervision and Curriculum Development.

ABOUT THE AUTHOR

Samuel Totten is currently a professor in the Department of Curriculum and Instruction at the University of Arkansas at Fayetteville. Before entering academia, he taught English and social studies at the secondary level in Australia, Israel, California, and Washington, D.C. He also served as a K–8 principal in northern California.

Prior to and several years into its operation, Totten served as an educational consultant to the United States Holocaust Memorial Museum. In the latter capacity, he coauthored (with William S. Parsons) *Guidelines for Teaching about the Holocaust* (Washington, DC: United States Holocaust Memorial Museum, 1993).

His essays on Holocaust education have appeared in such journals as *The British Journal of Holocaust Education, Canadian Social Studies, The Journal of Holocaust Education*, the *Journal of Curriculum and Supervision, Social Education*, and *The Social Studies*. He also served as coeditor (with Stephen Feinberg) of the 1995 special issue ("Teaching About the Holocaust") of *Social Education*, the official journal of the National Council for the Social Studies.

Most recently he coedited (with Stephen Feinberg) *Teaching and Studying the Holocaust* (Boston: Allyn & Bacon, 2001) and edited *Teaching Holocaust Literature* (Boston: Allyn & Bacon, 2001). Currently, he is completing two books, one entitled *Remembering the Past, Educating for the Future: Educators Encounter the Holocaust* (Westport, CT: Greenwood) and another entitled *Pioneers of Genocide Studies* (New Brunswick, NJ: Transaction Publishers).

1

The Significance of Rationale Statements in Developing a Sound Holocaust Education Program

SAMUEL TOTTEN

STEPHEN FEINBERG

WILLIAM FERNEKES

When preparing to teach about the Holocaust, it is essential to establish a solid set of rationales. Holocaust lessons and units bereft of controlling principles often lack a sound historical focus, including the critical need to address the "whys" of the historical events versus focusing solely on the "whats" of the history. Ultimately, a sound set of rationales helps teachers to design and implement clearly delineated goals, objectives, content, and assessment strategies.

In this chapter, we discuss numerous concerns regarding rationale statements including but not limited to the following: their purpose, their use in developing goals and objectives, their value in guiding content selection, their influence in selecting pedagogical strategies and resources, their use in avoiding pitfalls common to many studies of the Holocaust, and the critical need to revisit them throughout the study.

The Purpose of Rationales

In his essay, "Toward a Methodology of Teaching about the Holocaust," Henry Friedlander (1979), a scholar and survivor of the Holocaust, expressed great concern about the sudden proliferation of courses of study and curricula about the Holocaust:

The problem with too much being taught by too many *without focus* [italics added] is that this poses the danger of destroying the subject matter through dilettantism. It is not enough for well-meaning teachers to feel a commitment to teach about genocide; they also must know the subject. . . . The problems of popularization and proliferation should make us careful about how we introduce the Holocaust into the curriculum; it does not mean we should stop teaching it. But we must try to define the subject of the Holocaust. Even if we do not agree about the content of the subject, we must agree on its goals and on its limitations. (Friedlander, 1979, pp. 520–521, 522)

The issues raised by Friedlander in 1979 remain central concerns today, perhaps even more so. Within the last decade there has been an even greater surge in the development of curricula, teacher guides, resources, and organizational programs addressing the subject of the Holocaust. Although many of the resources and programs are engaging and pedagogically sound, many are not (Totten and Parsons, 1993, pp. 27–47). In particular, rationales for some curricula are extremely weak, often providing superficial justifications for the study of the Holocaust. That poses a serious problem to teachers and students alike, making the need for sound rationales, goals, and objectives for teaching about the Holocaust that much more significant.

As the authors of the United States Holocaust Memorial Museum's *Guidelines for Teaching about the Holocaust* note:

Because the objective of teaching any subject is to engage the intellectual curiosity of the student in order to inspire critical thought and personal growth, it is helpful to structure lesson plans on the Holocaust by considering throughout questions of rationale. Before addressing what and how to teach, one should contemplate the following: Why should students learn this history? What are the most significant lessons students can learn about the Holocaust? Why is a particular reading, image, document, or film an appropriate medium for conveying the lessons about the Holocaust which you wish to teach? (Parsons and Totten, 1993, p. 1)

Issues of rationale are not emphasized enough in most classrooms. For example, some teachers plunge into their courses without asking students questions such as, "Why study the Holocaust?" or "Why study this particular aspect of the Holocaust?"

Regardless of whether the teacher is experienced or inexperienced in teaching about the Holocaust, questions of rationale should always be considered. Teachers should constantly ask themselves, "Why am I teaching this subject in the first place?" "What are the most essential topics/questions that need to be addressed within this subject matter, and why is that so?" "Is this topic, reading, audiovisual material, or resource speaker truly appropriate for this study?"

It is impossible, of course, to teach all history, so each community, school, and individual educator must select and organize those historical events and deeds that best assist students to understand the past as well as the world they live in today. This means that rationale statements must clearly identify why a particular period of history should be incorporated into the school curriculum. If this is not done, there is the danger that this history may become marginal and irrelevant to the students. As Friedlander (1979) suggests, equally significant is the need for the teacher (hopefully in conjunction with the students) to decide what aspects of the history should be taught and why. Developing clearly stated rationales will assist teachers in emphasizing particular aspects of the history, thus helping to assure that the study is neither so broad or so limited that it becomes meaningless.

All that said, to ignore the history of the Holocaust is to distort the history of humanity and, particularly, that of the twentieth century. Indeed, we are in complete agreement with Eisner's (1979) perceptive thesis that

> . . . what schools do not teach may be as important as what they do teach. I argue this position because ignorance is not simply a void; it has important effects on the kinds of options one is able to consider, the alternatives one can examine, and the perspectives with which one can view a situation or problem. (p. 83)

Finally, those teachers who have understood the importance of rationales for teaching the Holocaust have sound responses and answers to those individuals—students, parents, administrators, school board members, or other citizens in the community—who question the importance of teaching about the Holocaust. When teachers are asked why they are teaching something that may be perceived as "outside the curriculum" and/or controversial, they often lack sound explanations for curricular decisions. The development of sound rationales can help to alleviate this painful situation.

Developing Rationale Statements

When developing rationale statements, teachers find it helpful to ask themselves a series of questions:

- Why is the Holocaust important to study?
- What do I perceive as the most important lesson(s) to be learned from a study of the Holocaust, and why?
- If I have time to teach only five different topics/aspects of the Holocaust, what would they be and why?
- What do I want my students to walk away with after a study of the Holocaust, and why?
- If I can plant only one seed about the Holocaust in my students' minds for them to ponder over the long haul of their lives, what would it be and why?

When developing rationale statements, one should concentrate on both cognitive and affective levels—the mind, knowledge, and thinking, as well as the heart, dispositions, and feelings. To address one of those components and not the other is likely to result in an incomplete curriculum, one that is bereft of the essential components that make us human.

If, after designing a series of rationale statements, one discovers that the focus is on the "whats, wheres, and whens" of the history as opposed to the "whys," then it behooves the teacher to reconsider the goals, objectives and content for the lesson or unit. Likewise, if one discovers that the focus is solely on a series of facts versus the importance this history has for both the individual and post-Holocaust society, then it would be wise to consider adding components that are likely to engage students in pondering long and hard what meaning this history has for their own lives and the world in which they live. Indeed, this process is imperative. As historian Yehuda Bauer (1978) has stated: ". . . [T]he crucial problem is how to anchor the Holocaust in the historical consciousness of the generation(s) that follow it" (p. 45). And, we would add, moral consciousness.

By examining the causes and consequences of the policy decisions made by the Third Reich, as well as those by other societies during the Holocaust period, we help students gain a deeper understanding of how governmental policies can lead to persecution, discrimination, and the destruction of human life. The moral and ethical dimensions of Holocaust study, often embedded in the context of memoirs, diaries, and other first-person accounts, help students reexamine their own values and actions, and provide opportunities for reflection on genuinely caring responses to patterns of prejudice and discrimination.

If a key goal in teaching the Holocaust is to "make a student both knowledgeable and different" (Lipstadt, 1995, p. 29), then teachers need to consider how to accomplish this. A key place to begin this process is in the development of their rationale statements. As Rosenberg and Bardosh (1982–1983) correctly assert:

> There is a fundamental distinction between the process of learning and the process of integrating the meaning and implications of an important event into consciousness and conscience. One can learn about an event by consuming and assimilating the factual details that have gone into its making. But learning does not necessarily indicate understanding. The latter is the result of integration. By integration we mean that the actions of individuals who have successfully absorbed an event into their moral and intellectual world will display an awareness of that event in their everyday activities. (p. 3)

Examples of Rationale Statements for Teaching the Holocaust

If the study of genocide is not also the study of humanity and inhumanity, if it does not add to our understanding of human behavior, then what is its purpose in the curriculum?

—Margaret Drew

Over the past twenty years, a number of thought-provoking rationales have been generated by educators in regard to the question: "Why teach about the Holocaust?" Those that we find the most thought-provoking and/or valuable are as follows:

- to study human behavior;
- to teach students why, how, what, when, and where the Holocaust took place, including the key historical trends/antecedents that led up to and culminated in the "final solution" (Totten, n.d.);
- to explore concepts such as prejudice, discrimination, stereotyping, racism, antisemitism, obedience to authority, the bystander syndrome, loyalty, conflict, conflict resolution, decision making, and justice;
- "to illustrate the effects of peer pressure, individual responsibility, and the process of decision making under the most extreme conditions" (Schwartz, 1990, p. 101);
- to become "cognizant that 'little' prejudices can easily be transformed into far more serious ones" (Lipstadt, 1995, p. 29);
- to "make students more sensitive to ethnic and religious hatred" (Lipstadt, 1995, p. 29);
- to develop in students an awareness of the value of pluralism and diversity in a pluralistic society;
- to reflect on the roles and responsibilities of individuals, groups, and nations when confronting life in an industrial/technological/information age, including the abuse of power, civil and human rights violations, and genocidal acts;
- "to develop a deeper appreciation of the relationship of rights and duties, and to realize that human rights and the corresponding duties they entail are not the birthright of the few but the birthright of all—every man, woman, and child in the world today" (Branson and Torney-Purta, 1982, p. 5);
- to examine the nature, structure, and purpose of governments;
- to "become sensitized to inhumanity and suffering whenever they occur" (Fleischner, in Strom and Parsons, 1982, p. 6);
- to provide a context for exploring the dangers of remaining silent, apathetic, and indifferent in the face of others' oppression;
- "to teach civic virtue . . . [which is related to] the importance of responsible citizenship and mature iconoclasm" (Friedlander, 1979, pp. 532–533);
- to understand that the Holocaust was *not* an accident in history; it was not inevitable (Parsons and Totten, 1993, p. 1);
- to develop an understanding that the Holocaust was a watershed event not only in the twentieth century, but in the entire history of humanity (Parsons and Totten, 1993, p. 1);
- to demonstrate how a modern nation can utilize its technological expertise and bureaucratic infrastructure to implement destructive policies ranging from social engineering to genocide;

■ to illustrate that the Holocaust resulted from a cumulative progression of numerous historical events and deeds, *and* that it was not an event in history that was inevitable (Parsons and Totten, 1993, p. 3).

Teachers—in conjunction, if they wish, with their students—need to decide what the focus of the study will be, and then develop appropriate rationale statements. Just as each class of students is unique, each study of the Holocaust by necessity will be unique. To a certain extent this is likely to be dictated by the teacher's knowledge base, what the teacher perceives as being of the utmost significance vis-à-vis the history, the levels and the abilities of the students, the time alloted for the study, the type and amount of resources available, and/or a combination of these concerns.

Although some teachers explain why the subject of the Holocaust is important to their students, they do not always encourage student responses. This approach is apt to set a "preachy" tone that may cause students some consternation and/or even to question the motive(s) of the teacher. This style of teaching also signals to students that their views and thoughts are not as important as those of the teacher.

Finally, some educators (particularly curriculum developers) have a tendency to borrow noble-sounding rationales from others and posit them as goals for their own curricula. *To use other educators' rationale statements in this fashion is the same as never designing a rationale statement in the first place.*

The Need for Careful Use of Language in Rationales

The language used in creating the rationale(s) is critical. Of the utmost importance is that rationales *not* constitute "comparisons of pain." That is, one should *not* assert that "The Holocaust is the most horrific example of genocide in the history of humanity." To make such an assertion minimizes the horror and suffering experienced by humans in other genocides.

Terms such as *"unimaginable"* or *"unbelievable"* are often used when speaking about the Holocaust, but these terms may send a message to students that the Holocaust was so "unreal" that it is pointless to try and learn about what happened. Indeed, students may end up believing that the Holocaust was a one-time aberration, and that it has no message for humanity today. The simple but profound fact is that the Holocaust did happen. It was systematically planned and implemented by human beings, and thus it is not "unimaginable" or "unbelievable." As Holocaust scholar Lawrence Langer (1978) states:

> What does it mean to say that an event is beyond the imagination? It was not beyond the imagination of the men who authorized it; or those who executed it; or those who suffered it. Once an event occurs, can it any longer be said to be "beyond the imagination"? Inaccessible, yes; . . . contrary to "all those human values on

which art is traditionally based," of course. What we confront is not the unimaginable, but the intolerable, a condition of existence that so diminishes our own humanity that we prefer to assign it to an alien realm. (p. 5)

One should also avoid the use of clichés in rationale statements. Too often teachers and curriculum developers have mindlessly latched on to such phrases as "Never Again," "Always Remember," "Never Forget," and "Those Who Do Not Remember History are Condemned to Repeat It," without giving ample thought and consideration as to their meaning.

Spoken by survivors, these admonitions are powerful and meaningful. That is not true, however, when they are spoken by politicians, after-dinner speakers, conference participants, and teachers who neglect to acknowledge the fact that genocide has been perpetrated, time and again, since 1945.

If and when curriculum developers use such phrases as "Never Again," they should ask themselves what they mean by them. That is, do they mean that the Holocaust, involving the same people (in which Jewish men, women, and children are the victims and the Nazis are the tormentors and executioners) must never take place again? Or, do they mean that no genocide should ever take place again?" Both, of course, are legitimate goals and something that everyone should strive for and be vigilant about.

To use such phrases simply because they sound good is problematic at best. (For a more detailed discussion of this issue, see Chapter 9, "The Imperative to Avoid Clichés.")

Factors Influencing the Focus of Rationale Statements

Among the most important factors influencing the focus of rationale statements are: (1) one's aims in teaching the history; (2) one's knowledge of the history of the Holocaust; (3) the particular course one is teaching; (4) the levels and abilities of one's students; (5) the available time for study of the Holocaust; and (6) the instructional resources available.

Quite obviously, the major factor influencing the focus of one's rationale statements is one's aim in teaching this history. Is it to provide a deep understanding of how Germany became a fascist, totalitarian, and genocidal state? Is it to focus on both the incremental nature of the assault against the Jews and others and the extermination process? Is it to focus on the complexity and danger of the bystander syndrome both within and outside the Nazi sphere of influence and power? Is it to focus on the literature (fiction, poetry, drama) of the Holocaust? Is it to teach lessons about living in a world where genocide is still perpetrated on a regular basis?

On a different note, even those who have a working knowledge of this history need to seriously consider what their goals are for such a study. In doing so, it is wise to consult key historical works, pedagogical essays, comprehensive chronologies of the Holocaust, and the most accurate and pedagogically sound lessons and curricula available on the Holocaust, in order to develop strong rationale statements. If, on the other hand, one has an extremely limited knowledge of the history then *it is imperative that the teacher educate himself or herself about this history prior to teaching it.*

The particular course one teaches will also dictate the focus of the rationale statements. For example, the rationale statement in a history course will differ from one in a literature course, because the focus of each is bound to be fundamentally different. That said, overlap in the content of the rationale statements can be expected. The study of human behavior could very well be the focus of both a historical and literary rationale statement. On the other hand, a social studies teacher emphasizing the study of change over time may develop rationale statements that stress the impact of the past on present societal conditions and decision making, or on how contemporary democratic institutions reflect the relative success or failure of citizens to embody democratic values and processes in their daily lives.

In developing a course on the Holocaust, it is vital to take into consideration the levels, abilities, and backgrounds of one's students. The factors inherent in these concerns will dictate the sophistication and depth of the study, the resources used, and the pedagogical strategies and learning activities employed. To neglect these issues is pedagogically unsound. Further, it is an invitation to a study that will likely be too sophisticated or too simplistic. For students with limited reading ability, one can create a study of the Holocaust through a blend of graphic, visual, and audio resources, as well as appropriate reading materials that are accurate but not beyond their ability to comprehend. Many resources, including those available on selected Internet sites, can be utilized effectively with those who have reading difficulties, particularly when in-depth discussion of the resources is regularly employed to facilitate student comprehension and an understanding of how specific cases (i.e., personal audio testimonies) are illustrative of larger historical trends.

Time is always a critical factor in the classroom. Many teachers are extremely limited in how much time they can allot to this history, necessitating some difficult decisions about what one can and cannot include in such a study. An in-depth study of fewer topics is generally preferable to superficial coverage of a plethora of topics. As Newmann (1988) states, ". . . less in this context does not mean less knowledge or information, for depth can be achieved only through the mastery of considerable information. Rather, less refers to less mastery of information that provides only a superficial acquaintance with a topic" (p. 347). As he eloquently frames this problem:

> . . . we usually try to teach too much. . . . We are addicted to coverage. This addiction seems endemic in high school, especially in history. . . . Beyond simply wasting time or failing to impart knowledge of lasting value, superficial coverage has a more insidious consequence: it reinforces habits of mindlessness. Classrooms become places in which material must be learned—even though students find it nonsensical because their teachers have no time to explain. Students are denied

opportunities to explore related areas that arouse their curiosity for fear of straying too far from the official list of topics to be covered.

. . . The alternative to coverage, though difficult to achieve, is depth: the sustained study of a given topic that leads students beyond superficial exposure to rich, complex understanding. (Newmann, 1988, p. 346)

Teachers who do not consider the issue of time when developing rationale statements may be in for a rude awakening when it comes to teaching the course predicated on such rationale statements.

The instructional resources a teacher has available for a study of the Holocaust will likely influence the focus of the study; and that, in turn, will likely impact the type of rationale statements one devises. Simply stated, one can develop all the rationale statements one wants, but if one does not have the resources to teach the information, concepts, and issues, then it is likely that the focus and intent of the rationale statements will not be realized. Given that the range of available instructional resources will influence classroom practices, the development of rationales should coincide with a determined effort to expand available resources to encompass the broad goals of the course. Although this is time-consuming and costly, over time a comprehensive set of instructional resources, including books, first-person accounts, primary documents, online resources, computer software, audiovisual materials, and fiction and poetry can be developed to support curricular rationales and programs.

The Use of Rationale Statements to Develop Goals and Objectives for the Study

Limited value exists in developing rationale statements if they do not influence the actual goals and objectives of the course. Together, the rationale statements, goals, and objectives will assist one in developing the content, the pedagogy, the resources, and the learning activities to be employed.

Learning objectives should take into consideration the developmental level of prospective students in the course, address all levels of Bloom's taxonomy or a comparable taxonomy of thinking or cognitive operations, include both content and process concerns, and provide opportunities for extension of learning beyond the classroom so that other "communities" experience the benefits of what students have learned in the course.

Rationales Should Direct the Content Used in the Study

Over the course of the past five years, both educators (Shawn, 1995) and noted scholars (Dawidowicz, 1992; Lipstadt, 1995) have criticized the content of courses being offered on the Holocaust in many of our nation's public schools. In doing so, they have addressed everything from the weakness of curricular goals and objectives to the weaknesses inherent in the depiction of the history in various curricula.

In an article entitled "Current Issues in Holocaust Education," educator Karen Shawn (1995) argued that "The ill-considered rush to educate may lead to the trivialization and distortion of the memory of the Holocaust. This is evident in the recent alarming proliferation of poorly conceived and executed textbooks, teaching aids, and lesson plans flooding our schools" (p. 18). She concluded her article by stating ". . . today Holocaust education is threatened by ignorance, arrogance, superficiality, and commercialism" (p. 18).

Teachers need to carefully select from the mass of topics and information available materials that specifically and accurately address the emphases in their rationale statements. The key here is to narrow the information without watering it down, and to strive for depth over superficial coverage. (See the annotated bibliography at the end of this text for a list of many of the best resources available for conducting a study of the Holocaust.)

In addition to the question, "Why teach about the Holocaust?," there are several other key questions that teachers must ask themselves prior to engaging their students in a study of the Holocaust: "What are the most important lessons we want our students to learn from the Holocaust?" (Parsons and Totten, 1993), and, as the Coalition of Essential Schools personnel (1989) continually ask in the course of their pedagogical efforts, "So what? What does it [the information and new-found knowledge] matter? What does it all mean?" (p. 2). This process should guide teachers to develop and implement a study that is relevant and meaningful for their students, as well as assist them in shaping an unwieldy and massive amount of information into something more manageable.

Historian Lucy Dawidowicz (1992) correctly asserts that presently most Holocaust curricula are "better at describing what happened during the Holocaust than explaining why it happened" (p. 69). In a survey of twenty-five curricula, Dawidowicz (1992) found that "most curricula plunge right into the story of Hitler's Germany; a few provide some background on the Weimar Republic, presumably to explain Hitler's rise to power. Though all curricula discuss Nazi anti-Semitism, preferring generic terms like 'racism' and 'prejudice' instead of the specific 'anti-Semitism,' fifteen of the twenty-five never even suggest that anti-Semitism had a history *before* Hitler. Of those that do, barely a handful present coherent historical accounts, however brief. . . . A small number of curricula include lessons which survey the pre-Nazi history of Jews in Europe, presumably to humanize the image of the Jews depicted in Nazi propaganda" (p. 69).

In regard to the issue of antisemitism—which is often the issue that most curricula developed for use by secondary-level teachers neglect to address—Dawidowicz (1992) persuasively argues that avoidance of that topic, "and especially its roots in Christian doctrine" (p. 71), skews history and provides a distorted picture of the cause of the Holocaust. "To be sure, Christianity cannot be held responsible for Hitler, but the Nazis would not have succeeded in disseminating their brand of racist anti-Semitism had they not been confident of the pervasiveness, firmness, and durability of Christian hatred of Jews" (Dawidowicz, 1992, p. 71). "Omitting all references to Christian anti-Semitism is one way some curricula avoid the sensitivities of the subject. The more acceptable and common pedagogic strategy is to generalize the highly particular nature and history of anti-Semitism by subsuming (and camouflaging) it under general rubrics like scapegoating, prejudice, and bigotry. . . . These abstract words suggest that hatred of the Jews is not a thing in itself, but a symptom of 'larger' troubles, though no explanation is given as to why the Jews, rather than dervishes, for instance, are consistently chosen as the scapegoat" (Dawidowicz, 1992, p. 73).[1] (For additional insights into similar as well as other problems in various Holocaust curricula, see Totten's and Riley's [in press] "The Problem of Inaccurate History in State Developed/Sponsored Holocaust and Genocide Curricula and Teacher Guides: A Challenge to Scholars of the Holocaust and Genocide.")

The complexity of the subject matter of the Holocaust is daunting. The era itself, without even considering major antecedents or postwar issues, spanned a period of twelve years (1933-1945), the geographic area covered all of continental Europe and beyond, and the people involved numbered in the millions. Numerous "parties" were involved, including the perpetrators, collaborators, the bystanders, and the victims—none of whom were monolithic. Inherent in the above are such issues and concerns as the Nazis' rise to power, the life of the Jews in Germany and Europe prior to the Holocaust period, and so on. Over and above that there are the host of critical historical trends (antisemitism, racism, social Darwinism, extreme nationalism, totalitarianism, industrialism, and the nature of modern war) that one needs to be conversant with in order to even begin to understand the Holocaust (Niewyk, 1995, p. 175). It is imperative that teachers provide students with a solid knowledge base regarding the antecedents of the Holocaust as well as the whys, hows, whens, and wheres.

It is also essential to place the study of the Holocaust within a historical context that will allow students to see the relationship of political, social, and economic factors that had an impact on the times and events which resulted in that history (Totten and Feinberg, 1995, p. 325). The content that teachers and other curriculum planners select for a study of the Holocaust should facilitate the understanding of the historical context of the period. For example, depending on the emphasis in one's course, familiarizing students with the history of antisemitism, the impact of the German defeat in World War I, or the consequences for Germany of the Great Depression will greatly influence the construction of a unit on the Holocaust. If emphasis is placed almost exclusively on the political factors leading to the rise of the Nazis, while scant attention is paid to a social phenomenon such as antisemitism, the ultimate organization of the unit and its historical context will be directly affected. Similarly, creating a context that primarily emphasizes the economic misery brought on by the Depression as the *main* "cause" of the Nazis' assumption of power to the exclusion of the social and political factors that motivated large and significant segments of the German public will, likewise, influence the final organization of the teaching unit. The development of historically accurate lessons and units on the Holocaust demands that teachers and curriculum planners attempt to thoroughly and accurately integrate the political, economic, and social factors associated with this history. The role of the rationale in guiding content selection is crucial.

It is also incumbent on teachers to show that behind the statistics are real people, comprised of families of grandparents, parents, and children. First-person accounts provide students with a way of "making meaning" of collective numbers. Although students should be careful about overgeneralizing from first-person accounts such as those from survivors, journalists, relief workers, bystanders, and liberators, personal accounts can supplement a study of the Holocaust by moving it "from a welter of statistics, remote places and events, to one that is immersed in the 'personal' and 'particular'" (Totten, 1987, p. 63). And as Friedlander (1979) has noted, one of the best ways to study human behavior in such extreme situations as genocide is "to consult the memoir literature as an original source" (p. 526). Again, if rationale statements focus on individuals as well as groups, it will be more likely that teachers and students will come to understand and appreciate that real people are behind the mind-numbing statistics.

In some cases, teachers focus on one or two aspects (pieces of the history, issues, perspectives) of the Holocaust to the exclusion of other key issues. For example, some focus on the crimes of the perpetrators but not the antecedents of the history; the actions of the perpetrators but not the lives of the victims; the fact of the death camps versus the ever increasing discrimination that marginalized and isolated the Jews and other victims in the first place; the role of the rescuers to the exclusion of the policies and/or actions of the perpetrators, victims, and bystanders; the passivity of Jews but not the varied forms of resistance they put up; the notion that Jews allowed themselves to be herded into ghettos, camps, and gas chambers, but nothing about the deceit and overwhelming power of the Nazis, the abject fear experienced by the potential and actual victims or the "choiceless choices" people were forced to make; and, the obedience to authority but nothing about the terror induced by the Nazis.

By developing strong rationale statements that focus on the whys and hows of the Holocaust as well those pertaining to the whats, wheres, and whens, teachers are more likely to not only include absolutely critical information about the Holocaust, but also a more well-rounded perspective of the events. Concomitantly, they are also more likely to include a balanced and accurate view of the perpetrators, collaborators, bystanders, rescuers, and victims. To skip over this initial work (e.g., developing rationale statements that provide an accurate and comprehensive view of the history) is to enter a study blind.

Developing a rationale statement, however, is simply the first step. Once teachers and students develop rationale statements, they must carefully scrutinize them in regard to the type of study they are about to undertake. If, after developing a set of rationale statements, the teacher and the class discover that their primary focus is going to be on just the victims or just the perpetrators or just the rescuers or simply the what and whens of the Holocaust but not the whys and hows, then they need to ask themselves the following: Is this sensible? If not, why not, and what can we do to rectify the situation? Is such a study valuable? If so, how and why? And if not, why not? Will such a study provide the students with a solid sense of the history of the Holocaust? What is the point of focusing on one aspect of the Holocaust to the exclusion of another that is equally important? Is there a way to balance the study in order to make it more inclusive, more comprehensive, more valuable?

Thoroughly examining and weighing rationale statements assists the teacher in determining whether a course of study is comprehensive, thorough, and historically accurate, versus one that is unduly limited in some form or manner.

Using Rationales to Guide the Type of Pedagogy and Resources Used During the Study

Strong rationales should guide the selection of effective pedagogical strategies and appropriate instructional resources. To develop rationales and then ignore them when developing or selecting teaching strategies, learning activities, and resources is likely to weaken the value of the overall study.

The complexity and emotionally charged nature of this history dictates that not just any instructional strategy, learning activity, or resource will do. Each must be of the highest quality, thought-provoking, and not comprised of those that, even inadvertently, minimize, romanticize, or simplify the history. As Totten (1991) noted, "a major flaw endemic to much of the current curricula on [the Holocaust], at least at the secondary level, is that the suggested teaching methods are routine and predictable, and the learning activities are comprised of memorizing facts and pencil-and-paper exercises that call for answers to lower level cognitive questions" (p. 198). Numerous Holocaust curricula also include activities as "word scrambles" or crossword puzzles, many of which may lead to the creation of a "fun and games" atmosphere, rather than one of serious study. In turn, this tends to trivialize the importance of studying this history (Parsons and Totten, 1993, p. 7).

Some teachers have a propensity to engage their students in simulations where they, the students, supposedly act out actual situations experienced by the perpetrators, victims, and others. As the authors of the United States Holocaust Memorial Museum's *Guidelines for Teaching about the Holocaust* state, this is a dubious practice: "Even when teachers take great care to prepare a class for such an activity, simulating experiences from the Holocaust remains pedagogically unsound. The activity may engage students, but they often forget the purpose of the lesson, and even worse, they are left with the impression at the conclusion of the activity that they now know what it was like during the Holocaust . . . The problem with trying to simulate situations from the Holocaust is that complex events and actions are over-simplified, and students are left with a skewed view of history" (Parsons and Totten, 1993, pp. 7, 8).

There is absolutely no way that students will *ever* be able to experience what it was like for victims of the Holocaust to be forced from their homes, herded into ghettos, crammed into suffocatingly hot or freezing cattle cars for days on end, or subjected to torture and murder at the hands of the Nazis. Simulations that purport to provide students with such experiences trivialize and mock the experiences of those who were killed and those who survived.

Those teachers who are prone to use simulations as part of a unit on the Holocaust should ask the question, "Why should simulations be used when there already exists a wealth of actual case studies?" It is one thing for a teacher to broaden student perspectives by asking, "What might you have done?" (which is more appropriate than asking,"What would you have done?"), and quite another to launch a class into a simulation that attempts to recreate choices and human behavior that almost defy the imagination. Statements of rationale hopefully will prod teachers to reflect on the content and purposes of classroom practices.

Strong rationales can also assist with the opening and closing of lessons and units on the Holocaust, critical stages in any study of the Holocaust because they set the tone and context for the entire course. For example, if one of the rationales for the study is "to help students think about the use and abuse of power, and the roles and responsibilities of individuals, organizations, and nations when confronted with civil rights violations and/or policies of genocide," an opening can easily be tailored to begin to explore such issues. Additionally, strong openings are able to dispel misinformation students may hold prior to the study of the Holocaust; set a reflective tone whereby students come to appreciate the need to make careful distinctions when weighing various ideas, motives, and behaviors; indicate to the students that their ideas and opinions about this history are important; tie the history to the students' lives; and/or establish that the history has multiple interpretations and ramifications. On the other hand, a strong closing can encourage students to synthesize the various aspects of their study, connect this history to the world they live in today, and encourage them to continue to examine this history. (For a detailed discussion of various ways to begin a lesson or unit on the Holocaust, see Chapter 2, "Establishing a Foundation for a Study of the Holocaust"; and for a detailed discussion of various ways to close a lesson or unit on the Holocaust, see Chapter 8, "Closing a Lesson or a Unit on the Holocaust: Assisting Students to Synthesize and Reflect upon What They Have Learned.")

The pedagogy used in such a study should be one that is student-centered; that is, one in which the students are not passive, but rather actively engaged in the study. It should be a study that, in the best sense of the word, complicates the students' thinking, engages students in critical and creative thought, and involves in-depth versus superficial coverage of information. It should also involve students in reading and examining primary sources (e.g., contemporaneous documents issued during the Holocaust period, diaries and letters written by the victims and others, and so on). Using first-person accounts and other primary sources about the Holocaust (e.g., documents, photographs, trial records, spoken-word recordings, and documentary film footage) helps students establish direct connections with the ideas of those who experienced this historical period, thus helping them examine the broader historical themes in a more personal dimension. The vast scope and complexity of the Holocaust can be difficult to comprehend; therefore, it is critical that teachers choose resources that not only facilitate the achievement of course goals, but that help students grapple with the choices and decisions made by perpetrators, bystanders, victims, and rescuers in this era. This is also true of the many "choiceless choices," as Lawrence Langer refers to them, that the victims were often forced to make.

Because the history itself as well as many of the primary sources available on the Holocaust have the power to generate powerful emotional responses in students, the use of personal journals is highly recommended to provide a means for young people to express their feelings privately to the teacher about the information and issues they are encountering. At appropriate junctures, the teacher can determine if journal entries should be shared with other students, but this is clearly a pedagogical decision that requires careful consideration. (For ideas along this line, see Chris M. Anson and Richard Beach [1995] *Journals in the Classroom: Writing to Learn.* Norwood, MA: Christopher-Gordon.)

Clearly stated and well-thought-out rationale statements are not only capable of assisting a teacher in selecting appropriate resources, they can also help to avoid materials that detract from the study, diminish its importance, and/or move the study far afield. Unfortunately, in an ostensible effort to engage students' interest, some curriculum developers have incorporated such questionable pieces as Mick Jagger's "Sympathy for the Devil," Lenny Bruce's "My Name is Adolf Eichmann," "The Boomtown Rats," and "I Never Loved Eva Braun" into their curricula on the Holocaust. Because a wealth of powerful resources on the Holocaust exists that students find extremely thought-provoking and engaging, marginal materials are to be avoided. The latter materials, although possibly interesting at first glance, tend to trivialize and oversimplify the study of the Holocaust, reducing its significance to the level of a popular culture artifact when taken out of context. In contrast, poetry, fiction, and artwork that reflects deeply on the Holocaust and its legacy is highly appropriate for use, because it illustrates and deepens understanding of core themes without resorting to artistic techniques or conventions that transform the Holocaust into just another topic of mass popular culture, devoid of deep meaning or long-term significance. (Note: For a discussion of appropriate and powerful literary, artistic and musical responses to the Holocaust, see the chapters in Totten's and Stephen Feinberg's [2001] *Teaching and Studying the Holocaust* by Karen Shawn, Totten, Shari Werb, Belarie Zatzman, and Roselle Chartock.)

Involving Students in the Development of Rationales

A good place to begin with the development of rationale statements for a study of the Holocaust is with the students themselves. This immediately encourages them to begin thinking about why one would want or need to study this history; and in doing so, begins to personalize the study for them. It may also motivate them to become more engaged in the study and to begin to see the relevance it has for their own lives as well as the society, country, and world in which they live.

Initially, the teacher can ask the students to think of reasons why young people *should* study the Holocaust. After the students record their responses in journals or on a sheet of paper, the teacher can write a selection of the responses on the board or overhead projector. Later, these can be transferred to a bulletin board, where they could remain during the course of the study to highlight and draw attention to them. As the unit progresses and students learn more about the actual history of the Holocaust, the class can return to the initial responses, during which they could reexamine and, if need be, revise their initial rationales.

An even more engaging way to get the students involved in the development of rationale statements is to have them write down those questions they have about the Holocaust and/or that they wish to have answered during the course of the study. For example, during a special week-long, four-hour-a-day, summer course on the Holocaust, a group of high school students came up with the following questions (all quoted exactly as they were written):

- Why exactly did the Holocaust happen?
- What was the main factor that caused this genocide?
- What percent of Germany's population was Jewish during the time of the Holocaust's beginning?
- Why were Jews blamed in the first place?
- How many people actually survived the Holocaust?
- How did Hitler get into office?
- Why did Hitler have so much power?
- What was Hitler's main motive for killing all the Jews?
- How did the Jews become so hated?
- Did this affect America?
- Why are we usually only taught that Jews were persecuted?
- Why didn't all the people in the camps rebel at once, so that their [sic] may have been a hope for freedom?
- Who else was eventually included with the Jews, and why?
- Was there any dissention [sic] among the German ranks regarding following orders which lead to the mass extermination of Jews?
- Why didn't the U.S. try and step in sooner?
- What are the warning signs of something like the Holocaust , and how can we stop it from happening again?
- Why???

Many of the student questions penetrate to the core of the tragedy of the Holocaust, while others are more concerned with key facts (chronology, the number of people who were murdered by the Nazis, number of survivors). Students could take such questions as the above and fashion them into rationale statements. These statements, in conjunction with the teacher's, could set the stage for the study.

Using Rationale Statements to Avoid Pitfalls During the Course of Study

Another use of rationale statements is to safeguard against some of the many pitfalls (e.g., assaulting students with one shocking image after another, minimizing
the horrific nature of the Holocaust, romanticizing the Holocaust, skewing the history by under- or overstating key situations or aspects of the history, providing
simple answers to complex questions/situations) that have plagued Holocaust
lessons and units. As one can readily ascertain, teaching this history involves, at
least to a certain extent, a "balancing act" of sorts.

Teachers need to be judicious in their approach to the Holocaust and be sure
that in teaching about the history, they do not constantly bombard their students
with one horrific image after another, to the point where the students are overwhelmed. Students are essentially a "captive audience." Assaulting them with
horrific images outside of any constructive context is antithetical to good teaching.
The assumption that students will seek to "understand" human behavior after
being exposed to horrible images is a fallacy. Instead of becoming engaged with
the history, students may tend to ignore it or "shut down" their attention to protect
themselves from the ghastly images.

Teachers also need to avoid denying the reality of the Holocaust by minimizing the fact that the perpetrators committed ghastly crimes against the Jews and
others. What is required is a very fine balancing act. To attempt to teach the Holocaust without presenting the facts is miseducational. As Darsa (1991) stated, the
facts of the Holocaust may be uncomfortable for the students to learn [because]
"in discomfort there is struggle and growth" (p. 181). When the horror is
explored, it should be done only to the extent necessary to achieve the objective(s)
of the lesson.

Some teachers have a tendency—often inadvertently—to "romanticize" the
Holocaust. For example, some teachers try to leave the students with a rosy view;
that is, they place an inordinate emphasis on the themes of hiding and rescue.
Many place a heavy emphasis on the Allies' liberation of the camps, while ostensibly ignoring the fact that for years and years stories about the fate of the Jews fell
on deaf ears. Still others tend to conclude the study in a way that leaves students
with a sense that "all is well with the world." This is often done by focusing on the
postwar trials of the Nazis and insinuating that, in the end, "justice was done."

The fact that some people reached out to support or rescue Jews is vitally significant, but to place it at the center of such a study skews the history. Teachers and
students need to keep the facts in mind, and the fact is "at best, less than one-half
of one percent of the total population [of non-Jews] under Nazi occupation helped
to rescue Jews" (Oliner and Oliner, 1991, p. 363). And although the "liberation" of
the camps was a monumental event, it is also true that the liberation of the camps
was never really an objective of the Allies so much as a duty they more or less
encountered as they drove toward the unconditional surrender of Germany and
her allies. It is also a deplorable fact that the vast majority of the perpetrators and
collaborators never were brought to trial. And, of course, all did not end well. Six

million Jews perished at the hands of the Nazis, and five million others (including Gypsies, the physically and mentally handicapped, Soviet prisoners of war, Poles and other Slavs) also had their lives taken by the Nazis. Many Jews lost entire families and had neither homes nor communities to which they could return when World War II ended. Others tried to return to their towns but were met with everything from contempt to outright antagonism to murder. And over fifty years later, many survivors remain traumatized by the events they experienced and the losses they suffered. Students need to learn the hard facts of the Holocaust, and rationale statements should reflect that.

Many teachers tend to present the Holocaust as a totally unique event in the history of humanity, or, as a vehicle for universal statements about humanity. There are aspects of the Holocaust that are unique and there are key aspects that are of universal significance. There is a critical need to examine both the uniqueness of the Holocaust as well as its universal nature. This must be done by avoiding the pitfall of establishing a false dichotomy between the two. The latter simply degenerates into a situation that removes the students from the history and the myriad ramifications it has for them and the world in which they live.

Why is it important to consider the issue of the uniqueness of the Holocaust? As this history is taught or studied, some are apt to equate it to the long and tortured history of man's inhumanity to man. Yet one must recognize that, while other groups throughout history have been persecuted and murdered, the complete and total physical annihilation of an entire people as official state policy brings a solitary character to the study of the Holocaust. As Steven T. Katz (1994) writes, "It is this unconstrained, ideologically driven imperative that *every* Jew be murdered that distinguishes the Sho'ah (Holocaust) from prior and to date subsequent, however inhumane, acts of collective violence, ethnocide, and mass murder" (p. 26). And as Elie Wiesel (1979) has noted: "While not all victims [of the Nazis] were Jews, all Jews were victims, destined for annihilation solely because they were born Jewish. They were doomed not because of something they had done or proclaimed or acquired but because of who they were: sons and daughters of the Jewish people" (p. iii). Few statements graphically illustrate the systematic, sustained, and unprecedented nature of this genocidal act as well as the following one by Wiesel (1984):

> The Nazis' aim was to make the Jewish shrink—from town to neighborhood, from neighborhood to street, from street to house, from house to room, from room to garret, from garret to cattle car, from cattle car to gas chamber.
>
> And they did the same to the individual—separated from his or her community, then from his or her family, then from his or her identity, eventually becoming a work permit, then a number, until the number itself was turned into ashes. (p. 1)

Similarly, while various scholars have demonstrated that the Holocaust was a "phenomenologically unique" historical era (e.g., Katz, 1994), it is also important to focus on the universal dimensions and significance of the era. Although it was undeniably unique within the context of human civilization, those who fell victims to the Nazi reign of terror experienced prejudice, discrimination, scapegoating, denial of fundamental human rights, barbarous treatment, and other lawless actions against them, just as did victims of other genocides.

When selecting content, every effort should be made to avoid depicting groups (Jews, Gypsies, Germans, Poles, rescuers, bystanders, etc.) as one-dimensional. The multifaceted aspects of all groups must be acknowledged. Simplistic views and stereotyping takes place when groups are viewed as monolithic in attitudes and actions. Thus, while Jews have been the target of antisemitism and were the central victims of the Nazi regime, students should not view Jews as solely being victims. Jewish resistance should also be examined. Likewise, Germans should not be perceived only as Nazis or perpetrators, nor should Poles and Ukrainians be characterized solely as collaborators. To focus exclusively or almost totally on the role of the rescuers to the exclusion of role of the bystanders is to distort the history. While the role of the rescuers is vital to address, it is also critical to acknowledge and ponder the fact that many more stood by and allowed the events to unfold that ultimately culminated in the Holocaust.

It is also important to keep in mind that generalizations without modifying and qualifying words (e.g., sometimes, usually, and so on) tend to stereotype group behavior and historical reality (Parsons and Totten, 1993, p. 4).

When teaching any piece of history, it is imperative to avoid allowing simple or simplistic answers or notions to explain complex behavior or situations. This is even more significant when myths or misnomers abound about a subject—as it does with the Holocaust. *Common knowledge of a historical event does not constitute accurate knowledge.* Rather, accurate knowledge of a historical event is based on the collection of accurate data. Its effective interpretation is predicated on using organizing principles and concepts drawn from legitimate scholarship. It is this type of information and data that should be used in the classroom. A good method to assess the accuracy of information is to do ample reading of the major historians of the Holocaust and to check and cross-check their sources against the best sources available.

In an attempt to make history relevant to students, some curricula have a tendency to distort it. As Lipstadt (1995) has noted, certain Holocaust curricula "elide the differences between the Holocaust and all manner of inhumanities and injustices." [Such curricula often] "address a broad array of injustices" (p. 27), and many other types of mass murder. Some tend to suggest that all genocidal acts are the same in their genesis and/or implementation. Some also draw direct or near direct parallels between Nazi Germany and the issue of racism, prejudice, and economic and social disenfranchisement in the United States.

Although it is pedagogically sound to make connections between the historical and moral issues of the Holocaust and contemporary life, it is pedagogically unsound to equate the Holocaust with any and all civil and human rights violations. Rationale statements that clearly delineate the distinctions are more likely to result in a study that is both historically accurate and pedagogically sound.

Too often the Holocaust is simply taught because teachers think it might prove to be a "hook" to engage students' interest, or because they are interested in the subject matter. A case in point is the fact that many teachers in the late 1990s were swayed by popular culture that "Schindler's List" was "the thing to do/see," and thus took their students to see the film without providing them with any background information in which to contextualize or understand it. With such sensitive subject matter this is both egregious and unconscionable. Once again, this highlights the need for educators to establish well-thought-out rationales before proceeding with the study of the Holocaust.

Revisiting Rationales Throughout the Study of the Holocaust

It is vital to revisit issues of rationale throughout the study. This is especially important during an in-depth study of the Holocaust because learners can lose sight of why they are studying and concentrating on the experiences of a particular group.

As teaching about complex human behavior often results in examining multiple aspects of events and deeds, students need to continuously think about why they are studying this history. By repeatedly highlighting questions of rationale throughout a course, a signal is sent to students that *this is not simply another piece of history to wade through,* but that it has important lessons for both contemporary and future generations. What those lessons are will have to be extrapolated, discussed, and wrestled with by the teacher and the students. Finally, by continually revisiting and wrestling with issues of rationale, students will more likely gain a greater understanding as to how and why the Holocaust is important to their own lives as well as to society.

Denial

Finally, it is worth addressing the issue of denial here—if for no other reason than the fact that some students are apt to broach the issue in class, either because they have received misinformation at home or from friends or have come across denier's sites on the Internet. *It is our firm belief that the discussion of denial has no place in the classroom during a study of the Holocaust.* There are numerous reasons for this, but those we consider most significant are as follows: First, we strongly believe that it is ludicrous to "give time" to such foolish and totally fallacious assertions. The deniers are not, despite their incorrect and euphemistic use of the term "revisionism," historians; instead, they spew outright lies that deserve no attention by clear-thinking individuals. The fact of the matter is, deniers are antisemitic individuals who are out to poison the minds of others. Second, to devote time to the deniers' words in class constitutes, quite literally, a waste of time. This is true for the very simple but profound reason that most teachers do not have enough time as it is to address any subject matter in depth, let alone one as complex and detailed as the Holocaust. Thus, to take time to address the issues the deniers raise sucks precious time away from the study of critical issues germane to the Holocaust. If even a half or a quarter of a period is allocated to address deniers' falsifications, it likely means that another topic is not going to be addressed at all or will be discussed in less depth than it could or should have been. Third, students who either believe in or are enamored of the arguments of deniers often sound "authoritative" in what they have to say, when, in fact, most are talking off the top of their heads, and are largely ignorant of the historical record. For a teacher to attempt to engage such individuals in a "discussion" is futile, not to mention counterproductive.

Realizing that some teachers may feel compelled to "offset" or argue against the deniers' assertions, we are in total agreement with Ronnie S. Landau, author of *Studying the Holocaust: Issues, Readings and Documents* (New York: Routledge, 1998) when he says, ". . . the most effective ways of countering the potentially harmful influence of Holocaust deniers . . . are to keep in mind the following: that care should be taken not to dignify their opinions, accusations and assertions. . . . In other words, it is quite unnecessary and probably counter-productive to write a book, teach a class or deliver a lecture with the *express* purpose of refuting their work; a corollary of this is that every serious word that *is* written or uttered on this subject is *implicitly* working counter to the revisionists' aims and desires. In short, we should guard against . . . providing the very publicity they seek . . ." (p. 11).

For those students insistent on learning more about issues of denial, teachers would be wise to refer them to the Anti-Defamation League (823 United Nations Plaza, New York, NY 10017) for information. They should also be encouraged to read such works as Deborah Lipstadt's thought-provoking and instructive *Denying the Holocaust: The Growing Assault on Truth and Memory* (New York: The Free Press, 1986). Despite making such recommendations, teachers should make it clear that the students are to do this on their own time and that such issues will not be addressed in class.

Conclusion

Well-constructed rationales for Holocaust study represent the foundation for successful curriculum design, instructional planning, selection of curricular resources, instruction, and evaluation of student progress. The ongoing refinement of rationales is a critical dimension of reflective practice, because it fosters a critical approach to the improvement of Holocaust education and can engage both students and teachers in dialogues about the significance and meaning of the Holocaust in contemporary society.

REFERENCES

Anson, Chris M., and Beach, Richard. (1995). *Journals in the Classroom: Writing to Learn.* Norwood, MA: Christopher Gordon.
Bauer, Yehuda. (1978). *The Holocaust in Historical Perspective.* Seattle: University of Washington.

Branson, Margaret S., and Torney–Purta, Judith (Eds.). (1982). *International Human Rights, Society, and the Schools.* Washington, DC: National Council for the Social Studies.

Coalition of Essential Schools. (1989, June). "Asking the Essential Questions: Curriculum Development." *Horace, 5*(5):1–6.

Darsa, Jan. (1991). "Educating About the Holocaust," pp. 175–193. In Israel Charny (Ed.) *Genocide: A Critical Bibliographic Review.* Volume Two. London: Mansell.

Dawidowicz, Lucy S. (1992). "How They Teach the Holocaust." In Lucy S. Dawidowicz, *What is the Use of Jewish History?* New York: Schocken.

Eisner, Elliot. (1979). *The Educational Imagination: On the Design and Evaluation of School Programs.* New York: Macmillan.

Friedlander, Henry. (1979). "Toward a Methodology of Teaching About the Holocaust." *Teachers College Record, 80*(5): 519–542.

Katz, Stephen. (1994). *The Holocaust in Historical Context: Volume 1: The Holocaust and Mass Death Before the Modern Age.* New York: Oxford University Press of New England.

Langer, Lawrence L. (1978). *The Age of Atrocity: Death in Modern Literature.* Boston: Beacon Press.

Langer, Lawrence L. (1995). *Admitting the Holocaust: Collected Essays.* New York: Oxford University Press.

Lipstadt, Deborah. (March 6, 1995). "Not Facing the History." *The New Republic,* pp. 26–27, 29.

National Council for the Social Studies. (1991, February). Special Issue ("Teaching About Genocide") of *Social Education, 55*(2). [Edited by Samuel Totten and William S. Parsons.]

Newmann, Fred. (1988, January). "Can Depth Replace Coverage in the High School Curriculum?" *Phi Delta Kappan,* pp. 345–348.

Niewyk, Donald L. (1995). "Holocaust: The Genocide of the Jews," pp. 167–184. In Samuel Totten, William S. Parsons, and Israel W. Charny (Eds.) *Genocide in the Twentieth Century: Critical Essays and Eyewitness Accounts.* New York: Garland.

Oliner, Pearl M. and Oliner, Samuel P. (1991). "Righteous People in the Holocaust," pp. 363–385. In Israel Charny (Ed.) *Genocide: A Critical Bibliographic Review.* London and New York: Mansell Publishing and Facts on File.

Parsons, William S., and Totten, Samuel. (1993). *Guidelines for Teaching About the Holocaust.* Washington, D.C.: United States Holocaust Memorial Museum.

President's Commission on the Holocaust. (1979). *Report to the President.* Washington, D.C.: Author. [One page handout.]

Rosenberg, Alan, and Bardosh, Alexander. (Fall/Winter 1982–1983). "The Problematic Character of Teaching the Holocaust." *Shoah,* pp. 3–7, 20.

Schwartz, Donald. (1990, February). "Who Will Tell Them After We're Gone?": Reflections on Teaching the Holocaust." *The History Teacher, 23*(2):95–110.

Shawn, Karen. (1995). "Current Issues in Holocaust Education." *Dimensions: A Journal of Holocaust Studies, 9*(2):15–18.

Sizer, Theodore R. (1984). *Horace's Compromise: The Dilemma of the American High School.* Boston: Houghton Mifflin.

Strom, Margot Stern, and Parsons, William S. (1982). *Facing History and Ourselves: Holocaust and Human Behavior.* Watertown, MA: Intentional Educations.

Totten, Samuel. (1987). "The Personal Fate of Genocide: Curricula and Inservice Training." Special issue of the *Social Science Record* ("Genocide, Issues, Approaches, Resources") *24*(2):63–67.

Totten, Samuel. (1991). "Educating about Genocide: Curricula and Inservice Training," pp. 194–225. In Israel W. Charny (1991) *Genocide: A Critical Bibliographic Review*. Volume 2. London: Mansell.

Totten, Samuel. (1991). *First-Person Accounts of Genocidal Acts Committed in the Twentieth Century: An Annotated Bibliography*. Westport, CT: Greenwood Press.

Totten, Samuel, and Parsons, William S. (Spring 1992). "State-Developed Teacher Guides and Curricula on Genocide and/or the Holocaust: A Succinct Review and Critique." *Inquiry in Social Studies: Curriculum, Research, and Instruction. The Journal of the North Carolina Council for the Social Studies*, 28(1):27–47.

Totten, Samuel. (Summer 1994). "The Use of First-Person Accounts in Teaching About the Holocaust." *The British Journal of Holocaust Education*, 3(1): 53–76.

Totten, Samuel. (1994, November). "Educating About Genocide: Progress is Being Made, But Much Still Needs to be Done." *Internet on the Holocaust and Genocide*, Special Triple Issue, 51/52/53.

Totten, Samuel, and Feinberg, Stephen. (1995, October). "Teaching About the Holocaust: Rationale, Content, Methodology, & Resources." *Social Education*, 59(6):323–327, 329, 331–333.

Totten, Samuel. (1998, February). "The Start Is as Important as the Finish in a Holocaust Study." *Social Education*, 62(2):70–76

Totten, Samuel. (Spring 1999). "Teaching the Holocaust: The Imperative to Move Beyond Clichés." *Canadian Social Studies*, 33(3):84–87

Totten, Samuel. (in press). "Nothing About a Study of the Holocaust Should Be Perfunctory, Including Its Close: Suggestions for Closing a Lesson, Unit or Study on the Holocaust." *Social Education*.

Totten, Samuel, and Riley, Karen (n.d.). "The Problem of Inaccurate History in State-Developed/Sponsored Holocaust and Genocide Curricula and Teacher Guides: A Challenge to Scholars of the Holocaust and Genocide."

United States Holocaust Memorial Museum. (1995). "Frequently Asked Questions About the Holocaust." Handout. Washington, DC: Author.

Wiesel, Elie. (1984). "All Was Lost, Yet Something Was Preserved." Review of *The Chronicle of the Lodz Ghetto, 1941–1944*. *New York Times Book Review*, pp. 1, 23.

Wiesel, Elie. (1979). Preface. *Report to the President*. Washington, DC: President's Commission on the Holocaust.

Wiesel, Elie. (1978). "Then and Now: The Experiences of a Teacher." *Social Education*, 42(4): 266–271.

NOTES

1. Speaking of the need to address the issue of antisemitism but taking a different slant than that of Dawidowicz, Friedlander (1979) has suggested that: "Studies of modern anti-Semitism are more useful. They analyze the social roots and political uses of modern anti-Semitism; they trace the birth of the anti-Semitic parties and of their transformation into totalitarian movements. They show how the new anti-Semitism based on race differed qualitatively from the preceding type based on religion. They thus delineate the radical nature of modern anti-Semitism. But because they usually do not include the demonic, they fail to provide a fully satisfying explanation of how this ideology could lead to genocide" (p. 528).

CHAPTER

2 Establishing a Foundation for a Study of the Holocaust: Assessing the Students' Knowledge Base

As with any study, it is vitally important to ascertain the knowledge base possessed by students before examination of the subject begins. To neglect to do so may result in a waste of time (e.g., possibly addressing information the students already know), not to mention frustration on both the students' part (e.g., their attempting to learn something that doesn't mesh with their present understanding) and the teacher's (e.g., not accomplishing one's goals and objectives). Also important is for students to express their interests and concerns about the subject. Toward these ends I have designed a series of opening activities with the express purpose of discovering:

- students' current knowledge base about the Holocaust, including their knowledge of basic facts as well as any inaccurate information and misconceptions they hold;
- students' depth of knowledge about the Holocaust, including their understanding of connections between and among key issues, events, and personages;
- students' crucial questions and concerns about the Holocaust; that is, what they most want to learn or discover in the course of this study.

In this chapter I delineate four types of opening activities that can help frame a study of the Holocaust. Quite obviously, they are not the only procedures available for assessing student knowledge of the subject, but all have been effective in setting the stage for an in-depth study of the Holocaust.

Developing a Cluster/Mind-Map

An engaging and effective strategy for ascertaining the depth of student knowledge vis-à-vis the Holocaust (or for that matter, any topic) is to have them develop a cluster (alternatively referred to as a mind-map, web, or conceptual map) around the "target" word/event "Holocaust." A cluster has been defined as "a nonlinear brainstorming process that generates ideas, images, and feeling around a stimulus word until a pattern becomes discernible" (Rico, 1987, p. 17). More graphically, teacher Michael O'Brien (1987) defined clustering in the following manner: "Think of them as flowers. Clusters do, after all, resemble flowers whose petals burst forth from the central corolla. Note that clusters do beautifully in both remedial and advanced classes. . . ." (p. 25).

To develop a cluster, have students write the term "Holocaust" in the center of a piece of paper (a minimum of 8½" by 11"), circle it, and then draw spokes out from the circle on which to place related terms or ideas. Each time a term is added, they should circle it and draw new spokes for relating it to other terms and concepts. Each new or related idea may thus lead to a new clustering of ideas. As Rico (1987) points out: "A cluster is an expanding universe, and each word is a potential galaxy; each galaxy, in turn, may throw out its own universes. As students cluster around a stimulus word, the encircled words rapidly radiate outward until a sudden shift takes place, a sort of 'Aha!' that signals a sudden awareness of that tentative whole . . ." (p. 17). Furthermore, "Since a cluster draws on primary impressions—yet simultaneously on a sense of the overall design—clustering actually generates structure, shaping one thought into a starburst of other thoughts, each somehow related to the whole" (Rico, 1987, p. 18).

Clustering is a more graphic, generally easier and more engaging way to delineate what one knows about a topic than outlining it. (For excellent and thought-provoking discussions by classroom teachers regarding the clustering method, see Carol Booth Olson, *Practical Ideas for Teaching Writing as a Process.* Sacramento: California State Department of Education, 1996.)

To help students understand both the purpose for and the method of clustering, the teacher should choose a topic and demonstrate the development of a cluster, progressing from simple to more complex stages. More specifically, the teacher should first create a simple, almost perfunctory, cluster and then a more complex cluster on the same topic. The two clusters should be used as a nonexemplar (e.g., the simplistic cluster) and an exemplar (the more complex cluster). *It is important not to develop a cluster on the Holocaust, as students may be tempted to (or simply unable not to) replicate the same kinds of information and connections that the teacher has demonstrated.*

In directing students to develop a cluster, teachers should encourage them to create the most detailed, comprehensive, and accurate one possible. At the same time, the students should be encouraged to strive to delineate the connections between or among key items/concepts/events/ideas. *If such directions are not given and emphasized, many students are likely to develop very simple, if not simplistic, clusters.*

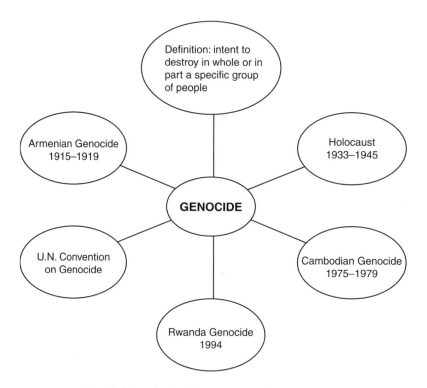

FIGURE 1   Simple/Simplistic Cluster or Mind-Map

Once each student has completed a cluster, groups comprised of three to four students should meet in order to share and discuss their individual clusters. Each student should be given time (two to three minutes) to explain his or her cluster by giving:

- a quick overview of key points
- reasons why these ideas were chosen
- an explanation of the connections between or among the various ideas

As students present their clusters, others in the group may add items to their own clusters in a color other than the one originally used in order to indicate the number and type of ideas shared. At the end of this session, all of the clusters may be taped to the classroom wall or stored for revisiting during the course of the Holocaust study.

Developing clusters serves a number of key purposes. First, it may assist a student to recognize what he or she does and does not know about the subject. Second, the teacher gains a vivid illustration of a student's depth of knowledge, as well as the sophistication of his or her conceptual framework, of the subject. Third, the teacher is able to pinpoint specific inaccuracies, misconceptions, and/or myths

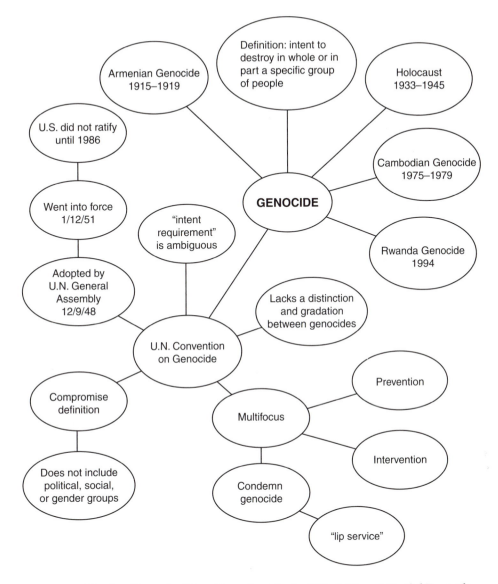

FIGURE 2   Moving Toward a More Complex Cluster/Mind-Map: A Partial Example

that students hold about the Holocaust. In other words, the activity serves as a powerful preassessment exercise.

Clustering also provides students with a unique method to express their ideas; and in doing so, it allows them to tap into an "intelligence" (e.g., spatial) other than the typical one of writing (linguistic). (For an informative discussion on how to incorporate multiple intelligences into the classroom, see also Thomas

Armstrong, *Multiple Intelligences in the Classroom*. Alexandria, VA: Association for Supervision and Curriculum Development, 1994.)

At the conclusion of the study (and/or at a midway point), students could be asked to complete another cluster. Doing so provides both the students and the teacher with a vivid sense as to the students' new acquisition of increased knowledge, insights, and connections between and among topics, and whether this new-found knowledge is of a greater depth and sophistication than at the outset of the study. This, of course, serves as a powerful way of conducting a postassessment (and/or formative) exercise.

As a postassessment exercise, the same kind of small group discussion that began the study could take place. Alternatively, students could be asked to individually compare and contrast their clusters (initial, midpoint, and final) by addressing one or more of the following questions:

- What is the most pronounced difference between these clusters, and what does this tell you about your knowledge base in regard to the Holocaust?
- What items on your final cluster do you think a person must definitely know in order to begin to understand the Holocaust? Why?
- What was the most revelatory insight you gleaned from your study of the Holocaust? Why?

Using the Cluster to Develop a Working Definition of the Holocaust

Next, using the information (facts, concepts, connections) they have included in their clusters, I have each student develop a working definition of the Holocaust. In doing so, I suggest that they look carefully at all of the components of their cluster and then make every effort to develop the most comprehensive and accurate definition they possibly can. I also inform them that as they refine their definition, if they discover they have left out key facts or concepts or failed to make certain connections, then they should add such information to their clusters.

Once everyone has developed a definition, I place the students in groups of three to four (the original or new groups) to share their definitions. A recorder in each group is chosen to take down the salient points of the discussion that ensues as each definition is read. At the conclusion of the small group discussions, we hold a general class discussion during which we place any questions or points about which students are unsure on a large sheet of paper with the heading "Holocaust: Issues to Resolve and/or Examine in More Detail." I explain that as we proceed with our study we will return to these questions/concerns and attempt to answer them. In doing so, I explain, we will attempt to clarify our understanding of what the Holocaust was (and/or wasn't) as well as come to a more comprehensive and accurate definition.

To simply provide the students with an accepted definition of the Holocaust (for example, the one used by the United States Holocaust Memorial Museum) would be easier and faster but less pedagogically sound than the method I've described. By using their own knowledge and insights to construct a definition, students are likely to develop an understanding of why scholars too wrestle over definitions—and why definitions are so important in framing an understanding of complex issues and events. This process, of course, does not preclude the examination of various scholars' definitions of the Holocaust at a later time. Doing so often deepens the students' thinking about the historical process as well as their understanding of the Holocaust.

Again, as with the clusters, the development of such student definitions provides the teacher with valuable insights into his or her students' understanding of the Holocaust, including their depth of knowledge, misconceptions, and so on. This, of course, serves as another powerful preassessment exercise.

What follows are samples of the definitions that high school students (grades 10, 11, and 12) developed at the outset of one study of the Holocaust. These examples are purposely grouped in sets according to the types of information found in them.

The initial set includes those definitions that were the *least inaccurate* among the definitions developed by the students. (Note: The wording "least inaccurate" has been used to highlight the fact that *all* of the following definitions lack key ideas or information as to why the Holocaust was implemented. *On another note, the following definitions are not included here as a form of criticism; rather, they are enumerated in order to illustrate the type of misconceptions that some students may hold about the Holocaust. Such information is valuable for teachers to know, for it avails them of key issues that need to be addressed at some point during the study.*)

> *Holocaust:* When the Nazis decided the Jews were the cause of Germany's problems. In World War II the Nazis tortured and killed Jews. The Nazis wanted a genocide of the Jews.

> *Holocaust:* To gain political power, Hitler blamed the Jews for Germany's hardships after World War I. This created much of the negative sentiment necessary for Hitler to come to rule Germany. He began imprisoning Jewish people in concentration camps. Eventually millions were murdered and treated like animals.

> *Holocaust:* The persecution and/or extermination of people of primarily Jewish background by the Nazis during World War II, involving the creation of Jewish ghettos, forced labor forces, and concentration camps.

> *Holocaust:* Persecution of Jews during the 1940s in Germany and near areas of Europe; led by Adolf Hitler, a Nazi dictator; took place during World War II; many Jews died in concentration camps due to crowded housing and gas chambers. They were cremated.

> *Holocaust:* A time during World War II when Hitler's Nazi party punished the Jews for "causing all of Germany's problems." The Jews were forced to wear the yellow Star of David and had virtually no rights. Many were sent to concentration camps, and many died.

Holocaust: Hitler forced Jews into hiding and killed six million Jews in concentration camps. Jews were forced to wear the Star of David, and be segregated from others because Hitler believed that the Germans were the supreme race.

When comparing the above definitions with that used by the United States Holocaust Memorial Museum (1994), one can readily discern the gaps in the students' definitions:

The Holocaust refers to a specific event in 20th-century history: the state-sponsored, systematic persecution and annihilation of European Jewry by Nazi Germany and its collaborators between 1933 and 1945. Jews were the primary victims—six million were murdered; Gypsies, the handicapped, and Poles were also targeted for destruction or decimation for racial, ethnic, or national reasons. Millions more, including homosexuals, Jehovah's Witnesses, Soviet prisoners of war, and political dissidents, also suffered grievous oppression and death under Nazi tyranny. (p. 3)

In addition to leaving out a good number of key concerns, very few of the students' definitions display awareness of the major historical trends that contributed to the Holocaust. As scholar Donald Niewyk (1995) has pointed out: "A number of historical trends combined to make the Holocaust possible: anti-Semitism, racism, social Darwinism, extreme nationalism, totalitarianism, industrialism, and the nature of modern war. The absence of any one of these trends would have made the genocide of the Jews unlikely" (p. 175). Also obvious is the fact that some students confused "concentration camps" with "death camps," or at least didn't distinguish between the two. That said, the students who developed these definitions were at least on the right track in regard to what Nazi Germany was about and who was victimized. Still, the students have a tremendous amount to learn about why and how the Holocaust was implemented.

The next set of definitions not only are bereft of key information but are all flawed in major ways. More specifically, many include various inaccuracies and misconceptions:

Holocaust: The destruction of an entire race by a pathological maniac who felt he was in his right as playing God destroying one race and creating a better one.

Holocaust: The Germans boycotted the Jews and Adolf Hitler had his army ship them off to concentration camps where they were starved to death.

Holocaust: Discrimination against Jews by Germans in which they were forced into concentration camps, tortured, murdered, gassed, and it caused a world war. Hitler ran the Nazis party.

Holocaust: A time in history many of us wish we could forget. The Nazi German type of people were beaten, raped, murdered, put in concentration camps and shot just because they look [sic] different or other things.

Holocaust: The Holocaust was between 1939–1945. It was when Hitler gathered people (mostly Jews) and put them into death camps, or just killed them. Jews were educated people, and when they started taking most of the jobs, that's when the trouble started. Millions of people died and families were torn apart.

Holocaust: During World War II Nazi Germany had a problem with Jews. The Holocaust was when the Nazis killed 45 million Jews during that time period.

As one can ascertain, the inaccuracies and misconceptions of some of the students are, to say the least, glaring. Some refer to the Jews as a race (which they are not, although the Nazis referred to them as such; see Chapter 5 in this book for a discussion of this issue). Several believe that the Holocaust was the result of one man's efforts (when, in fact, it involved the Nazi hierarchy, the SS who ran the camps, and tens of thousands of others who contributed in various ways). Others suggest that the destruction of the Jews was *the* cause for the world to go to war (it wasn't the persecution of the Jews, but rather the Nazis' bellicosity and Nazi Germany's attacks on other nations); that the Jews were prospering in Germany when no one else was and/or at everyone else's expense (which is simply flat wrong); that the Nazis killed 45 million Jews (in fact, they killed approximately six million Jews and five million other people); and that the sole mistreatment of the Jews was their starvation by the Nazis (they were murdered in numerous ways, including being shot, hanged, starved to death, beaten to death and, of course, gassed).

The most glaring misconception, of course, is that of the student who totally misconstrues who the victims and perpetrators were (e.g., "the Nazi German type of people were beaten, raped, murdered, put in concentration camps, and shot just because they look [sic] different or other things"). Worth noting again is the fact that not a single student mentions the issue of antisemitism, let alone the rabid and poisonous form of deadly antisemitism practiced by the Nazis. Nor do any mention the critical issue of racism and how the Nazi philosophy was predicated on race.

Positing Gnawing Questions about the Holocaust

After the students have developed and discussed their clusters and their definitions of the Holocaust, I have each student write down (anonymously) three to five "gnawing questions" they have about the Holocaust. I explain that their questions can be about any and all facets of the Holocaust, and that throughout our study, we will wrestle with and attempt to find answers to their questions. I also explain that certain questions may never be answered—that both scholars and survivors are still wrestling with many thorny questions and that in certain cases no answers may ever be found. In such cases, I explain, we will try to figure out why.

Soliciting students' questions and concerns helps to make the study of the Holocaust more focused and personal. Moreover, it encourages students to become active researchers in a class, as opposed to passive participants. By raising their own questions, students can actively seek answers to their questions and to the conundrums in history.

Although I request that students submit at least one question, the majority come up with at least three. This, I believe, is indicative of their genuine interest in the subject matter and their appreciation of having their own concerns and questions solicited for the express purpose of helping to frame the study.

Among the many questions (all quoted exactly as they were written) that students have posited are:

- Why exactly did the Holocaust happen?
- What was the main factor that caused this genocide?
- What percent of Germany's population was Jewish during the time of the Holocaust's beginning?
- Why were Jews blamed in the first place?
- How many people actually survived the Holocaust?
- How did Hitler get into office?
- Why did Hitler have so much power?
- What was Hitler's main motive for killing all the Jews?
- How did the Jews become so hated?
- Did this effect [sic] America?
- Why are we usually only taught that Jews were persecuted?
- Why didn't all the people in the camps rebel at once, so that their [sic] may have been a hope for freedom?
- Who else was eventually included with the Jews, and why?
- Was there any dissention [sic] among the German ranks regarding following orders which lead [sic] to the mass extermination of Jews?
- Why didn't the U.S. try and step in sooner?
- What are warning signs of something like the Holocaust, and how can we stop it from happening again?
- Why???

Many of these questions penetrate to the core of the tragedy of the Holocaust. Others are more concerned with key facts (chronology, number of people who were murdered by the Nazis, number of survivors). Some questions, not listed here, were indicative of some of the misconceptions that the students have (for example, that Hitler was the only person behind the genocide of the Jews). Whatever the nature of the question, it is acceptable, as the purpose of the study is to help students gain a deeper, more accurate, and ultimately more profound understanding of the tragedy of the Holocaust.

Some teachers may perceive the soliciting of such questions and concerns as an added burden. I see the task as an opportunity to help me frame the study in a way that becomes even more meaningful than it might be otherwise. Further, addressing such concerns can be done in a host of ways—none of which are particularly onerous; for example, using key readings, lectures, or guest speakers, activities such as the Jigsaw cooperative learning strategy, individual and/or group research projects, and so on.

At the conclusion of the study, it is wise to ascertain whether all of the students sense that their questions have been, if not answered, at least examined in some detail. Those questions that are still unexamined should have a period or two dedicated to them, if possible.

Questionnaire: Another Option

At the conclusion of the above activities, I have the students answer a short questionnaire about the Holocaust. Some teachers may consider this to be going a bit overboard; however, I find the additional information it provides to be useful. Indeed, throughout the study, I refer to the questionnaires to refresh my memory as to what we need to be sure to address.

It is also worth noting that some educators may find such a questionnaire reductive or simplistic. Some may even claim that by setting up questions in such a fashion (true/false, multiple choice, short answer), one is setting up students to want simple (if not simplistic) answers later. Personally, I disagree with both arguments. Again, one needs to understand and appreciate that this is simply a "quick and dirty" preassessment aimed at establishing the students' basic knowledge. Using such an instrument at the outset of the study does not dictate that the subsequent study should be directed at providing simple answers to complex questions and/or issues during the course of the rest of the study. Not only would that be counterproductive, but it would constitute miseducation. That said, if one looks askance at the use of such instruments, then he or she should not use them.

It is worth noting that the questionnaire below includes some key questions (e.g., those that are critical to gaining a deeper understanding of the Holocaust) that many students did not address in their clusters, definitions, and discussions of the Holocaust. Depending on the group of students, it can be as sophisticated and detailed as the teacher sees fit. A sample of a questionnaire that I used with a combination of tenth-, eleventh-, and twelfth-grade students is as follows:

Questionnaire—Holocaust

1. What does the word "holocaust" mean? (When answering this question, don't tell what the Holocaust was but rather tell what the word "holocaust" actually means.)

2. What was the Holocaust? (When answering this question, try to tell what actually happened, who was involved, why it took place, when it took place, etc.)

3. During what time period did the Holocaust take place?
   A. _____ 1833–1845   B. _____ 1915–1925
   C. _____ 1933–1945   D. _____ 1945–1956

4. Place a "x" next to each of the historical trends that combined to make the Holocaust possible (you may mark as many or as few as necessary):

A. _____ antisemitism   B. _____ racism
C. _____ social Darwinism   D. _____ extreme nationalism
E. _____ totalitarianism   F. _____ industrialism
G. _____ the nature of modern war   H. _____ others

5. What were the Nuremberg Laws? (Try to answer each of the following: the purpose of the laws, who implemented them, the date when they were implemented, and the type of restrictions imposed by the laws.)

6. Jews constitute a race.
   True _____   False _____   Not Sure _____

6a. Please explain your answer to #6.

7. The Holocaust was not inevitable. In other words, it did not have to happen. Rather, it occurred because individuals, organizations, and governments made choices which not only legalized discrimination, but which allowed prejudice, hatred, and ultimately, mass murder to occur.
   True _____   False _____   Not Sure _____

7a. Please explain your answer to #7.

8. All concentration camps were designated "killing centers."
   True _____   False _____   Not Sure _____

8a. Please explain your answer to #8.

9. Whereas not all victims of the Nazis were Jews, all Jews were victims, destined for annihilation simply because they were born Jewish.
   True _____   False _____   Not Sure _____

10. At best, less than one-half of one percent of the total population (of non-Jews) under Nazi occupation helped to rescue Jews.
   True _____   False _____   Not Sure _____

11. The Jews were the only people whom the Nazis purposely murdered.
   True _____   False _____   Not Sure _____

11a. Please explain your answer to #11.

12. The Holocaust was a result of the fact that the Jews did something wrong and thus were being punished by the Nazis.
   True _____   False _____   Not Sure _____

12a. Please explain your answer to #12.

13. Define the term/concept "genocide." Be as accurate and comprehensive as possible.

14. Since the conclusion of World War II, and the end of the Holocaust, no genocide has taken place in the world.
   True _____   False _____   Not Sure _____

14a. Please explain your answer to #14.

A Chronological Approach

Still another approach to introducing a study of the Holocaust is one that Steve Feinberg, a former middle school teacher in Wayland, Massachusetts and now a Holocaust educator at the United States Holocaust Memorial Museum, used with his students. This chronological approach aims at assessing students' knowledge base of the Holocaust while generating an initial discussion of various aspects of Holocaust history. On one side of the blackboard, Feinberg wrote the dates 1933–1939, and on the other side he wrote 1939–1945. The Holocaust period is, generally speaking, divided into these two periods (1933–1939 being the rise of the Nazis to power, and 1939–1945 being the dates of World War II as well as part of the period during which the "Final Solution" was implemented). Then, as he called out a series of items (an event, the imposition of a law or act, the establishment of a ghetto or camp, etc.), one at a time, he asked his students which heading each belonged under. As a student called out an answer, Feinberg asked whether there was agreement or disagreement with the student's decision. If there was disagreement, a discussion ensued during which Feinberg encouraged the class members to share their ideas. He interjected information when appropriate. Ultimately, he transferred the information to butcher paper and hung it up for the duration of the study.

This ostensibly simple process is in fact a thought-provoking jumping off point for a study of the Holocaust. It also provides the students with a visual aid that they can revisit during the course of the study and to which they can add additional information as they grapple with this complex history.

Examining One's Own Life in Relation to Issues of Prejudice, Discrimination, and Abuse of Power

Jan Darsa, a longtime associate of the noted Facing History and Ourselves program in Brookline, Massachusetts, suggests that one of the more powerful ways that she has found to begin a study of the Holocaust is to have students examine their own lives in regard to such issues as peer pressure, scapegoating, power, abuse of power, blind obedience, justice, and survival. As she says:

> It is often easy for students to distance themselves from the events of forty years ago; to see themselves as somehow a superior generation incapable of such crimes. Yet, all students can recount instances when they were bullied, when they participated in bullying, or when they didn't speak up about cruelty that they witnessed. Perhaps this should be the first part of any course in genocide, so that as students examine themselves, they will understand how their lives today relate to the events of the Holocaust. If students understand that the Holocaust involved average people making decisions and everyday choices, then they can reflect on the consequences of their own actions and begin to see themselves as participants in history. (Darsa, 1991, p. 181)

The key, of course, is to help the students make vital distinctions between what the victims of the Holocaust suffered and why and what the students themselves have personally experienced. What teachers *must not* do in attempting to help their students make connections between the history and their own lives is "elide the difference between the Holocaust and all manner of inhumanities and injustices" (Lipstadt, 1995, p. 27).

Conclusion

Experience has taught me that a study of the Holocaust that begins with a thorough examination of what the students know, don't know, and want to know ultimately contributes to a more potent and meaningful understanding of this tragic event. The activities described in this chapter are only a few of the many effective ways a teacher can initiate this study. My ultimate goal is to devise a study of the Holocaust in which *all* students are left with something to ponder for the rest of their lives. Then and only then, it seems, will such a study be worth the time, effort, and agony of confronting such horrific events and issues.

REFERENCES

Armstrong, Thomas. (1994). *Multiple Intelligences in the Classroom.* Alexandria, VA: Association for Supervision and Curriculum Development.

Darsa, Jan. (1991). "Educating About the Holocaust," pp. 175–193. In Israel W. Charny (Ed.), *Genocide: A Critical Bibliographic Review.* Volume II. New York: Facts On File.

Gardner, Howard. (1983). *Frames of Mind: The Theory of Multiple Intelligences.* New York: Basic Books.

Gardner, Howard. (1993). *Multiple Intelligences: The Theory in Practice.* New York: Basic Books.

Lipstadt, Deborah. (March 6, 1995). "Not Facing History." *The New Republic,* pp. 26–27, 29.

Niewyk, Donald. (1995). "Holocaust: Genocide of the Jews," pp. 167–207. In Samuel Totten, William S. Parsons, and Israel W. Charny (Eds.), *Genocide in the Twentieth Century: Critical Essays and Eyewitness Accounts.* New York: Garland.

O'Brien, Michael. (1987). "Propagating Clusters," p. 25. In Carol Booth Olson (Ed.), *Practical Ideas for Teaching Writing As a Process.* Sacramento: California State Department of Education.

Parsons, William S., and Totten, Samuel. (1993). *Guidelines for Teaching About the Holocaust.* Washington, DC: United States Holocaust Memorial Museum.

Rico, Gabrielle. (1987). "Clustering: A Prewriting Process," pp. 17–20. In Carol Booth Olson (Ed.), *Practical Ideas for Teaching Writing As a Process.* Sacramento: California State Department of Education.

United States Holocaust Memorial Museum. (1994). "Guidelines for Teaching About the Holocaust," pp. 1–15. In *Teaching About the Holocaust: A Resource Book for Educators.* Washington, DC: Author.

CHAPTER

3 Selecting Essential Issues and Topics for a Study of the Holocaust

With a limited amount of time to teach about any topic, teachers often agonize over which aspects constitute essential information and thus merit the most attention. This dilemma becomes particularly acute when teaching an event as complex as the Holocaust—an event that spanned twelve years, engulfed dozens of countries and millions of people in innumerable ways, and involved such issues as racial antisemitism, social Darwinism, totalitarianism, industrialism, and bureaucratic structures. Whether a teacher is teaching a three-day unit, a two-week unit, or a semester-long unit on the Holocaust, he or she will inevitably face making critical and difficult decisions regarding what to address and not address during the course of the study.

An "essential topic" is largely determined by the specific aspects of the Holocaust to be examined. The latter is dictated largely by a teacher's rationales, goals, and objectives and whether he or she is teaching a single lesson, a weeklong unit, or semester-long study. It is also contingent on the age and developmental level of the students. Ultimately, the availability of resources also comes into play. Before making a final decision about what to teach, it is imperative for the teacher to consider the full scope of the Holocaust and the myriad issues that comprise the event. Then and only then will teachers likely teach something of value to their students.

The purpose of this chapter is threefold: (1) to highlight effective ways for teachers to familiarize themselves with key issues and topics of the Holocaust; (2) to delineate essential topics teachers need to consider prior to developing and teaching a lesson or unit on the Holocaust; and (3) to provide concrete suggestions as to how teachers can begin to narrow the selection of topics for specific units of study.

Examining Historiographical Essays and Major Historical Works in Order to Familiarize Oneself with Key Topics

Familiarizing Oneself with Key Issues and Topics

Prior to selecting essential topics for a study, teachers must develop rationales, goals, and objectives that complement the focus of the study. (See Chapter 1 for a detailed discussion about rationales.) Developing sound rationales and goals naturally involves teachers in wrestling with why they wish to teach this history in the first place, and what they deem to be the most important aspects of the history and why that is so. *However, before making a decision about the goals and objectives, one needs to become conversant with the many and significant topics that are germane to that focus of the study.*

A good starting point for becoming conversant with key issues and topics—including historical trends that combined to make the Holocaust possible as well as more general facts (major figures, decisions, actions, regulations, dates)—is the examination of major historiographical essays on the Holocaust. By reading historiographical essays, educators are likely to gain a clear sense of the field's development. By immersing oneself in such literature, educators will: (1) become conversant with major aspects of the history; (2) ascertain what various scholars perceive as the major historical trends that combined to make the Holocaust possible, thus gaining key insights into the *whys* behind the "whats," "wheres," "hows," and "whos" of the Holocaust—something many teachers tend to overlook in their lessons and units; (3) gain insights into *how and why* various scholars interpret the events, thus recognizing that there is not total agreement about the "whys" behind the "whats"; and (4) begin to ascertain and wrestle with those aspects of the history that they think are most important for secondary level students to know about the Holocaust. Some may perceive this as a daunting task. *However, the significance of this event demands that those who teach this history be conversant with the key historical trends and major facts.* Those educators who do not take the time and effort to become conversant with such aspects of this history are liable to teach it in a watered-down, simplistic and, ultimately, miseducative manner. (Some valuable sources on the historiography of the Holocaust are: Abraham Edelheit [1990], "Historiography of the Holocaust"; Saul Friedländer [1997], "The Extermination of the European Jews in Historiography: Fifty Years Later"; Y. Gutman and G. Greif [1988], *The Historiography of the Holocaust Period*; Michael R. Marrus [1987], *The Holocaust in History*; Karen J. Greenberg [1996], "The Burden of Being Human: An Essay on Selected Scholarship of the Holocaust," and Michael Marrus [2001], "Historiography," in Walter Laqueur [Ed.], *The Holocaust Encyclopedia*.)

Reading Key Histories in the Field

Another effective way to become familiar with key issues and topics on the Holocaust is to read some of the more highly acclaimed histories of the Holocaust. If someone cares enough to teach about this event, then he or she should be willing to put in the time and effort to thoroughly prepare him or herself to do so as effectively as possible.

By reading key works by some of the more distinguished and respected scholars (e.g., Yehuda Bauer, 1982; Christopher Browning, 1995; Lucy Dawidowicz, 1986; Henry Friedlander, 1995; Saul Friedländer, 1997; Raul Hilberg, 1985; Michael R. Marrus, 1987; Sybil Milton, 1995; Donald Niewyk, 1995; Leni Yahil, 1990) in the field, teachers will gain a sense of the history and a deeper appreciation for the complexity of the issues. The latter will provide a road map for developing a unit of study around key ideas, concepts, and events.

Examining Major and Authoritative Chronologies of the Holocaust to Determine Essential Topics

An enlightening exercise for educators is to read each and every entry in an authoritative chronology of the Holocaust, noting significant topics (e.g., the Enabling Act, the Nuremberg Laws, the Anschluss, Kristallnacht, The Wannsee Conference) and trends (e.g., the ever-increasing discrimination against the Jews, which could be broken down into how they were defined, isolated, excluded, segregated, impoverished, and ultimately murdered by the Nazis; and the development and "sophistication" of the killing process of "the other") that an individual needs to be cognizant of to be fairly well informed about the history of the Holocaust. Prior to analyzing such a chronology, it is a good idea to develop a "legend" to assist oneself in differentiating between various topics and trends. This can be done by assigning colors (e.g., blue for topics and red for trends) or initials ("top" for topics and "tr" for trends) to each category that is to be highlighted. Once the topics and trends have been delineated, a new color or initialing system can be used to represent *specific sets* of topics and trends. Finally, to make full use of such information it is handy to incorporate it into a master chart or schematic diagram.

For this exercise, it is wise to select chronologies developed by leading historians, versus those created by curriculum developers, state departments of education, or individual teachers. In following the latter advice, an educator is more likely to use an accurate and comprehensive chronology as opposed to one that is derivative and possibly rife with errors. Unfortunately, many of the chronologies "developed" and/or used by curriculum developers, state departments of education, or individual teachers are often based on chronologies published in other educational materials and, more often than not, such materials are bereft of key decisions, promulgations, and events, and/or include incorrect dates and names of people and places. It should go without saying that it is pointless to use historically inaccurate information in such a study. (A good starting point for obtaining an accurate chronology is to request an official one developed by the United States Holocaust Memorial Museum, 100 Raoul Wallenberg Place, SW, Washington, DC

20024–2126, or Yad Vashem, The Holocaust and Martyrs' and Heroes' Remembrance Authority in Jerusalem, P.O.B. 3477, Jerusalem 91034, Israel).

Consulting Major Pedagogical Essays and Critiques of Holocaust Curricula/Units in Order to Determine Essential Topics

Other useful sources for determining essential issues and topics are *select* pedagogical essays on teaching the Holocaust and critiques of Holocaust curricula, units, and lessons. Among the most useful essays and critiques are those written by noted Holocaust historians, particularly those who have taught courses on the Holocaust and have wrestled with the most effective way for doing so. Essays by such individuals offer valuable insights into what educators should both avoid and strive for when developing curricula or teaching about this history. Three such pieces, one pedagogical essay and two critiques, each by a noted Holocaust historian, shall be highlighted herein.

Written in 1979, Holocaust scholar and survivor Henry Friedlander's essay "Toward a Methodology of Teaching About the Holocaust" remains one of the most valuable and insightful pedagogical pieces available on teaching the Holocaust. In his introduction, Friedlander (1979) asserts that "The problems of popularization and proliferation should make us careful about how we introduce the Holocaust into the curriculum; it does not mean that we should stop teaching it. But we must try to define the subject of the Holocaust. Even if we do not agree about the content of the subject, we must agree on its goals and on its limitations" (p. 522). In the rest of his essay, Friedlander discusses goals and objectives, key content issues and topics, and different approaches to teaching this history.

Friedlander's essay is packed with ideas regarding the selection of key issues and topics. Among the issues and topics he suggests teachers consider are: "the German historical setting that produced Hitler and the Nazi movement" (p. 534); totalitarianism; Nazi racial theory; "Jewish history, so that we can understand the victims and their response" (p. 536); "the behavior of the bystanders, the reaction of the outside world to the fate of the Jews" (p. 537); and "the Nazi concentration camps, the arena for the Holocaust" (p. 537). *This essay is a must read for anyone who plans to teach or is currently teaching about the Holocaust.*

As for critiques, both Lucy Dawidowicz and Deborah Lipstadt have written trenchant examinations of available resources that provide ample food for thought. In her essay, "How They Teach the Holocaust," Dawidowicz (1992) reviews twenty-five major Holocaust curricula. Early in her biting but informative critique, she reports that:

> Most curricula plunge right into the story of Hitler's Germany; a few provide some background on the Weimar Republic, presumably to explain Hitler's rise to power. Though all curricula discuss Nazi anti-Semitism, preferring generic terms like "racism" and "prejudice" instead of the specific "anti-Semitism," fifteen of the

twenty-five never even suggest that anti-Semitism had a history before Hitler. Of those that do, barely a handful present coherent historical accounts, however brief. (p. 69)

As previously suggested, if students are to learn the "whys" behind the "whats," it is critical for them to learn about the history of traditional Christian antisemitism through the ages, the advent of political antisemitism in the nineteenth century, and the influences of traditional Christian antisemtism and political antisemitism on the Nazis' virulent and deadly strain of racial antisemitism. As Dawidowicz (1992) states, "To be sure, Christianity cannot be held responsible for Hitler, but the Nazis would not have succeeded in disseminating their brand of racist anti-Semitism had they not been confident of the pervasiveness, firmness, and durability of Christian hatred of Jews. Antisemitism, in the words of the late Ben Halpern, is 'the name of a cumulative tradition of hostility'" (p. 71). To avoid teaching about antisemitism by either couching it in terms of simple prejudice or general bigotry or by "simply" neglecting to mention it is intellectually dishonest and, ultimately, miseducative.

Continuing, Dawidowicz (1992) notes that:

> In studying prejudice or any other generic substitute for anti-Semitism, most curricula focus on individual attitudes, beliefs, and opinions rather than their embodiment in public policy and law. This approach conceives of prejudice as a psychological or mental-health problem, a disease that can be cured: if only every bigot could be put on the analyst's couch, prejudice would be eliminated from society. The failure to distinguish between individual behavior and state policies may be attributable to the relatively benign American experience of anti-Semitism, which, with few exceptions, has been a history of individual prejudices expressed through words and acts in the private sector of society. Yet anti-Semitism as public policy is an essential aspect of what the Holocaust was about, and it too has a history. Whenever anti-Semitism has become the instrument of authority, and been incorporated in the very structure of government, Jews have been deprived of their rights, their property, and ultimately their lives. (p. 74)

If students are not assisted to understand that the Nazis—driven by the ideology of racial antisemitism and social Darwinism—used the official power of government in the development of their policies, then they do not have a clear, let alone true, sense of what was at work in the Nazi regime. Indeed, as Hilberg (1985) clearly delineates, government policies, driven by Nazi ideology, were used to define, expropriate, concentrate, and, ultimately, annihilate the Jews.

Dawidowicz (1992) further observes that ". . . most [curricula and teachers] do not stress the centrality of premeditated mass murder as an instrument of policy" (p. 71). This, too, constitutes a major oversight. It is imperative that an essential topic emerge from the fact that the mass murder perpetrated by the Nazis was premeditated rather than spontaneous; systematic rather than "hit and miss"; and a policy rather than the work of a group of vigilantes or thugs acting on their own, apart from the government. To leave students with the notion that the murder process was anything but systematic is to leave them with the sense that the Holocaust was carried out by a few renegades or "crazies," rather than by a government with its leaders, bureaucracy, laws, and manpower fully behind it.

In her essay, "Not Facing History," Lipstadt's (1995) major concern is with Holocaust curricula that "elides the differences between the Holocaust and all manner of inhumanities and injustices" (p. 27). Although specifically addressing the curriculum developed by Facing History and Ourselves, a major Holocaust education organization based in Massachusetts, Lipstadt's criticism is germane to other Holocaust curriculum as well. In part, she warns against attempting to inoculate students against prejudice by making false comparisons between what took place during the Holocaust period and the racism and violence that has been perpetrated in the United States. She argues persuasively that when curricula engage in such facile comparisons *and* attempt to be relevant to a wide variety of parties, they, intentionally or not, encourage teachers to draw historically fallacious parallels, which results in a distortion of history.

Lipstadt acknowledges the value of studying various genocides, even making comparisons between and among them, but she wisely warns that it is imperative that teachers and students plumb the depths of each separate event to understand both their cause and effect. More specifically, Lipstadt (1995) states,

> The issue is not who lost more people or a greater proportion of their society, but what was at the root of the genocidal efforts. . . . This is not a matter of comparative pain—an utterly useless exercise—but of historical distinction . . .
>
> To say that the Holocaust is not the same as other more local and less bureaucratized and single-minded examples of mass killing is not to rule out all points of comparison. Ultimately, the only way we learn is through comparison. (pp. 27, 29)

A Partial List of Essential Topics

What are some of the other essential issues and topics that educators should become conversant with, again knowing full well that different scholars accede varying degrees of significance to different issues and topics? At a minimum, educators need to grasp the many and complex historical trends that combined to make the Holocaust possible. Without such knowledge, instruction about the Holocaust may be bereft of a focus in regard to what motivated or influenced the decisions and actions of governments, groups, and individuals. In this regard, it is, again, important to ponder the following observation by historian Donald Niewyk (1995): "A number of historical trends combined to make the Holocaust possible: anti-Semitism, racism [including the concept of racial hygiene], social Darwinism, extreme nationalism, totalitarianism, industrialism, and the nature of modern war. The absence of any one of these trends would have made the genocide of the Jews unlikely" (p. 175). Although not all historians may agree with either the statement as a whole or with independent parts of it, it is a good starting point to begin to ascertain and weigh which topics and issues are of the utmost importance to focus on during a study of the Holocaust.

In addition, educators might consider the following topics as they develop their pedagogical plans:

- Jewish life in Europe prior to the Holocaust years
- the long history of traditional Christian antisemitism
- the advent of political antisemitism in the nineteenth century
- the key differences between traditional Christian antisemitisim, political antisemitism, and racial antisemitism
- Germany losing World War I and the imposition and ramifications of the Versailles Treaty on Germany
- the outrageous inflation in the 1920s, the Depression in the 1930s, and the ramifications of both regarding the rise of the Nazi party
- the rise of the Nazi party during the Weimar Republic
- the Nazi electoral victories based on grass roots support
- the Nazi takeover of Germany
- the bureaucratic nature of Nazi policies, including the "legalization" of "exclusionary" policies
- the initial (and ongoing) legislation depriving Jews of their legal rights
- the role of propaganda in the Nazis' effort to demonize, ostracize, and isolate Jews and others
- the totalitarian practices of the Nazis
- the use of terror by the Nazis to instill fear and dread
- the unique combination of religious, political, and the Nazis' virulent and deadly form of racial antisemitism (Friedländer, 1997, p. 7)
- the concept of "racial hygiene" (which was integral to the Nazis' virulent form of racial antisemitism) (Friedlander, 1995; Koonz, 1996, Proctor, 1988)
- the Nuremberg Laws
- the Anschluss
- Kristallnacht
- the signing of the Munich agreement
- the annexation of the Sudetenland by Germany and the establishment of the Czechoslovak Republic
- the invasion of Poland by Germany and the beginning of World War II
- key groups involved (Germans and non-Germans)—perpetrators, collaborators, bystanders, victims, and rescuers
- the "euthanasia" of the mentally and physically handicapped
- the ghettoization of the Jews
- resistance (varied and widespread as well as factors mitigating against it)
- Operation Barbarossa
- the mass killings by the Einsatzgruppen
- the gassing operations at Chelmno in which gas vans were used
- the Wannsee Conference, in which the "Final Solution" was discussed
- the establishment of the death camps
- various victim groups—while the Jews were the primary target group, the Gypsies were also targeted for total annihilation. Other targeted groups, each

of whom suffered greatly but in various and different ways at the hands of the Nazis, include the Poles, other Slavs, political prisoners, Communists, and the Russian prisoners of war

- death and life in the concentration and death camps
- rescue (limited but significant)
- the world's response (including the tightening of immigration policies by both Allied and neutral nations)
- liberation
- the Nuremberg Trials

For advanced classes, teachers might include the debate between two key schools of thought—the intentionalists and the functionalists—regarding the nature and development of the Nazi plan for the extermination of the Jews. As Marrus (2001) notes:

> Historians differ on the motivations behind anti-Jewish mobilization and on the degree to which Nazi anti-Jewish policies formed part of a coherent, predetermined program. Although few would dispute that Hitler had a key role in decisions concerning the Jews, historians differ on how closely he followed events, on the extent to which he directed Nazi Jewish policy, and on when he determined that comprehensive mass murder was the goal of Nazi policy toward the Jews. Debate over both the timing and the character of the decisions taken has been extensive, owing largely to a paucity of documentary evidence on the decision-making process.
>
> Intentionalists, such as Lucy Dawidowicz, Gerald Fleming, or Richard Breitman, see both Hitler's ideas about the Jews and the Nazis' anti-Jewish program of the mid-1930s as pointing deliberately to the genocide. War, according to this perspective, simply gave Hitler a pretext to carry out a long-considered, murderous objective on a grand scale. Some intentionalists have investigated the roots of Nazi antisemitism in the German or European past. These writers have different points of emphasis: some look to Christian anti-Jewish motifs common to many European societies; some have explored the *völkisch* or racist ideology of late nineteenth-century Germany, and still others have sought to associate anti-Jewish thinking with some of the deepest currents of German culture. In a recent return to a viewpoint commonly expressed in the immediate postwar period, Daniel Goldhagen has argued that Germany was the home of a particularly virulent anti-Jewish commitment, which he terms "eliminationist antisemitism," that permeated the culture and required the removal of the Jews from German society. In Goldhagen's view, Hitler launched a murderous program that countless Germans truly desired.
>
> Functionalists, including Hans Mommsen, Uwe Dietrich Adam, Christopher Browning, and Philippe Burrin, stress the evolution of Nazi policy toward Jews and contend that mass murder emerged as a realistic option only during the ideologically charged Barbarossa campaign. They see the Nazis as groping toward a "solution" of a "Jewish problem" that they themselves had defined. A comprehensive strategy of mass murder was adopted, they argue, only when other options were blocked and when, through trial and error, they had developed techniques by which an entire people could be destroyed. Several interpreters, notably Martin Broszat, point to the frustration of local decision makers with Berlin's inattention to

Jewish policy in the early years of the war, and to the intense competition among such officials to reach an ideologically sound outcome, as pivotal factors in the move toward genocide. Their initiatives, it is claimed, launched and extended the killing process to the point that it became a pan-European program during the course of 1942. Christopher Browning, Saul Friedländer, and others have criticized the notion of local initiatives even while agreeing with Broszat's picture of confusion and rivalry within the Nazi administration. Instead, they see the impulse for the Final Solution as coming rather from the center—from Hitler himself. (pp. 280–281)

(Other useful sources for information on the positions of the intentionalists and functionalists are: Michael R. Marrus, *The Holocaust in History*. New York: Meridian, 1987; Abraham J. Edelheit and Hershel Edelheit, "History of the Holocaust" in *A Handbook and Dictionary*. Boulder, CO: Westview Press, 1994; and Christopher Browning, "The Decision Concerning the Final Solution" in Francois Furet [Ed.], *Unanswered Questions: Nazi Germany and the Genocide of the Jews:* New York: Schocken, 1989, pp. 96–118.)

Focusing on the Specifics: Examining the Evolution of the Nazis' Strangulation of the Jews

The Nazis' aim was to make the Jewish universe shrink—from town to neighborhood, from neighborhood to street, from street to house, from house to room, from room to garret, from garret to cattle car, from cattle car to gas chamber.

And they did the same to the individual—separated from his or her community, then from his or her family, then from his or her identity, eventually becoming a work permit, then a number, until the number itself was turned into ashes.

—Elie Wiesel

First, Jews were categorized; then civil liberties were restricted and property confiscated. Next, Jews were dismissed from universities and civil service jobs, which often included school teaching, and were barred from the professions. Jewish businesses were taken over and Aryanized. Jews were then isolated, forced to wear the Jewish star and forbidden to use public facilities.

Finally, Jews were assembled, first in large cities and then in transit camps. From 1942 on, they were deported from these transit camps to the death camps in the east.

—Michael Berenbaum

Proceeding from the examination of historiograhical essays, major historical works, authoritative chronologies of the Holocaust, and pedagogical essays and critiques of curricula by scholars, teachers can begin to zero in on specific topics they wish to address. To gain a solid understanding of *specific issues and topics,* teachers need to consult and study the work of those historians who specialize in this history. In doing so, one needs to cull out key ideas and insights that help to illuminate the events themselves. The example provided here concerns the evolution of the Nazis' policies and actions against the Jews.

Prior to the formal announcement of the decision at the Wannsee Conference to actually implement a policy of extermination, or the Final Solution, there was a lengthy period (1933–1942) that saw the ever-increasing constriction of the freedom and rights of the Jews and others. Studying this early period provides students with unique insights into the bureaucratic, systematic, and evolving set of policies that ultimately resulted in the genocide of the Jews and others.

Where better to begin an examination of this issue than with Raul Hilberg (1985), the noted historian who delineated this policy in such great detail in his magisterial work *The Destruction of the European Jews.* More specifically, he asserts that:

> The process of destruction unfolded in a definite pattern. It did not, however, proceed from a basic plan. No bureaucrat in 1933 could have predicted what kind of measures would be taken in 1938, nor was it possible in 1938 to foretell the configuration of the undertaking in 1942. The destruction process was a step-by-step operation, and the administrator could seldom see more than one step ahead.
>
> The steps of the destruction process were introduced in the following order: At first the concept of Jew was defined; then the expropriatory operations were inaugurated; third, the Jews were concentrated in ghettos; finally, the decision was made to annihilate European Jewry. Mobile killing units were sent to Russia, while in the rest of Europe the victims were deported to killing centers. (Hilberg, 1985, p. 53)

Particularly worth noting is that the policy involved *"definition, expropriation, concentration, and annihilation"* (Hilberg, 1985, pp. 53, 54). Entire lessons or units could be developed around each of these actions. Taking these actions and combining them with the insights of survivors and scholars, such as Wiesel and Berenbaum, respectively, one could develop a very powerful and thought-provoking set of lessons.

Reviewing and Critiquing the Selection of Issues and Topics

Following the selection of the issues and topics for the lessons or unit, it is imperative to review them to ascertain whether they are actually germane to one's rationale, goals, and objectives. Issues and topics not germane to the study should be dropped and, if need be, replaced with more relevant material. Similarly, other rationales, goals, and objectives can be added to accommodate the introduction of new issues and topics.

At this point it is also critical to ascertain whether the issues and topics selected will result in historically accurate lessons and units. More specifically, educators need to ask themselves whether such issues and topics contribute to:

"contextualizing the history" (Parsons and Totten, 1993, p. 5), providing a balance regarding "whose perspective informs the study" (Parsons and Totten, 1993, p. 6), "avoiding the acceptance of simple answers to complex questions and issues" (Parsons and Totten, 1993, p. 3), and "avoiding stereotypical descriptions of groups of people" (Parsons and Totten, 1993, p. 4). If the answer to any of these points is no, then the educator must review and revise his or her selections.

Furthermore, one must determine whether the issues and topics selected avoid teaching lessons and units that focus on certain issues to the exclusion of others (e.g., the killing process but not the evolutionary process of the Nazis' treatment of the Jews) or on a single group instead of the many that were involved or impacted by the Holocaust (e.g., the perpetrators but not the victims, or the victims and not the perpetrators).

At this juncture, teachers and curriculum developers should consider positing questions for themselves to answer. Examining one's selection of issues and topics, one might ask: "Can students even begin to understand the Holocaust if they know only the 'whats' and 'wheres' of the event but not the 'whys'?" This, in turn, may lead to such questions as: "Can students truly understand what drove the Nazis to develop and implement the Nuremberg Laws and, ultimately, the Final Solution, if they (the students) do not understand the Nazis' theory of racial antisemitism?" And, "Can students even begin to understand the concept of the Nazis' virulent and deadly concept of racial antisemitism if they do not have some understanding of traditional Christian antisemitism and its impact on Nazi thought?" Or, "Can students be said to understand the killing process if they do not have an understanding of the Nazis' concept of race or such precursors to the gas chambers as the euthanasia of the mentally and physically handicapped beginning in 1939, the actions of the Einsatzgruppen, or the early experiments with gas vans?" Again, the answers to such questions may suggest that one has to add certain issues or topics to the study in order to provide the students with a sound sense of the history as opposed to one that is perfunctory, decontextualized, and ahistorical.

Conclusion

Before attempting to teach about the complex subject of the Holocaust, teachers need to know this history. Without such a foundation, lessons on the Holocaust are likely to be confusing, superficial, and ahistorical.

Once teachers have a fairly solid understanding of the history, including issues and topics germane to the history, they can begin to select those issues and topics they deem most significant for such a study. To accomplish the latter, however, teachers need solid rationales for those subjects they choose to include and exclude. Such a winnowing process can only help to strengthen the eventual study the students will experience.

(Note: For a detailed discussion on the significance and the development of "rationales" for teaching this history, see Chapter 1 of this book.)

REFERENCES

Bauer, Yehuda. (1982). *A History of the Holocaust*. Danbury, CT: Franklin Watts.

Berenbaum, Michael. (1993). *The World Must Know: The History of the Holocaust As Told in the United States Holocaust Memorial Museum*. Boston: Little Brown.

Browning, Christopher R. (1995). *The Path to Genocide*. New York: Cambridge University Press.

Dawidowicz, Lucy S. (1986). *The War Against the Jews, 1933–1945*. New York: Bantam.

Dawidowicz, Lucy S. (1992). "How They Teach the Holocaust," pp. 65–83. In Lucy S. Dawidowicz (Ed.), *What Is the Use of Jewish History?* New York: Schocken.

Edelheit, Abraham J. (1990). "Historiography of the Holocaust," pp. 666–672. In Israel Gutman (Ed.), *Encyclopedia of the Holocaust*. New York: Macmillan.

Edelheit, Abraham J., and Edelheit, Hershel (1994). *History of the Holocaust: A Handbook and Dictionary*. Boulder, CO: Westview Press.

Feig, Konnilyn. (1990). "Non-Jewish Victims in the Concentration Camps," pp. 161–178. In Michael Berenbaum (Ed.), *A Mosaic of Victims: Non-Jews Persecuted and Murdered by the Nazis*. New York: New York University Press.

Friedlander, Henry. (1979). "Toward a Methodology of Teaching About the Holocaust." February. *Teachers College Record*, 80(3):519–542.

Friedlander, Henry. (1995). *The Origins of Nazi Genocide: From Euthanasia to the Final Solution*. Chapel Hill: University of North Carolina Press.

Friedländer, Saul. (1997). "The Extermination of the European Jews in Historiography: Fifty Years Later," pp. 3–17. In Alvin H. Rosenfeld (Ed.), *Thinking About the Holocaust: After a Half Century*. Bloomington and Indianapolis: Indiana University Press.

Greenberg, Karen J. (1996). "The Burden of Being Human: An Essay on Selected Scholarship of the Holocaust," pp. 29–39. In Verne W. Newton (Ed.), *FDR and the Holocaust*. New York: St. Martin's Press.

Gutman, Y., and Greif, G. (Eds.). (1988). *The Historiography of the Holocaust Period. Proceedings of the Fifth Yad Vashem Historical Conference*. Jerusalem: Yad Vashem.

Hilberg, Raul. (1985). *The Destruction of the European Jews*. Three Volumes. New York: Holmes & Meier.

Hilberg, Raul. (1992). *Perpetrators, Victims, Bystanders: The Jewish Catastrophe 1933–1945*. New York: HarperCollins.

Koonz, Claudia (1996). "Genocide and Eugenics: The Language of Power, pp. 155–177. In Peter Hayes (Ed.), *Lessons and Legacies: The Making of the Holocaust in a Changing World*. Evanston, IL: Northwestern University Press.

Lipstadt, Deborah (March 6, 1995). "Not Facing History," *The New Republic*, pp. 27, 29.

Marrus, Michael R. (1987). *The Holocaust in History*. New York: Meridian.

Marrus, Michael. (2001). "Historiography," pp. 279–285. In Walter Laqueur (Ed.), *The Holocaust Encyclopedia*. New Haven, CT: Yale University Press.

Milton, Sybil (1995). "Holocaust: The Gypsies," pp. 209–264. In Samuel Totten, William S. Parsons, and Israel W. Charny (Eds.), *Genocide in the Twentieth Century: Critical Essays and Eyewitness Accounts*. New York: Garland.

Niewyk, Donald L. (1995). "Holocaust: The Genocide of the Jews," pp. 167–207. In Samuel Totten, William S. Parsons, and Israel W. Charny (Eds.), *Genocide in the Twentieth Century: Critical Essays and Eyewitness Accounts*. New York: Garland.

Parsons, William S., and Totten, Samuel (1993). *Guidelines for Teaching about the Holocaust*. Washington, DC: United States Holocaust Memorial Museum.

Proctor, Robert (1988). *Racial Hygiene: Medicine Under the Nazis*. Cambridge: Harvard University Press.

Totten, Samuel, and Feinberg, Stephen (2001). *Teaching and Studying the Holocaust*. Boston: Allyn & Bacon.

Wiesel, Elie (1979). "Preface." *Report to the President*. Washington, DC: President's Commission on the Holocaust.

Yahil, Leni (1990). *The Holocaust: The Fate of European Jewry, 1932–1945*. New York: Oxford University Press.

4 Common Misconceptions and Inaccuracies That Plague Teaching and Learning about the Holocaust

Not surprisingly, students often enter a study of the Holocaust with a host of misconceptions and inaccurate information about various aspects of this history. Much of their knowledge comes from sources not especially concerned with historical accuracy, including television shows, major motion pictures, computer games, and conversations with friends and family members.[1] In light of this situation, it is not only imperative for teachers to ascertain the misconceptions their students hold, but to address and dispel them. If teachers neglect to do this, then it is likely, even probable, that students will continue to cling to their misconceptions, no matter what they read, discuss, or are taught. Ultimately, that will prevent the students from gaining an accurate understanding of this history.

Although it is advisable for teachers to ascertain early on the major misconceptions their students hold regarding this history (see Chapter 1), in all likelihood, as the study unfolds, teachers will continue to discover additional misconceptions and myths held by students that must be addressed.

In this chapter, numerous misconceptions that students and others hold about the Holocaust will be raised and discussed. Accurate information will be provided to replace the misconceptions. *It is important to note and for the reader to realize that due to space constraints, as well as the complexity of the issues addressed, only a minimal amount of information is provided in response to each misconception. In many cases, it would take volumes to treat some of these issues adequately. Thus, in order to gain a deeper and more thorough understanding of the issues addressed herein, it is imperative that readers conduct further study into each of the issues by consulting the work of major historians who specialize in the Holocaust.*

Misconceptions and Inaccuracies Delineated and Corrected

The Holocaust Was Inevitable

Some students are under the false assumption that the Holocaust was inevitable. For example, early in a semester-long Holocaust course I taught, a high school student was adamant that "It [the Holocaust] was bound to happen sooner or later. That period of time was ripe for it." This "astrological approach" to history—all the stars were in order and thus it (whatever the event) was destined to happen—is simplistic, ahistorical and anti-intellectual.

To assume the Holocaust was inevitable suggests that no matter what anyone or any nation did, the Holocaust could not have been prevented. That, of course, is not so. Further, to assume that something like the Holocaust was inevitable suggests that virtually every event in history was and is inevitable and that the choices, decisions, and actions made by individuals, groups, communities, and nations have no bearing on history. Not only is such a perspective deterministic, it is simply not logical.

As the authors of the United States Holocaust Memorial Museum's *Guidelines for Teaching about the Holocaust* argue:

> Just because a historical event took place, and it was documented in textbooks and on film, does not mean that it had to happen. This seemingly obvious concept is often overlooked by students and teachers alike. The Holocaust took place because individuals, groups, and nations made decisions to act or not to act. By focusing on those decisions, we gain insight into history and human nature, and we can better help our students to become critical thinkers (Parsons and Totten, 1993, p. 3).

There Are One or Two Major Reasons Why the Holocaust Was Perpetrated

Many students are inclined to believe that the Holocaust was a result of one or two major factors. For example, Hitler hated the Jews or, an even more common belief, Jews were the cause of serious economic problems and were thus hated by the Germans. Not only are such beliefs simplistic; they are ahistorical and sorely inaccurate.

At the outset of the same course mentioned above, one student wrote: "Jews were educated people, and when they started taking most of the jobs, that's when the trouble started." Another said, "Jews were responsible for the Depression so Hitler had to find a way to get rid of them."

What students need to learn and appreciate is that there was *no single cause* for the Nazis' moves against the Jews, which ultimately resulted in genocide. As noted in the earlier chapters of this book, "[A] number of historical trends combined to make the Holocaust possible: anti-Semitism, racism, social Darwinism, extreme nationalism, totalitarianism, industrialism, and the nature of modern war. The absence of any of these trends would have made the genocide of the Jews unlikely" (Niewyk, 1995, p. 175). If students do not understand how each of these, as well as other, trends played an integral role in the Holocaust, then their understanding of the Holocaust is certain to be minimal.

In this regard, the authors of the United States Holocaust Memorial Museum's *Guidelines for Teaching about the Holocaust* recommend that teachers

> [a]llow students to contemplate the various factors which contribute to the Holocaust; do not attempt to reduce Holocaust history to one or two catalysts in isolation from the other factors which came into play. For example, the Holocaust was not simply the logical and inevitable consequence of unbridled racism. Rather, racism, combined with centuries-old bigotry, renewed by a nationalistic fervor which emerged in Europe in the latter half of the 19th century, fueled by Germany's defeat in World War I and its national humiliation following the Treaty of Versailles, exacerbated by worldwide economic hard times, the ineffectiveness of the Weimar Republic, and international indifference, and catalyzed by the political charisma, militaristic inclusiveness, and manipulative propaganda of Adolf Hitler's Nazi regime, contributed to the eventuality of the Holocaust. (Parsons and Totten, 1993, p. 3)

The Victims Did Something Wrong, and Thus Brought the Discrimination, Ostracism, and Eventual Murder Upon Themselves

Many students believe that, for anyone to be treated as horribly as the Jews were by the Nazis, they [the victims] must have done something to deserve the ill treatment. Nothing could be further from the truth. As Holocaust survivor and acclaimed author Elie Wiesel (1979) observed many years ago, all Jews were "destined for annihilation solely because they were born Jewish. They were doomed not because of something they had done or proclaimed or acquired but because of who they were: sons and daughters of the Jewish people" (p. iii).

Indeed, contrary to the disinformation disseminated by the Nazis, the Jews were not responsible for Germany's loss in World War I (or "the stab in the back," as the Nazis were wont to say). Neither were the Jews responsible for the imposition of the Versailles Treaty on Germany, which resulted in harsh provisions and reparations. Nor were the Jews responsible for the global economic depression or the concomitant massive unemployment and general hard times in Germany and elsewhere.

The ugly and profound fact, then, is that the Jews were not attacked for what they had done but *simply because they existed*. (And, of course, *no matter what*, there is never a rational reason for committing genocide against any group.) The Nazis deemed Jews the most "inferior race" and one that posed a danger to the "master (or "Aryan") race." In Hitler's and the Nazis' belief system,

> . . . as early as 1922, political parties [in Germany] encouraged the teaching of eugenics. Racial hygiene and eugenics united in a national and professional discourse that defined values, perceptions, and the approach to racial characteristics. German universities were filled with lectures, studies, and research regarding race and the fear that certain "races" [e.g., Jews, Gyspies and others] would pollute and destroy the Aryan strain. German officials seemed possessed with rebuilding a genetically fit race decimated by losses in World War I.
>
> . . . Theories of identifying and containing the racially impure were the subject matter of racial hygiene lectures through the 1930s. By the early 1940s it took little psychological effort for public health administrators to shift from focusing on cleaning up the ghetto environments to clearing them out.
>
> . . . This ideological/psychological construction, deriving from the obsession with racial hygiene, lay behind the Nazis' political vision of purifying the nation through the Holocaust. (Glass, 1997, pp. 31–33)

What students must come to understand in regard to the Nazis' racial policies vis-à-vis the Jews is the impact that the long history of Christian antisemitism through the ages and the advent of political antisemitism in the nineteenth century had on their thoughts. They also need to understand the reasons behind that long history of Christian antisemitism, including the misconceptions, myths, and the sheer ignorance that propagated it. Further, students must be assisted to understand how the Nazis' virulent and, ultimately, deadly racial antisemitism differed from earlier forms of antisemitism.

The Holocaust Took Place Sometime Between the Early 1920s and the 1950s

Teachers often note that events that took place in the 1960s and 1970s seem like "ancient history" to many secondary-level students. Thus, it is no surprise that events of the 1930s and 1940s are even more of a blur in the minds of many students. Student guesses on teacher-made questionnaires as to when the Holocaust took place have ranged from the 1920s to sometime in the 1950s.

The Holocaust period, of course, ranged from January 1933 (when the Nazis gained power in Germany) through May 1945 (when the Germans surrendered and the concentration and death camps were "liberated"). Although the actual mass killing by the Nazis began in 1941 and continued through 1945, students need to understand that for seven long years (1933–1940), the Nazis did everything in their power to disenfranchise the Jews and strip them of everything but their lives. (Some Jews, of course, had their lives taken during this period. During Kristallnacht, in November 1938, for example, ninety-six Jews were killed.)

The Persecution of the Jews Took Place
Solely During the 1940s

When thinking or teaching about the Holocaust, many tend to focus primarily, or solely, on the mass murders perpetrated by the Nazis versus the entire twelve-year span (1933–1945) of the Third Reich's actions against its victims. This is a major oversight for, as mentioned above, the Nazis' decisions and actions in the early years, including the "legalized" discrimination against the victims, set the stage for the murderous decisions and actions of the later years.

More specifically, students need to understand that between 1933 and 1939 Nazi Germany passed and implemented four hundred pieces of legislation whose express purpose was to define, isolate, exclude, and segregate German Jews (Berenbaum, 1993, p. 22). Additionally, the Nazis used terroristic tactics both to cow and instill fear into those they considered to be inferior and to be their enemies. More specifically, beginning in 1933,

> [a]nti-Jewish policy was put into effect on two parallel levels: by means of laws, decrees, and administrative terror; and by "spontaneous" acts of terror and incitement of the population to hostility against the Jews. The early anti-Jewish laws included the Law for the Restoration of the Professional Civil Service. The racist basis of that law was expressed by the Arierparagraph ("Aryan Paragraph"), which became the foundation for all anti-Jewish legislation passed before the enactment of the Nuremberg Laws in the fall of 1935. Other laws passed at that stage restricted the practice of law and medicine by Jews; a special law mandated that the number of Jews in an educational institution must not exceed that proportional to their percentage of the population; and Jews were excluded from cultural life and journalism. The only exception to these laws applied to Jews who had served as front-line soldiers in World War I.
>
> The main purpose of the legislation was to give formal expression to the ideology and policy of discrimination against and persecution of the Jews, but it was also meant to serve as a means of restraining "spontaneous" terror and stabilizing the status of the Jews in the Nationalist Socialist state. In particular, it was the conservative elements in the government coalition who in the second half of 1933 advocated such "stabilization," out of concern for the country's international standing and the adverse effect that unrestrained Nazi action against the Jews could have on efforts to restore the country's economy.
>
> The methods employed in the regime's terror campaign against its opponents consisted mostly of arrest and imprisonment in concentration camps. The percentage of Jews among the detainees was quite high, and they were singled out for particularly cruel and humiliating treatment, which in many instances resulted in death. (Kulka and Hildesheimer, 1995, p. 562)

It is important, then, for students not only to be knowledgeable about the period of the mass killing, but also the period that led up to it. To be conversant with the former but not the latter is to walk away with a skewed view of the chronology *and* the history of the period.

(In addition to referring to historical accounts to learn more about the myriad of Nazis' actions against the Jews throughout the 1930s, teachers and students should find the following extremely instructive and interesting: Victor Klemperer, *I Will Bear Witness: A Diary of the Nazi Years 1933–1941*. New York: Random House, 1998; and *I Will Bear Witness: A Diary of the Nazi Years 1941–1945*. New York: Random House, 1999. It is a two-volume diary that powerfully delineates the ever-increasing stranglehold that the Nazis applied to the German Jews in the early to mid-1930s and then to other groups of Jews as they [the Nazis] expanded their power base throughout Europe. Another extremely valuable book that delineates the early years of Nazi rule and the impact it had on the Jews and others is Marion A. Kaplan's extraordinarily informative and fascinating *Between Dignity and Despair: Jewish Life in Nazi Germany*. New York: Oxford University Press, 1998.)

World War II and the Holocaust Were Synonymous

Although the vast majority of the Nazis' mass murder took place during the war years (especially between 1941 and 1945), there was a distinct difference between World War II and the Holocaust. It is critical for students to understand that *the Holocaust was not the cause of World War II*. Equally significant, students must understand that neither the Allies nor other nations fought the Nazis due to the latter's murderous treatment of the Jews.

World War II was ignited as a result of the Nazis' aggression against its neighbors and others. Central to the Nazis' aggression was its perverted ideology (Bauer, 1995). More specifically, it was the Nazis' desire "to establish the predominance of the Germanic-Nordic peoples of the 'Aryan' race in Europe, and thereby to control, in effect, the world. For that purpose Lebensraum ('living space') was aspired to in eastern Europe, in line with Nazi ideology as formulated by Adolf Hitler and others. To achieve it, the perceived enemies of Germany—Bolshevik Russia, liberal France, plutocratic America—all of whom were controlled by 'international Jewry,' in Nazi eyes, ultimately had to be defeated" (Bauer, 1995, p. 1661).

As Bauer (1995) further notes:

> War was a desideratum of Nazi ideology both as a means and an end, in the spirit of Social Darwinism: only war would show who was strong and who therefore had the right to rule. In the end, it was not economic, military, or political reasons that instigated the most terrible of wars to date. Economically, by 1938 or 1939, Germany had largely recovered; militarily, it threatened others but was under no danger of attack; and politically, it was already the predominant power in Europe. Nazi Germany wanted a war for ideological reasons." (p. 1661)

As previously mentioned, students need to be aware of the early years of Nazi rule and the evolution of Nazi thought and actions as they related to the Jews. As Edelheit and Edelheit (1994) observe:

The ink of President von Hindenburg's signature [in 1933]—designating Hitler as the new German chancellor—had hardly dried when the Nazis began to institute their platform. [W]ith legal means at their disposal, the Nazis' long-pent-up rage against Communists, Jews, and all other opponents gave vent to a campaign of harassment, assault, and terror against real or perceived enemies. Foremost on their hit list was German Jewry. This seemingly annoying beginning would, within less than a dozen years, culminate in the murder of some 6 million European Jews and millions of others. (p. 41)

Dawidowicz (1986) has also perspicaciously observed that the Nazis carried out two wars—the war against its neighbors and other nations, and a war against the Jews—the latter of which was the planned and systematic destruction of an entire group of people.

The "One Man" or "Evil Man" Theory

As previously mentioned, many students are under the misconception that the Holocaust was a result of a single individual's (Hitler's) will, ideas, plans, and "drive." That simply is not so.

To assume that the Holocaust was perpetrated by a single individual constitutes a naive and simplistic view of history. Although Hitler played a central role in the Nazis' views of the Jews and served, as some historians have put it, as "the spiritual force" behind the Final Solution, he did not act alone. Acknowledging the broad support the Nazis had and the ultimate involvement of thousands of people in various aspects of the Final Solution, Berenbaum (1993) writes:

> *Nazi Germany* became a genocidal state. The goal of annihilation called for participation by *every arm of the government*. The policy of extermination involved *every level of German society* and marshaled *the entire apparatus of the German bureaucracy*. . . . Above all, the policy of extermination was sanctioned by law, decrees, and official directives. The legal system itself served as the instrument of oppression and death." (p. 106) (italics added)

Students also need to learn that:

> Parish churches and the Interior Ministry supplied the birth records that defined and isolated the Jews. The Post Office delivered the notifications of definition, expropriation, denaturalization, and deportation. The Finance Ministry confiscated Jewish wealth and property; German . . . firms fired Jewish workers and board members. . . . [U]niversities refused to admit Jewish students, denied degrees to those already enrolled, and dismissed Jewish faculty. Government transportation bureaus handled the billing arrangements with the railroads for the trains that carried Jews to their death. (Berenbaum, 1993, pp. 106–107)

The point is, without the support and active involvement of numerous and varied departments and organizations, including the legislative and judiciary bodies of the Third Reich as well as other aspects of its bureaucracy, *and* without the actions of innumerable individuals, there could not have been a Holocaust.

It is essential for students to understand this, for if the Holocaust is attributed to the sole efforts of a single man then it is easy to perceive the Holocaust as something that was an aberration, something that was the result of "one sick individual," and not something that was well planned and carried out by many. Put another way, placing stock in the "one man" or "evil man theory" relieves scores of high echelons of Nazis of their responsibility for planning and carrying out the Holocaust, not to mention the tens of thousands who played less visible but integral parts in the tragedy. It also relieves the responsibility of those "average Germans" and others who, early on, looked the other way as the Jews were stripped, piece by piece, of their basic civil and human rights.

The Nuremberg Laws and the Nuremberg Trials Are Synonymous

Many students confuse the Nuremberg Laws with the Nuremberg Trials. As for the Nuremberg Laws, they were

> two constitutional laws issued on September 15, 1935, that became the basis for the legal exclusion of Jews from German life and the ensuing anti-Jewish policy . . . The first of the two Nuremberg Laws, the Reich Citizenship Law, stated that only Germans or people with related blood could be citizens of the Reich. German Jews lost their political rights through this law, which made them state subjects, whereas the "Aryan" Germans were declared citizens of the Reich. The Reich Citizenship law was complemented by thirteen implementation ordinances issued from November 1935 to July 1943 that systematically excluded the Jews from German life. The second of the two laws, the Law for the Protection of German Blood and Honor, prohibited marriages and extramarital intercourse between Jews and Germans, the employment of German maids under the age of forty-five in Jewish households, and the raising by Jews of the German flag. (Bankier, 1995, p. 1076)

On the other hand, the term "Nuremberg Trials"

> is often used to describe four different criminal proceedings. The first was the trial of twenty-four indicted "major" German and Austrian war criminals, conducted by the International Military Tribunal (IMT) from October 18, 1945, until October 1, 1946. Only twenty-two of them were actually tried. . . . Judges from Great Britain, France, the Soviet Union, and the United States presided over the IMT, which tried defendants on charges of conspiracy, crimes against peace, war crimes, and crimes against humanity. Nuremberg was also the site of twelve ensuing trials of 177 members of organizations and groups alleged to have been of a criminal character. Former members of the Gestapo and the SS, as well as civil servants and industrialists, were among those tried. . . . The third type of "Nuremberg trial" was held in Tokyo, [which] involved the trials of Japanese military and political leaders. The trials of "minor" war criminals conducted by military and national courts were the

fourth type of Nuremberg proceeding. The trials were held in the zones of former Axis territory occupied by the victorious powers, or in the liberated territories, at or near the scenes of the crimes. (Jones, 1995, pp. 1488–1489)

"Jews Went to Slaughter Like Sheep"

For many years following the end of World War II, there was a widespread belief that the Jews went to slaughter like sheep, but scholars have marshalled ample evidence that disproves this perception. Still, all these years later, many students are ready to believe such a falsehood.

There are numerous problems with this misconception. First, to latch onto such a phrase and/or belief without examining the social, political, economic, and military context of the period is ahistorical. Without a solid understanding of the latter issues, one is not able to appreciate the numerous factors that influenced individuals' and groups' actions. Nor is one able to appreciate the factors that might have prevented or mitigated against resistance. Second, belief in such a notion neglects to take into account the fact that many German Jews left Nazi Germany early on while they were still able to do so. Third, it is blind to the actual and heroic resistance put up by many Jews.

As Edelheit and Edelheit (1994) state:

> The simple fact must be stated: The majority of European Jewry did not actively resist the Nazis; neither did all other Europeans under Nazi occupation. This does not . . . mean that Jews collaborated in their own destruction. The majority of Jews could not resist for a variety of reasons. Eight major factors came together to inhibit Jewish resistance: lawfulness; time; lack of arms; lack of trained men; lack of an outside source of aid; lack of a suitable place to fight; the Jewish view of the Germans; and collective responsibility.

(For a full discussion of each of these factors, see Edelheit and Edelheit, *History of the Holocaust: A Handbook and Dictionary*. Boulder, CO: Westview Press, 1994, pp. 96–100.)

Regarding the issue of collective responsibility, the Edelheits (1994) comment as follows:

> The resistance was continually plagued by [the] moral dilemma [of collective responsibility]. The Nazis . . . made one Jew responsible for the other. Thus, for instance, if one Jew dared to resist, all Jews in the community would be held responsible. This moral dilemma was foremost in the mind of potential resistance fighters . . . For by the act that offered their chance for survival they were virtually guaranteeing the destruction of their loved ones, friends, and neighbors. (p. 99)

Students need to understand that, despite great odds and a host of factors that mitigated against resistance, various individuals and groups of Jews did actively resist the Nazi juggernaut. Again, as Edelheit and Edelheit (1994) note:

The earliest manifestations of organized active resistance took place in the East. Spontaneous acts of resistance have been recorded in response to Einsatzkommando Aktionen . . . In other instances, Jewish survivors of murdered communities and escapees who fled before or during Nazi Aktionen took to the forests. These individuals banded together to form units of Jewish partisans. Moreover, young Jews incarcerated in some of the ghettos systematically escaped to the forest, with or without weapons, and tried to form additional partisan groups . . . Jewish partisan units . . . operated throughout Eastern Europe. (pp. 100, 101)

. . . Jewish resistance activities culminated in rebellions in seventeen East European ghettos . . . Of these revolts, none is better known than the Warsaw Ghetto uprising. (p. 101)

. . . Jewish undergrounds operated in a number of concentration, slave labor, and death camps as well; in at least three, there were full-scale uprisings: Jews rose up in Sobibor, Treblinka, and Auschwitz-Birkenau . . . At least twelve other camps had undergrounds and resistance activities that culminated in revolts and mass escapes in eleven of them. . . . (pp. 104, 105)

(For a full discussion of Jewish resistance efforts in eastern and western Europe, see Edelheit and Edelheit, *History of the Holocaust: A Handbook and Dictionary.* Boulder, CO: Westview Press, 1994, pp. 100–107.)

A refusal to acknowledge the facts, the truth, and the complexity of the situation facing the Jews during the Holocaust period constitutes yet another victimization of the victims.

Resistance Refers Solely to Physical Resistance

When students even contemplate the fact of Jewish resistance, most automatically think in physical terms. As important as physical resistance was, there were many other types of opposition that students should learn about.

Among the various types of resistance put forth by the Jews were:

- "smuggling food, clothing, medicine and other necessities" (Rozett, 1995, p. 1267);
- spiritual resistance, called by the Jews "sanctification of life" (Rozett, 1995, p. 1267). This involved the "creation of Jewish schools, theaters, and orchestras [which] helped Jews retain their dignity despite Nazi oppression in the ghettos" (Rozett, 1995, p. 1267). It also involved "Jewish religious observance in the face of laws or rules that forbade" (p. 1267). And on an "individual level, merely keeping oneself clean in a place such as Auschwitz was an assertion of human dignity and the human spirit. Their preservation often aided camp inmates to retain the will to live, which was crucial to their survival" (p. 1267);
- the writing and distribution of underground Jewish newspapers and pamphlets: "The press provided information about events and analyzed them; it buttressed Jewish morale by publicizing poems, fiction, and jokes; and finally, it called for acts of armed resistance" (Rozett, 1995, p. 1267);

- "rescue activity that Jews initiated or in which they cooperated with non-Jews. Individuals and groups tried to escape from the Nazis by crossing borders to safer lands; with the use of false identity papers; or by hiding—with non-Jews, or in any place where conditions permitted" (p. 1267);
- "individual noncompliance with specific Nazi demands. . . . Instances have been recorded when individual Jews cursed their persecutors, spat at them, or attacked them with their bare hands, when it became clear that they were about to be deported or executed." (pp. 1267–1268)

Students need to be aware of all forms of resistance to appreciate the courageous and inventive ways in which Jews acted to maintain their integrity and to attempt to foil the Nazi effort to dehumanize and, ultimately, murder each and every Jew across Europe.

Concentration and Death Camps Were One and the Same

Although there were thousands of camps located throughout German-occupied Europe, there were a total of six death camps (Auschwitz-Birkenau or Auschwitz II, Chelmno, Belzec, Sobibor, Majdanek, and Treblinka), all of which were located in Poland.

There was a distinct difference between "concentration" (and other types of camps) and the "death camps," and students need to be made aware of what separated them. As Pingel (1995) notes:

> Although the term "concentration camp" is sometimes used as a generic term for Nazi camps, not all the camps eventually established by the Nazis were designated as concentration camps proper. Their extensive camp system also included labor camps, . . . transit camps, . . . prisoner-of-war (POW) camps, . . . and extermination camps. . . .
>
> Concentration camps were an essential part of the Nazi regime of oppression. The regime imprisoned in such camps political adversaries and persons considered socially or racially undesirable. Forced labor performed by the prisoners became a central element of the imprisonment. . . . These [were essentially] detention installations.
>
> Late in 1941 Chelmno began operating as an extermination camp, and in the spring of 1942 the extermination camps Treblinka, Sobibor, and Belzec were established as part of Aktion Reinhard. Auschwitz-Birkenau (Auschwitz II) and Majdanek, which were existing concentration camps, had extermination centers established within them as well. These sites became the main places in which the Jews of Europe were killed. Chelmno and the three Aktion Reinhard camps were not part of the concentration camp system, whereas Auschwitz and Majdanek were both concentration camps and extermination centers. All the prisoners who were not killed immediately upon arrival in these two camps were considered concentration camp inmates. (pp. 308, 310)

As Arad (1995) notes, the death camps "had a single goal: the blanket murder of the Jews, irrespective of age or sex. . . . A total of some 3.5 million Jews were murdered in the extermination camps, as well as tens of thousands of Gypsies and Soviet prisoners of war" (pp. 461, 463).

There Was a Relatively Small Number of Concentration and Other Types of Camps

Many people, not only students, are under the misconception that there were only dozens or, at the most, hundreds of Nazi-organized and -run "camps." In fact, there were, as already mentioned, literally thousands of various types of camps strewn across the face of Europe. In fact, more than nine thousand camps were located across Nazi-occupied Europe (Berenbaum, 1993). The type and purpose of the camps was extremely eclectic. As Berenbaum (1993) notes, among the thousands of camps there were "transit camps, prisoner-of-war camps, private industrial camps, work-education camps, foreign labor camps, [and] police detention camps. . . . More than three hundred camps were for women only" (p. 119).

To gain an understanding of the pervasive nature of the Nazi terror and control over millions of lives, students need to appreciate how the Nazis attempted to forge greater Europe into a "prison state."

All Death Camps Were Located in Germany

Many are under the misconception that the "death camps" were located in Germany. As mentioned above, all of the death camps were located in Poland. Instead of killing their victims where they resided, the Nazis transported them from all over Europe to the death factories in Poland. As Hilberg (1985) notes, "The sites [for the death camps] were chosen with a view to seclusion and access to railroad lines" (p. 875). In large part, the camp sites were chosen in order to conduct the killing process in as much secrecy as possible. In this vein, Arad (1995) states that:

> The existence of the extermination camps and their operations were classified as top secret in the Third Reich, with the SS coordinating an elaborate system of diversion and deception around them. The camps were concealed, first of all, from the prospective victims, but also from the local population and from German authorities not directly involved in the "Final Solution." From the outside, the sites had the appearance of labor or concentration camps, and the gas chambers looked as though they contained showers and disinfection rooms. The Jews who were to be sent to the camps were told that they were going to labor camps somewhere in the East; when they arrived at their destination, they were informed that they had come to a transit camp or labor camp, and that they were to take a shower while their clothes were disinfected. As a further means of hiding the truth, the women and children were separated from the men. (p. 463)

(For a detailed discussion of the establishment of the camps, see Raul Hilberg, *The Destruction of European Jews*. Three Volumes, New York: Holmes & Meier, 1985, pp. 863–894.)

Only German Jews Were Targeted for Total Annihilation by the Nazis

Since Hitler was the chancellor of Germany, many students mistakenly assume that only German Jews were targeted for annihilation. Nothing could be further from the truth. As Browning (1995) notes, "the goal of the 'Final Solution,' which was the code name for the Nazis' comprehensive program to solve their 'Jewish question', was the 'murder of every Jew in Europe'" (p. 488). This mass murder was the Nazis' final answer as to how to accomplish their goal of "racial hygiene," or the "cleansing" of the German volk of "the handicapped, mental and moral defectives," Jews, Gypsies, and "less worthy races" (Koonz, 1996, p. 164), all of whom the Nazis perceived as "life unworthy of living" (Koonz, 1996, p. 165) for they were "genetically ill" (p. 165) and would poison the Aryan race.

More specifically, Browning (1995) reports that:

> Initiated by Adolf Hitler in the summer of 1941 in the euphoria of his greatest successes and his seemingly imminent victory over the Soviet Union, the "Final Solution" was the culmination of a long evolution of Nazi Jewish policy—from Hitler's earliest articulation of a solution to the "Jewish question" [e.g., initially, it was understood as the expulsion and exclusion of Jews from the Aryan population] in 1919, through the Nazi attempts to coerce Jewish emigration in the 1930s, to the schemes for mass expulsion after the outbreak of war, and, finally, the leap to mass murder with the Einsatzgruppen assault of Russian Jewry in 1941. (pp. 488–489)

From 1941 through 1945 the Nazis systematically murdered the Jews in any way they could, including the gassing of Jews in the gas chambers of the death camps in Poland.

(For a detailed discussion of this issue, see Christopher Browning's entry entitled "Final Solution" in the *Encyclopedia of the Holocaust*, pp. 488–493. See also Martin Gilbert, *Atlas of the Holocaust*. New York: Pergamon Press, 1991.)

Jews Were the Sole Group of Victims During the Holocaust

When students think about the Holocaust, they are most apt to think of the six million Jews who were murdered by the Nazis. However, there were many other groups that were terribly ill-treated as well as murdered by the Nazis, and students need to be informed of these "others."

Berenbaum (1990) succinctly delineates the many other groups that were looked down on and victimized by the Nazis:

> The historical record during the Third Reich demonstrates all too clearly that not all victims of the Nazis were Jews. Millions of other people were swept into the Nazi net of death. If one calculates all the civilian casualties—not including those killed as part of the systematic murder, or those who died as accidental victims of battles, air raids, and military operations, but only those categorized as *Untermenschen*

(subhumans) and killed as a result of conscious persecution—the number is staggering. The Nazi reign of terror brought suffering and death to Jews, Gypsies, Jehovah's Witnesses, the mentally and physically disabled, homosexual, Communists, Slavs, Poles, Russians, Ukrainians, political opponents, and others. In short, anyone who opposed or did not fit into the Nazi worldview was vulnerable. (p. xii)

Thus, while it is important to teach students the fact that the Jews were the primary targets of the Nazis, it is also important to teach them that many others also suffered horrible fates at the hands of the Nazis.

Not only should students be cognizant of the various groups victimized by the Nazis, but they need to understand why and how the various groups were illtreated. *Indeed, it is important for students to understand that just because a group was targeted by the Nazis that did not mean they were targeted for extermination.* A classic case in point is that of the Jehovah's Witnesses.

> After the Nazis came to power in January 1933, attacks on Jehovah's Witnesses escalated almost immediately because of their beliefs and their behavior, particularly their refusal to pay obeisance to the Nazi state or to join any subsidiary Nazi Party organization. The Witnesses' response was homogeneous and cohesive, in conformity with their comprehensive religious code. The Nazis misinterpreted such noncompliance as subversive: the Witnesses refused to raise their arms in the "Heil Hitler" salute, would not display the swastika flag, did not vote in Nazi elections or plebiscites, and would not permit their children to join the Hitler Youth. Jehovah's Witnesses were frequently detained and beaten, their offices searched and vandalized, their funds seized, their presses and publications censored and banned. Hundreds of Witnesses were interned in jails and concentration camps in so-called protective custody. In April 1933 Jehovah's Witness groups and publications were banned throughout the Reich.
>
> . . . During the first two years of Nazi rule Witnesses had lost their jobs as civil servants and as employees in private industry because of their refusal to join the Reich Labor Front, to use the "Heil Hitler" salute, or to vote in elections.
>
> . . . Between 1935 and 1939 Jehovah's Witnesses were often transferred from protective custody in prison to indefinite detention in concentration camps. By 1939 nearly 7,000 Witnesses from Germany, incorporated Austria, and Czechoslovakia were detained inside concentration camps. After 1938 the Witnesses were given the opportunity to be released from concentration camps and prison if they signed a statement recanting their faith and membership in the International Jehovah's Witness Association, promised to denounce coreligionists who contacted them, and agreed to perform military service. Few Witnesses signed such declarations, and their refusal resulted in the execution of more than 40 Witnesses in Sachsenhausen and brutal corporal punishment in Buchenwald in September 1940.
>
> . . . Even in the camps Witnesses, typically marked by an inverted purple triangle sewn on their prison jackets and trousers, continued to meet, pray, and make converts. About 2,500 of the 10,000 imprisoned Jehovah's Witnesses perished in the concentration camps. (Milton, 2001, pp. 347–350)

As for the plight of homosexuals, the United States Holocaust Memorial Museum (n.d.) notes that:

An estimated 1.2 million men were homosexuals in Germany in 1928. Between 1933–45, an estimated 100,000 men were arrested as homosexuals, and of these, some 50,000 officially defined homosexuals were sentenced. Most of these men spent time in regular prisons, and an estimated 5,000 to 15,000 of the total sentenced were incarcerated in concentration camps.

How many of these 5,000 to 15,000 . . . perished in the concentration camps will probably never be known. . . . One leading scholar, Ruediger Lautmann, believes that the death rate for [homosexuals] in the camps may have been as high as sixty percent.

. . . Homosexuality outside Germany (and incorporated Austria and other annexed territories) was not a subject generally addressed in Nazi ideology or policy. . . . During the war years, 1939 to 1945, the Nazis did not generally instigate drives against homosexuality in German-occupied countries.

Consequently, the vast majority of homosexuals arrested under Paragraph 175 were Germans or Austrians. Unlike Jews, men arrested as homosexuals were not systematically deported to Nazi-established ghettos in eastern Europe. Nor were they transported in mass groups of homosexual prisoners to Nazi extermination camps in Poland.

(For a detailed discussion of the non-Jewish victims of the Nazis, see Michael Berenbaum [Ed.], *A Mosaic of Victims: Non-Jews Persecuted and Murdered by the Nazis*. New York: New York University Press, 1990.)

Jews Were the Sole Group of Victims Targeted for Extermination During the Holocaust

There is a common misconception among many that Jews were the sole group of victims that the Nazis targeted for total annihilation. Although it is a vitally significant fact that *Jews were the primary target for Nazi annihilation*, the mentally and physically handicapped and the Gypsies were also targeted for extermination.

In a pamphlet, "Handicapped," issued by the United States Holocaust Memorial Museum (n.d.), the authors observe that:

Forced sterilization in Germany was the forerunner of the systematic killing of the mentally ill and the handicapped. In October 1939, Hitler himself initialed a decree which empowered physicians to grant a "mercy death" to "patients considered incurable according to the best human judgment of their state of health." The intent of the so-called "euthanasia" program, however, was not to relieve the suffering of the chronically ill. The Nazi regime used the term as a euphemism: its aim was to exterminate the mentally ill and the handicapped, thus "cleansing" the Aryan race of persons considered genetically defective and a financial burden to society. . . .

Outside of Germany, thousands of mental patients in the occupied territories of Poland, Russia, and East Prussia were also killed by the Einsatzgruppen squads (SS and special police units) that followed in the wake of the invading German Army.

In all, between 200,000 and 250,000 mentally and physically handicapped persons were murdered from 1930 to 1945 under the T–4 and other "euthanasia programs."

Further, in an essay entitled "Holocaust: The Genocide of Disabled Peoples," Hugh Gregory Gallagher (1995) states the following:

[S]everely disabled and chronically mentally ill patients . . . were said by their doctors to be "useless eaters"—persons with "lives not worth living."

[M]ost of its victims were neither terminally ill nor in unbearable pain, nor were they anxious to die. The program's proponents advanced various arguments in its justification—compassion, eugenics, economics, racial purity. The official program was halted by Hitler in the summer of 1941, in the face of a rising wave of protests from disabled people, their families and friends, and religious officials. Even so, many doctors, acting largely on their own counsel, continued killing patients in hospitals and institutions throughout Germany.

The mass murder techniques developed in the euthanasia hospitals were later utilized against Jews. (p. 265)

As for the fate of the Gypsies (Roma and Sinti), in an essay entitled "Holocaust: The Gypsies," Holocaust historian Sybil Milton (1995) asserts that

To be sure, the "Jewish Question" loomed larger than the "Gypsy Plague" in Nazi ideology, since Roma and Sinti were socially marginal whereas Jews were increasingly assimilated in German society and culture; the Gypsies were also far fewer in number, representing about 0.05 percent of the 1933 German population. Nevertheless, there is a striking parallelism between the ideology and process of extermination for Jews and Gypsies.

. . . Initially, the Nazis developed parallel racial regulations against Jews, Gypsies, and the handicapped. Gypsies were included as "asocials" (an aggregate group including—but not limited to—prostitutes, beggars, shirkers, and any persons the police designated as "hooligans") in the July 1933 Law for the Prevention of Offspring with Hereditary Defects and in the November 1933 Law Against Habitual Criminals. The first law resulted in their involuntary sterilization, while the second permitted their incarceration in concentration camps. . . . Following passage of the 1935 Nuremberg racial laws, semiofficial commentaries interpreting these laws classified Gypsies, along with Jews and Blacks, as racially distinctive minorities with "alien blood."

. . . Hitler was preoccupied with racial purity, and was determined to cleanse the gene pool of the German nation. He demanded the exclusion of the unfit and the alien. In cooperation with racial scientists, the Nazi party and German government bureaucrats defined the groups to be excluded. From the beginning in 1933 these bureaucrats focused on the handicapped, Jews, and Gypsies, advancing solutions for exclusion that became progressively more radical. Before the final solution of mass murder became feasible, these bureaucrats proposed sterilization and deportation (or emigration) as solutions. The handicapped were thus sterilized before they were killed, and this also applied to many Gypsies. Even during the war, Nazi functionaries continued to search for an easy method that would make mass sterilization of Jews possible. When emigration or expulsion was no longer feasible but before the killings commenced, the Nazis instituted the deportation of Jews and Gypsies as a means of exclusion. Sterilization, deportation, and killings thus reflected the evolving policy of exclusion and was applied to the handicapped, Jews, and Gypsies.

    . . . In October 1947, Otto Ohlendorf, who had headed the *Einsatzgruppen* that operated in southern Russia and the Crimea, testified at Nuremberg that the basis for killing Gypsies and Jews in Russia had been the same. In similar fashion the Reich Commissar for the Ostland in July 1942 informed the Higher SS and Police Leader in Riga that "treatment of Jews and Gypsies are to be placed on equal footing." (pp. 209, 210–211, 220, 227–228)

Jews Are a Race

Many are under the misconception that Jews constitute a race unto themselves. That is not so.

Related to this issue is that many students are under the false impression that the Holocaust involved one "race" (the "Aryan race") exterminating another "race" (the "Jewish race"). The fact is, there is no such entity as an "Aryan race" or a "Jewish race," let alone a "superior" or "inferior" race. That said, *according to the Nazis' mind-set*, which was comprised of a bizarre set of ideas and notions, the Holocaust did in fact constitute a "race war."

As for the misconception that Jews constitute a race, Kleg, Rice, and Bailey (1970) correctly note that:

> Race is a biological term. Synonyms which could be used for race are variety, breed, stock, and strain. Just as there are different varieties of cattle (one species), there are different varieties of man (one species). The confusion in the use of the word race results from the fact that it has been applied to religion (e.g., "Jewish race"); language (e.g., "Semitic," "Aryan"); and other cultural traits.
>
>   Is there a Jewish race? No. Jews are followers of Judaism, the name of the Jewish religion. Another name for Jew is Hebrew. Jews have many different physical characteristics according to geographic location. Some are light skinned, blue eyed, with blond hair; others have darker skin, brown eyes, and straight, black hair. In Northwest Europe, Jews resemble other Northwest European people. In Yemen, the Jews resembled the Muslim residents. Just as Christians and Muslims (followers of Islam) come in various shades of black, yellow, red and white, Jews come in many different colors (p. 149).

(For a solid introduction to the issue of race, racism, why and how Jews came to be falsely considered a race, and the Nazis' racial ideology, see George Mosse, "Racism" in *The Encyclopedia of the Holocaust*. New York: Macmillan, 1995. For a detailed discussion of the myth that Jews are a race, see Chapter 5, "Do the Jews Constitute a Race? An Issue Holocaust Educators Must Get Right.")

There Is an "Aryan Race"

A driving force of the Nazis' belief system was that the Jews and various other groups constituted inferior races that "polluted" the "Aryan race." Such beliefs were pure nonsense, for just as the Jews do not constitute a race, there was and is no such entity as an Aryan race. Furthermore, there is no superior group of people, except in the minds of racists.

Tellingly, "Nazi ideology failed to formulate a precise definition of the Aryan race" (Yahil, 1990, p. 307). Students need to understand that "'Aryan' was a term originally used by anthropologists and linguists to describe people who speak an Indo-European dialect, [but it is] a term that was perverted by the Nazis to mean a so-called master race" (Epstein and Rosen, 1997, p. 14). Moving beyond the linguistic meaning of the term, early German "anthropologists of rank and standing popularized [though fallaciously] the belief in two separate races, Aryans and Semites, with opposed physical, mental and moral traits. Aryans [were described as] fair-skinned, long-skulled, and light of eye [and] were an agricultural and warrior people, Semites a swarthy, roundheaded, dark-eyed trading race" (Weiss, 1996, p. 130).

Speaking of the Nazis' concept of an Aryan race, Gutman (1990) writes:

> In Germany, racism [racial antisemitism], more than any other theory (aside from nationalism), was the substance of National Socialism. . . . The authorities of the Third Reich were faced with the challenge of defining who was an Aryan and determining who was a Jew. They never attempted to define a person's race by means of elements in his blood, the shape of his skull or nose, his hair color or body type, and so on, realizing that such criteria would undoubtedly lead to many Nazis being defined as Jews and many Jews being considered pure Aryans. Therefore the Nazis turned to religion as the measurement of race, even though Hitler had claimed many times that the Jews did not constitute a religion but a race, and that it was race which determined their identity as Jews. (p. 69)

In order to understand the perverted nature of the Nazis' belief system, students need to understand the above—otherwise they are apt to believe that there are such entities as an Aryan race and a Jewish race. Indeed, not to comprehend these issues leads one to a skewed understanding of the Holocaust.

All or Most German Jews Were Rich and Controlled the Economy

Many students are under the mistaken impression that German Jews were uniformly wealthy, controlled the economy, and were the cause of the Great Depression, which resulted in widespread misery for the rest of German society and beyond. Many students also believe that the main cause of the Holocaust was the economic straits in which Germany found itself in the late 1920s and early 1930s.

The simple facts are: The Jews did not control the German economy, they were not the cause of the Depression, and although the poor economy did play a central role in the Nazi rise to power, it was not the driving reason for the Nazis' perpetration of genocide against the Jews.

First, although many Jews who lived in major cities "were mainly involved in brokerage, finance, and commerce, though toward the end of the Weimar period their influence in a number of branches of commerce began to decline" (Yahil, 1990, p. 22), *[f]or the most part the Jews belonged to the middle class and were self-employed, in various branches of business and in the professions"* (italics added) (Kulka and Hildesheimer, 1995, p. 560). Further, "some 20 percent of Germany's Jewish population" lived in small towns and villages, and [t]hey were employed mostly in the traditional crafts, petty trade, and in providing services to local farmers" (Yahil, 1990, p. 21). The point is, the vast majority of German Jews were not rich. Significantly, "[t]he only people who were able to maintain their standard of living were the moneyed upper middle classes, particularly owners of large commercial enterprises, department stores and chain stores" (Yahil, 1990, p. 16).

Second, the causes of resentment among non-Jewish Germans toward German Jews were twofold. To begin with, "[a]s a rule the Jewish craftsman and tradesman were better off than their German counterparts" (Yahil, 1990, p. 22) who did not have a craft or trade and were, in general, laborers. Tellingly, "[l]aborers composed 46.3 percent of the German work force in Germany, whereas 46 percent of the Jews were self-employed" (Yahil, 1990, p. 22). Additionally, once the laborers were laid off due to the economic plunge caused by the Depression, they had nothing to fall back on, whereas those with a trade or craft and/or who were self-employed had more flexibility in making a living.

Nazi propaganda, including its ugly and vicious stereotyping of Jews, perpetuated the falsities that the Jews wanted to totally control the world economy, were the cause the Great Depression, and were the prime cause of Germany's economic misery.

The Holocaust Was Implemented Solely in Germany

Some are under the misconception that the Holocaust took place solely in Germany, and thus was carried out solely by Germans against German Jews. The Holocaust was planned and largely implemented by the leaders and followers of Germany's Third Reich from 1933–1945, but the actions and events of the Holocaust engulfed all of Europe and had ramifications far beyond Europe. More specifically,

> . . . Every Jew in Europe was targeted by the Nazis. At the Wannsee Conference [Reinhard] Heydrich [head of the SS Reich Security main Office and the convenor of the Wannsee Conference] noted that the Final Solution would have to deal with eleven million Jews, including those in Britain and Ireland . . . Jews were hunted down throughout Europe, . . . There were more than nine thousand camps scattered throughout German-occupied Europe . . . and between 1942 and 1945, trains carrying human cargo from every corner of Nazi-occupied Europe rolled into death camps. (Berenbaum, 1993, pp. 105, 112, 119)

As noted earlier, all of the death camps were located in Poland, and trains transported their human cargo from all over Europe to these death factories.

Many Reached Out to Assist the Jews and Did So As a Result of Altruism

Thinking the best of people, students often assume that large numbers of individuals and groups offered assistance to Jews throughout the years the Nazis were in power (1933–1945). Nothing could be further from the truth. When addressing rescuers in the classroom, it is important to inform students of the fact that "at best, less than one-half of one percent of the total population [of non-Jews] under Nazi occupation helped to rescue Jews" (Oliner and Oliner, 1991, p. 363). It is also important to note that there were individuals who acted courageously and assisted others no matter what the consequences had they been caught. Finally, it is imperative to inform students as to the reasons why people may not have acted to save those in peril.

The factors that influenced the attitudes and behavior of rescuers ranged from altruism and care for the others to outright greed. As Oliner and Oliner (1991) state:

> [R]escues were not necessarily the consequences of noble concerns. In several cases, political opportunism alone sometimes motivated government officials who nonetheless saved many Jews. Thus, for example, while acknowledging that the Soviet Union saved tens of thousands of Jews, [it is argued by some] that Soviet policy toward Jews (as well as toward the rest of the population) was purely self-serving, that it was designed to serve the political, military, and economic interests of the Soviet Union at that moment. Self-interested opportunism, rather than humanitarian considerations, also explains Bulgaria's resistance to turning over Jews to the Nazis during the waning days of the war. . . . On the individual level, several rescuers clearly exploited those they helped, sometimes betraying them or even murdering them when their resources were depleted.
>
> Self-serving interests are also sometimes ascribed to religious rescuers, particularly to those who either sought to convert those they helped or actually did so. (pp. 367–368)

Due to the Nazis' Dominance No Nation in Europe Would Dare Help the Jews

Some students are under the impression that because of the Nazis' dominance, no nation or group would even consider helping the Jews. That, however, was not entirely the case.

Although most nations and many religious bodies (including the Roman Catholic Church, which ardently protested the euthanasia policy of the Nazis but did not protest against the murder of the Jews) for all intents and purposes ignored the plight of the Jews, it is also a fact that thousands of people throughout Nazi-controlled Europe provided assistance to Jews—even though they risked death in doing so. In certain remarkable instances, entire communities reached out to Jews and provided places of hiding and sustenance. A classic example was the populace of the French town of Le Chambon-Sur-Ligon. The town's people sheltered thousands of Jews during most of the Nazi occupation. More specifically,

> The town's overwhelmingly Protestant population responded to the call of Pastor André Trocmé, who with his wife, Magda, initiated and presided over [a] vast rescue operation (with the help of interdenominational organizations). Refugee Jews were housed in public institutions and children's homes or with local townsmen and farmers, for various periods of time. Then, with the help of others, some were taken on dangerous treks through French towns and villages and under assumed French names to the Swiss frontier. They were surreptitiously smuggled across it and into the waiting hands of other Protestant supporters on the Swiss side. It is estimated that some three thousand to five thousand Jews found shelter in Le Chambon and its environs at one time or another between 1941 and 1944. (Paldiel, 1995, p. 859)

Remarkably, an entire nation, Denmark, also came together to save its Jewish citizens from deportation.

> On the night of October 1–2, 1943, the German police began arresting Jews. Reports of the planned deportation of the Jews were leaked to various Danish circles by several German sources. The reaction was spontaneous. The Danes alerted the Jews, helping them move into hiding places and from there make their way to the seashore, and, with the help of Danish fishermen, cross into Sweden. At first this was an unorganized and spontaneous operation, but soon the Danish resistance joined in and helped to organize the massive flight that followed the Swedish government's proclamation that it was ready to take in all the refugees from Denmark. In Denmark, all groups of the population went into action in order to save the Jews. The operation went on for three weeks, and in its course seventy-two hundred Jews and some several hundred non-Jewish relatives of theirs were taken to Sweden. (Yahil, 1995, p. 364)

Different nations, groups, and individuals acted the way they did for a variety of reasons. Much depended, of course, on the time period; the location of the nation, group, or individual; the other socioeconomic and political events of the period; and so on. For example, nations in close proximity to Nazi Germany were wary of the latter's actions. Also, in the early 1930s, many nations across the world were suffering from the Great Depression. Further, from 1939 onward, many nations were engulfed in World War II. What also needs to be taken into consideration is the extent to which a nation, group, or individual was antisemitic. This is not to make excuses for any nation, group, or individual; however, as the authors of the United States Holocaust Memorial Museum's *Guidelines for Teaching about the Holocaust* state:

Events of the Holocaust, and particularly how individuals and organizations behaved at that time, must be placed in an historical context so that students can begin to comprehend the circumstances that encouraged or discouraged these acts. [Teachers must] frame [their] approach to specific events and acts of complicity or defiance by considering when and where an act took place; the immediate consequences to oneself and one's family of assisting victims; the impact of contemporaneous events; the degree of control the Nazis had on a country or local population; the cultural attitudes of particular native populations historically toward different victim groups, and the availability, effectiveness, and risk [of different actions]. (Parsons and Totten, 1993, p. 5)

As Nechama Tec (1998) has written:

The most formidable barrier to Jewish rescue was the degree to which Nazi occupying forces controlled the governmental machinery. Where the Germans were in complete control, they were prepared to do whatever was necessary to annihilate the Jewish populations. . . . Another condition affecting Jewish rescue was the level of antisemitism within a given country. Where a strong antisemitic tradition prevailed, denunciations of Jews and their protectors were more common. In addition, in a society hostile to Jews, Jewish rescue by Christians was likely to invite disapproval, if not outright censure from . . . countrymen. Also, in areas of pervasive antisemitism, . . . Christian helpers themselves could be influenced by long-taught anti-Jewish images and values. . . . Additionally, the sheer number of Jews within a particular country and the degree to which they were assimilated also affected their chances of rescue. . . . The easier it was for Jews to blend in, the less dangerous it was for others to shield them. . . . These facts . . . came together in an almost limitless number of combinations. (p. 651)

In speaking about the rescue of Jews in Poland, where both huge Nazi-organized ghettos and all the death camps were located, Tec (1991) points out that:

[T]o rescue Jews, Poles had to overcome a number of formidable barriers. Foremost among them were the Nazi policies of Jewish annihilation. In Poland these polices were introduced early and with a high degree of ruthlessness. Among the measures aimed at Jewish destruction was a 1941 decree that made any unauthorized move out of a ghetto a crime punishable by death. The same punishment applied to Poles who helped Jews move to the forbidden Christian world, the so-called Aryan side. This law was widely publicized and strongly enforced. Executions of Christians and Jews followed, and the names of the executed were widely publicized. Since the Nazis followed the principle of collective responsibility the same punishment applied to the family members of those who defied this law. There are many cases on record where entire families of Poles were murdered, including infants, only because one of them had protected Jews.

. . . [T]he cultural climate of Poland was [also] antagonistic toward Jews. [P]ervasive Polish antisemitism was often translated into opposition and hostility to Jewish rescue, and Poles who were eager to save Jews knew that by following their inclinations they would be inviting the censure of their fellow citizens.

. . . Non-assimilation of the Polish Jews also interfered with their protection. For centuries Poles and Jews lived apart. . . . Each felt like a stranger in the other's world, and distinctions between them permeated all aspects of life. One [was] speech. In the last prewar census of 1931, only 12 percent of the Jewish population identified Polish as their native tongue, 79 percent chose Yiddish, and the rest Hebrew.

. . . [C]ultural differences were among other serious drawbacks. These differences permeated all aspects of life, including such matters as eating and drinking. For example, onion and garlic were defined as Jewish foods. For anyone who wanted to pass for a Pole, it was safest to profess a dislike for both. (pp. 211, 212, 213)

(For information about those individuals, organizations, and nations that reached out to assist the Jews, see Leo Goldberger, *The Rescue of the Danish Jews: Moral Courage Under Stress*. New York: New York University Press, 1987; Leni Yahil, *The Rescue of Danish Jewry*. Philadelphia: Jewish Publication Society, 1969; Philip Hallie, *Lest Innocent Blood Be Shed: The Story of the Village of Le Chambon and How Goodness Happened There*. New York: Harper & Row, 1979; Per Anger, *With Raoul Wallenberg, Missing Hero of the Holocaust*. New York: Viking, 1981; Nechama Tec, *When Light Pierced the Darkness: Christian Rescue of Jews in Nazi Occupied Poland*. New York: Oxford University Press, 1986; Susan Zuccotti, *The Italians and the Holocaust: Persecution, Rescue, Survival*. New York: Basic Books, 1987; and Ivo Herzer, *The Italian Refuge: Rescue of Jews During the Holocaust*. Washington, DC: Catholic University Press, 1989.)

At Least Early On, No One Amongst the Allied Nations Knew about the Planned and Actual Annihilation of the Jews by the Nazis

Students are often apt to excuse or rationalize the fact that the Allies did not come to the direct and immediate assistance of the millions that were being brutally persecuted and murdered by the Nazis. In doing so, they often assert, incorrectly, that no one really knew, until it was too late, about the mass murder of the Jews.

In an essay entitled "What Did They Know and When," Holocaust scholar Randolph L. Braham (1981) reports that as early as December 1941 and January 1942, novelist Thomas Mann disclosed in BBC radio broadcasts information that he had about the mass killings of Jews (p. 111). Braham (1981) also reports that "[I]n May 1942 the Jewish Socialist party of Poland, the 'Bund,' transmitted a detailed report to London informing the world that the Germans had 'embarked on the physical extermination of the Jewish population on Polish soil'" (p. 111). Braham subsequently notes that "the report was broadcast over the BBC on June 2 and 26, 1942; details were also published by the *Daily Telegraph* on June 25 as well as by the Jewish press" (p. 111).

In his book *While Six Million Died: A Chronicle of American Apathy*, Arthur D. Morse (1968) reports that:

On July 1, [1942] . . . the Polish government-in-exile had released a report from underground sources to the Allied governments and the press detailing the massacre of seven hundred thousand Jews since the German invasion in September 1939. It included a city-by-city roll call of death and revealed the first use of mobile gas vans, at Chelmno. Ninety Jews at a time had been packed into each van and asphyxiated by carbon monoxide. (p. 5)

Morse (1968) also reveals that:

> On August 1, 1942 . . . Gerhart Riegner, the representative in Switzerland of the World Jewish Congress, learned from a leading German industrialist that many months before, Hitler had ordered the extermination of all the Jews in Europe. *Riegner, like the governments of the United States and Great Britain, had been receiving a constant flow of information about the deportation of Jewish men, women and children to Poland. He knew, and they knew, about the mass executions of Jewish nations in Poland and Russia;* since the German invasion of the Soviet Union in 1941, hundreds of thousands of Jews had been shot by the Einsatzgruppen, the mobile killing units which followed the Nazi armies for just that purpose . . . *Detailed reports of their operations had reached the United States and its allies, and, in fact, had been published in daily newspapers* (italics added). (pp. 3–4)

In early August 1942, Riegner provided both the consulates of the United States and Great Britain with a cable that detailed the aforementioned information and asked that the report be forwarded to the World Jewish Congress. The U.S. State Department chose to suppress the cable; the British Foreign Office, however, did provide the London branch of the World Jewish Congress with a copy of the cable (Morse, 1968, pp. 7–9).

Using new evidence from recently released intelligence archives, Richard Breitman (1998), in his *Official Secrets: What the Nazis Planned, What the British and Americans Knew,* reports the following about when and what the British government knew regarding the Nazis' extermination of Jews in Soviet territories:

> On August 28 [1941], Winston Churchill learned that Police Battalion 314 had shot 367 Jews; he circled the total. Two days later he read that Battalions 45 and 314 shot a total of 355 Jews, and the Police Squadron another 113. On August 31, the First SS Brigade killed 283 Jews, and Police Regiment South was credited with 1,342.
>
> . . . Even with the ambiguous and camouflaged terminology for the victims, the number of Jews reported killed was staggering—and produced some skepticism. Between August 23 and August 31 alone, British decoders revealed that the German SS and Order Police units (not the Einsatzgruppen, the details of whose activities were probably still unknown) killed 12,361 Jews. The intelligence summary issued on September 12 contained a disturbing projection: the actual number of executions was probably double the recorded number, because the code breakers had succeeded only about half of the time, it said. A short but pointed paragraph followed:
>
>> The execution of "Jews" is so recurrent a feature of these reports that the figures have been omitted from the situation reports and brought under one heading (3.d). Whether all those executed as "Jews" are indeed such is of course [!] doubtful; but the figures are no less conclusive as evidence of a policy of savage intimidation if not of ultimate extermination. (pp. 94, 96)

These are just a few of the many examples of the early reports that were available to key agencies and, in certain cases, the general public, regarding the mass atrocities being perpetrated by the Nazis.

(For a detailed discussion of which nations knew what when, see Richard Breitman, *Official Secrets: What the Nazis Planned, What the British and Americans Knew*. New York: Hill & Wang, 1998; Walter Laqueur and Richard Breitman, *Breaking the Silence*. New York: Simon & Schuster, 1986; Walter Laqueur, *The Terrible Secret: Suppression of the Truth About Hitler's "Final Solution."* New York: Penguin Books, 1983; Randolph L. Braham, "What Did They Know and When?" In Yehuda Bauer and Nathan Rotenstreich [Eds.], *The Holocaust as Historical Experience: Essays and a Discussion*. New York: Holmes & Meier, 1981; and Arthur D. Morse, *While Six Million Died: A Chronicle of American Apathy*. New York: Hart, 1968.)

The United States Helped to Save the Jews from Annihilation

Wishing to think the best of their country, many secondary level students in the United States tend to believe that the United States did all it could to assist the Jews during the Holocaust period. Unfortunately, sadly, and tragically, that simply was not the case. As Holocaust scholar Henry Feingold (1995) states:

> The United States government's response to the antisemitic policy of the National Socialist regime in Germany is best viewed in the context of the long-range contours of American foreign policy and the stringencies of the domestic economic crisis of the 1930s. During the refugee phase of the crisis (1933–1941), there was a reluctance to accept Jewish refugees. Only in 1939, after the Evian Conference, were the existing quotas fully utilized. . . . [Be that as it may,] a bill to admit ten thousand Jewish refugee children outside the quota (the Wagner-Rogers Bill) introduced in 1939 and again in 1940, did not emerge from committee. During World War II, the "Jewish question" maintained the low priority it had before the war.
>
> The initial context of the United States' relationship to Germany was its policy of isolationism, which meant in practice a rejection of all the responsibilities of being a world power while not eschewing commercial relations. Disillusionment with America's entry into World War I was of primary importance in this consideration. Strong isolationist sentiment prevented the Roosevelt administration from assuming an effective interventionist policy.
>
> . . . The existing indifference to the refugees extended, after Pearl Harbor, to the question of rescuing those in camps. Even when it became clear that Berlin had actually embarked on the "Final Solution" the State Department tried for a time to suppress confirmation of the news, which emanated from Leland Harrison, its own consul in Bern, Switzerland.
>
> . . . Between 1942 and the end of the war in Europe in 1945, the Allies gave no priority in their war aims to the rescue of Jews. Repeated suggestions for retribution, negotiations, or ameliorating the situation, such as sending food packages to camps or changing the designation of their inmates to that of prisoners of war, were rejected because it was felt that such steps would interfere with the prosecution of

the war. The processed murder of the Jews was not mentioned at any of the Allied war conferences held at Tehran, Casablanca, and Yalta. (pp. 1546–1547)

Nazis Who Refused to Kill Jews Were, Themselves, Murdered

Many are under the misconception that individual Nazis did not have a choice whether they became perpetrators or collaborators in the systematic murder of the Jews. As a result, some students tend to rationalize away the guilt of the perpetrators.

In *Ordinary Men: Reserve Battalion 101 and the Final Solution in Poland,* Holocaust scholar Christopher Browning (1992) writes the following about the lack of severe punishment for those who refused to kill unarmed civilians:

> Quite simply, in the past forty-five years no defense attorney or defendant in any of the hundreds of postwar trials has been able to document a single case in which refusal to obey an order to kill unarmed civilians resulted in the allegedly inevitable dire punishment. The punishment or censure that occasionally did result from such disobedience was never commensurate with the gravity of the crimes the men had been asked to commit. (p. 170)

Further, in an article entitled "Those Who Said 'No!': German Soldiers, SS, and Police Who Refused to Execute Civilians During World War II," historian David Kitterman (1991) writes:

> Could a Nazi soldier refuse to participate in the round-up and murder of Jews, Gypsies, and other unarmed groups of men, women, and children during World War II and survive without getting shot or put into a concentration camp? Conventional wisdom among German soldiers held that any order to shoot unarmed civilians must always be obeyed. Failure to carry out this order would have drastic results. Many students of Nazi history have the same view, even today.
>
> We may never learn the full answer to the above question. Yet ample documentary evidence exists of over 100 cases in which individuals or groups within Germany's armed forces, even SS or police units, refused participation in the shooting of unarmed civilians or POWs. None of them paid the ultimate penalty—death! Very few even suffered any other serious consequence! There are no proven cases where any of them were shot or physically harmed for refusing such orders. (p. 113)

(For a more detailed discussion, see Kitterman's article by the same title in *German Studies Review,* XI [2], May 1988, pp. 241–254.)

Conclusion

When teaching about the Holocaust, it is essential that teachers have a clear perception of their students' basic understanding of the history—including any misconceptions and inaccurate information they may hold. Those who neglect to ascertain *and* address such information do so at the peril of teaching information and concepts that students may end up rejecting, not believing, or not understanding because their personal knowledge base "suggests" the situation during the Holocaust was otherwise than what they are being taught.

Note: Teachers are encouraged to obtain a copy of the Simon Wiesenthal Center's *The Holocaust, 1933–1945: Educational Resources Kit,* for it includes a section, "36 Questions and Answers," that complements the ideas and concerns highlighted in this chapter. Write to: Simon Wiesenthal Center, 9760 West Pico Boulevard, Los Angeles, CA 90035–4792.

REFERENCES

Arad, Yitzhak. (1995). "Extermination Camps," pp. 461–463. In Israel Gutman (Ed.), *Encyclopedia of the Holocaust.* New York: Macmillan.

Bankier, David. (1995). "Nuremberg Laws," pp. 1076–1077. In Israel Gutman (Ed.), *Encyclopedia of the Holocaust.* New York: Macmillan.

Bauer, Yehuda. (1995). "World War II," pp. 1661–1679. In Israel Gutman (Ed.), *Encyclopedia of the Holocaust.* New York: Macmillan.

Berenbaum, Michael. (1990). *A Mosaic of Victims: Non-Jews Persecuted and Murdered by the Nazis.* New York: New York University Press.

Berenbaum, Michael. (1993). *The World Must Know: The History of the Holocaust as Told in the United States Holocaust Memorial Museum.* Boston: Little, Brown.

Braham, Randolph L. (1981). "What Did They Know and When?" In Yehuda Bauer and Nathan Rotenstreich (Eds.), *The Holocaust as Historical Experience: Essays and a Discussion.* New York: Holmes & Meier.

Breitman, Richard. (1998). *Official Secrets: What the Nazis Planned, What the British and Americans Knew.* New York: Hill and Wang.

Browning, Christopher. (1992). *Ordinary Men: Reserve Police Battalion 101 and the Final Solution in Poland.* New York: HarperCollins.

Browning, Christopher. (1995). "Final Solution," pp. 488–493. In Israel Gutman (Ed.), *Encyclopedia of the Holocaust.* New York: Macmillan.

Browning, Christopher. (1995). *The Path to Genocide: Essays on Launching the Final Solution.* New York: Cambridge University Press.

Dawidowicz, Lucy. (1986). *The War Against the Jews 1933–1945.* New York: Bantam.

Dawidowicz, Lucy. (1992). "How They Teach the Holocaust," pp. 65–83. In Lucy S. Dawidowicz (Ed.), *What Is the Use of Jewish History?* New York: Schocken.

Edelheit, Abraham, and Edelheit, Hershel. (1994). *History of the Holocaust: A Handbook and Dictionary.* Boulder, CO: Westview Press.

Eliach, Y. (1984). "Defining the Holocaust: Perspectives of a Jewish Historian," pp. 11–23. In A. J. Peck (Ed.), *Jews and Christians After the Holocaust.* Philadelphia: Jewish Publication Society.

Epstein, Eric Joseph, and Rosen, Philip. (1997). *Dictionary of the Holocaust: Biography, Geography, and Terminology.* Westport, CT: Greenwood Press.

Feingold, Henry L. (1995). "United States of America," pp. 1546–1549. In Israel Gutman (Ed.), *Encyclopedia of the Holocaust.* New York: Macmillan.

Gallagher, Hugh Gregory. (1995). "Holocaust: The Genocide of Disabled Peoples," pp. 265–298. In Samuel Totten, William S. Parsons, and Israel W. Charny (Eds.), *Genocide in the Twentieth Century: Critical Essays and Eyewitness Accounts*. New York: Garland.

Glass, James M. (1997). *"Life Unworthy of Life": Racial Phobia and Mass Murder in Hitler's Germany*. New York: Basic Books.

Gutman, Israel. (1990). "Antisemitism," pp. 55–74. In Israel Gutman (Ed.), *Encyclopedia of the Holocaust*. New York: Macmillan.

Hilberg, Raul. (1985). *The Destruction of the European Jews*. Three Volumes. New York: Holmes & Meier.

Jones, Priscilla Dale. (1995). "Trials of War Criminals, General Survey," pp. 1488–1489. In Israel Gutman (Ed.), *Encyclopedia of the Holocaust*. New York: Macmillan.

Kitterman, David. (February 1991). "Those Who Said 'No!': German Soldiers, SS, and Police Who Refused to Execute Civilians During World War II." In a special issue of *Social Education* ("Teaching About Genocide"), edited by William Parsons and Samuel Totten, 55(2):113.

Kleg, Milton, Rice, Marion J., and Bailey, Wilfrid C. (1970). "Appendix D. A Catechism on Race and Racial Prejudice," pp. 149–155. In Milton Kleg, Marion J. Rice, and Wilfrid C. Bailey, (Eds.) *Race, Caste, and Prejudice*. Athens: University of Georgia.

Koonz, Claudia. (1996). "Genocide and Eugenics: The Language of Power," pp. 155–177. In Peter Hayes (Ed.), *Lessons and Legacies: The Meaning of the Holocaust in a Changing World*. Evanston, IL: Northwestern University Press.

Kulka, Otto Dov, and Hildesheimer, Esriel. (1995). "Germany," pp. 557–575. In Israel Gutman (Ed.), *Encyclopedia of the Holocaust*. New York: Macmillan.

Milton, Sybil. (1995). "Holocaust: The Gypsies," pp. 209–264. In Samuel Totten, William S. Parsons, and Israel W. Charny (Eds.), *Genocide in the Twentieth Century: Critical Essays and Eyewitness Accounts*. New York: Garland.

Milton, Sybil. (2001). "Jehovah's Witnesses," pp. 346–350. In Walter Laqueur (Ed.), *The Holocaust Encyclopedia*. New Haven, CT: Yale University Press.

Morse, Arthur D. (1968). *While Six Million Died: A Chronicle of American Apathy*. New York: Hart.

Mosse, George. (1995). "Racism," pp. 1206–1217. In Israel Gutman (Ed.), *Encyclopedia of the Holocaust*. New York: Macmillan.

Niewyk, Donald. (1995). "Holocaust: The Genocide of the Jews," pp. 167–207. In Samuel Totten, William S. Parsons, and Israel W. Charny (Eds.), *Genocide in the Twentieth Century: Critical Essays and Eyewitness Accounts*. New York: Garland.

Oliner, Pearl M., and Oliner, Samuel P. (1991). "Righteous People in the Holocaust," pp. 363–385. In Israel W. Charny (Ed.), *Genocide: A Critical Bibliographic Review*. London and New York: Mansell and Facts On File, respectively.

Paldiel, Mordecai. (1995). "Le Chambon-Sur-Lignon," pp. 859–860. In Israel Gutman (Ed.), *Encyclopedia of the Holocaust*. New York: Macmillan.

Parsons, William S., and Totten, Samuel. (1993). *Guidelines for Teaching About the Holocaust*. Washington, DC: United States Holocaust Memorial Museum.

Pingel, Falk. (1995). "Concentration Camps." In Israel Gutman (Ed.), *Encyclopedia of the Holocaust*, pp. 308–317. New York: Macmillan.

Rozett, Robert. (1995). "Resistance, Jewish." In Israel Gutman (Ed.), *Encyclopedia of the Holocaust*, pp. 1265–1268. New York: Macmillan.

Supple, Carrie. (1998). "Issues and Problems in Teaching About the Holocaust," pp. 17–59. In Geoffrey Short, Carrie Supple, and Katherine Klinger (Eds.), *The Holocaust in the School Curriculum: A European Perspective*. Strasbourg, Germany: Council of Europe Publishing.

Tal, U. (1979). "On the Study of the Holocaust and Genocide." *Yad Vashem Studies* 12: 7–52.

Tec, Nechama. (1991). "Helping Behavior and Rescue During the Holocaust," pp. 210–224. In Peter Hayes (Ed.), *Lessons and Legacies: The Meaning of the Holocaust in a Changing World*. Evanston, IL: Northwestern University Press.

Tec, Nechama. (1998). "Reflections on Rescuers," pp. 651–662. In Michael Berenbaum and Abraham J. Peck (Eds.), *The Holocaust and History: The Known, The Unknown, The Disputed, and The Reexamined*. Bloomington: Indiana University Press.

United States Holocaust Memorial Museum. (n.d.). *Homosexuals*. Washington, DC: Author.

Weiss, John. (1996). *Ideology of Death: Why the Holocaust Happened in Germany*. Chicago: Ivan R. Dee.

Wiesel, Elie. (1979). "Preface." *Report to the President*. Washington, DC: President's Commission on the Holocaust.

Yahil, Leni. (1990). *The Holocaust: The Fate of European Jewry*. New York: Oxford University Press.

Yahil, Leni. (1995). "Denmark," pp. 362–365. In Israel Gutman (Ed.), *Encyclopedia of the Holocaust*. New York: Macmillan.

NOTES

1. In an essay entitled "Issues and Problems in Teaching About the Holocaust," Supple (1998) provides one startling example of this phenomena: "[I]t has recently been reported that in Germany ten percent of children play Nazi computer games which include the gassing of Jews and Turks as part of the 'fun' . . . And a recent poll of ten- to nineteen-year-olds in Austria revealed that twelve percent owned at least one of these games" (Supple, 1998, p. 18).

5 Do the Jews Constitute a Race? An Issue Holocaust Educators Must Get Right

From the standpoint of scientific classification, from the standpoint of physical anthropology, and from the standpoint of zoology, there is no such thing as a Jewish physical type, and there is not, nor was there ever, anything even remotely resembling a Jewish "race" or ethnic group . . . It is, in fact, as incorrect to speak of a "Jewish race" or ethnic group as it would be to speak of a Catholic, Protestant, or Moslem "race" or ethnic group.

—Ashley Montagu

However much medieval Christians hated Jews, and however much some of them were prepared to do to express their hate, [a]ny stigma that might attach to Jewishness was not a permanent characteristic of those born Jewish. It could be washed off in the waters of baptism. A Jewish convert to Christianity was a Christian in the fullest sense, no longer a Jew.

—William Nicholls

Are Jews a race, or not? At first blush, this issue may seem somewhat inconsequential or rather arcane to those who are interested in teaching about the Holocaust. However, when one realizes that the Nazis not only perceived the Jews as a race but were intent on expunging that "race" from the face of the world in order to purify their own "race," the so-called "Aryan race," the significance of this racial issue becomes paramount for anyone studying this history. That is also true in light of the fact that many people, including students, the parents of students, and even many teachers continue to believe that the Jews constitute a race unto themselves.

The Misconceptions That Some Teachers and Students Hold Regarding Jews Constituting a Race

Repeatedly, both in the classroom and at conferences, I have come across high school students, university students, and educators who are adamant in their belief that Jews constitute a race. For example, during a discussion of Nazi racial policies at a Holocaust education conference in Hot Springs, Arkansas, an audience member raised her hand and asserted: "My mother is Jewish and my father is part Gypsy and I am Caucasian, and so I am of the Jewish race." A historian in the audience responded, "Over and above the fact that race is a concept now eschewed by anthropologists and biologists, an individual can convert to Judaism but one cannot convert from being a white or a black so there can hardly be a Jewish race." The woman retorted: "I consider myself a member of the Jewish race. Period!" Another member of the audience said, "Are you saying that you, a single person, have two races?" The woman replied, "Yes, exactly." When provided additional information why Jews do not constitute a race and why, and that race is a bogus concept, the woman responded, "Well, that's your opinion and it's not one I have to believe."

In another venue, this time during the early stages of a semester-long high school course on the Holocaust that I cotaught, student after student referred to Jews as a race. On a preassessment examination, each student was required to define, in his or her own words, the Holocaust; and in doing so, many referred to the Jews as a separate race:

> During 1933 to 1945, Adolf Hitler, dictator of Germany, led the extermination of six million Jews and five million others by Nazi concentration camps. He convinced the German people that the Jewish race was draining the economy of Germany.

> For some reason Hitler didn't like the Jewish race, and tried to make it extinct.

> Holocaust: The genocide of an entire race of people.

> Holocaust—A time where a ruler tried to take over a country and the world by means of violence and threatening [sic] and torture against another race. At this time it was Hitler trying to completely wipe out the Jews by killing them. A lot of people died and they wiped out three-fourths of Europe's Jewish population.

> The destruction of an entire race by a pathological maniac who felt he was in [sic] his rights playing as God, destroying one race while creating another.

> The Holocaust was an inhuman, disgusting plan of one man and his army to wipe out an entire race of people any way he could. He would kill in ways that he could experiment on them to try to create the perfect race.

The Holocaust was the murdering of the Jews and many other races to turn the world into an Arian [sic] race. Adolf Hitler was the head of this and it took place during WW II. I don't know too much more than this.

One section of the preassessment exercise asked the students to list and comment on those questions/issues that they definitely wished to address during the course of the semester. Here again, many students referred to the Jews as a race:

- Why did Germany pick the Jewish race as a scapegoat?
- What other races, beside the Jews, were killed?
- I am curious about what other kinds of races besides the Jews got killed in the holocaust [sic].

If teachers neglect to correct students' false assumptions that Jews constitute a race, then the students' ultimate understanding of the Holocaust is destined to be skewed. This is true for numerous reasons. First, when students read anything in which the Nazis refer to the Jews as a race, they are likely to accept, at face value, that the Jews are a race. Second, if students think of Jews as a race, they may be apt to accept the Nazis' misconceived and inaccurate notion that there actually is an "Aryan race" and a "Semitic race." Third, thinking of the Jews as a race plays into the Nazis' way of thinking, especially when it is applied to their view of "racial science" *and* their worldview as determined or driven by social Darwinism. At one and the same time, such a misconception is bound to interfere with the students' understanding of the critical differences between traditional history of antisemitism, political antisemitism, and the Nazis' virulent and deadly strain of racial antisemitism.

The imperative to clearly understand this issue becomes even more evident when one realizes that the Nazis perceived the Jews as a lethal danger to the body politic, and how the Nazis planned to "ameliorate" that danger. (The latter issues will be discussed later in this chapter.)

The Misunderstood Concept of "Race"

In his book *Hate Prejudice and Racism*, Milton Kleg (1993) asserts that "The word 'race' is one of the most misunderstood and explosive words in any language, so much so that one anthropologist, Ashley Montagu, suggested that 'The idea of "race" represents one of the most dangerous myths of our time, and one of the most tragic'" (pp. 64–65). Even a cursory study of the history of the past two centuries—the nineteenth and twentieth—corroborate Kleg's assertion.

Although most lay people speak and act as if the concept of race is a given—in fact, to such an extent that most probably never question its viability as a concept or a categorization—a vast majority of anthropologists, geneticists, and biologists today view the concept of "race" as being specious and nonsensical. One may be reasonably expected to ask: "But how can that be? With my own eyes, I can see Caucasians, African Americans, Asians, Hispanics." In an essay entitled "The Meaninglessness of the Anthropological Conception of Race," anthropologist Ashley Montagu (1941) addressed this very issue:

> Certainly, I had always taken the idea [of race] for granted, and I think all of us have done so. Indeed, the idea of race is one of the most fundamental, if not *the* most fundamental of the concepts with which the [early] anthropologist[s] ha[d] habitually worked. To question the validity of this fundamental concept upon which we were intellectually brought up as if it were an axiom, was something which simply never occurred to one. One doesn't question the axioms upon which one's science . . . are based—at least, not usually. One simply takes them for granted." (pp. 1–2)
>
> [That said,] the indictment against the anthropological concept of race is (1) that it is artificial; (2) that it does not agree with the facts; (3) that it leads to confusion and the perpetuation of error, and finally for all these reasons, it is meaningless, or rather more accurately, such meaning as it possesses is false. (p. 9)

Many years ago, Montagu (1965) cogently explained why the concept of race is not only a myth but fallacious and unscientific: "It is generally agreed among students of the evolution of man that all men have originated from a common stock and belong to the same species, *Homo sapiens* . . . [T]he so-called 'races' simply represent the adaptive responses to the different challenges of the environments in which these different peoples or so-called 'races' originating from a common stock found themselves" (p. 51). Continuing, Montagu (1965) explains that:

> If . . . as all the evidence indicates, man [sic] originated from a single stock, how is the variety which he presents to be accounted for? In broad outline, the answer to that question is as follows: As the result of the migration of individuals and families away from the common *sapiens* homelands, and the long continued isolation of the migrants from the parent and similar related groups . . . , the inherent variability of the genetic system in random manner produced in the course of time certain patternings of genes differing from those exhibited by the other groups. Furthermore, living in different environments, some under the unremitting action of intense sunlight, and others in areas of reduced sunlight, those individuals possessing genes that would enable them to respond in adaptation to the challenges of the environment would be more likely to leave a larger progeny to perpetuate the group than those not possessing the necessary adaptive fitness.
>
> This, in a few words, is the explanation for the differences that characterize the varieties of mankind [sic]—an explanation which for this and the many other traits that cannot be dealt with here it would take volumes to treat of adequately. The evolutionary factors I have implicitly referred to are migration, isolation, genetic drift, mutation, culture, hybridization, social selection, and natural selection. (pp. 55–56)

Montagu (1965) concludes by asserting that, "Evolutionary change is a dynamic process, not a static one and that constitutes yet another reason why the idea of a 'race' as a group of similar individuals is quite hopeless, for such an artificially created entity would be incapable of change, being hardened immodifiably by the criteria of the taxonomist's preserving spirit" (p. 115).

In his introduction to *The Concept of "Race" in Natural and Social Science*, E. Nathaniel Gates (1997) delineates recent thinking vis-à-vis various scholars' conception of "race," and in doing so delineates why it is a concept that has fallen into disfavor with most geneticists, biologists, and anthropologists:

> The first serious challenge to the racial taxonomies that undergirded these early forms of racialized hierarchy arose in 1859 with the publication of Charles Darwin's *On the Origin of the Species by Means of Natural Selection*. In contrast to most of his predecessors, Darwin was more interested in the dynamic processes of biological change than in the static nature of formal taxonomies. . . . Yet, the full impact of Darwin's evolutionary theory could not be fully appreciated or explored until the subsequent emergence of the science of genetics, which firmly established the biological basis of evolutionary processes. Only when it became possible to examine and analyze biological attributes invisible to the human eye did genetic science gradually shift its attention away from superficial morphological differences such as skin coloration. By the 1960s, partly as a result of this shift in emphasis, it was generally accepted among geneticists that the nineteenth-century view of "race" as a fixed taxonomy, based upon selected morphological features such as skin color or hair texture, no longer possessed real scientific utility or meaning. For these and other reasons too complex to examine here, a growing number of physical anthropologists and other biology-dependent social scientists concluded concurrently that there was no demonstrable causal relationship between physical or genetic characteristics and alleged "cultural" characteristics. The incremental advance of genetic science demonstrated definitively that "races," as conceived and defined by men of science from the late eighteenth century onward, had no scientifically verifiable referents. (pp. vii–ix)

Gates (1997) goes on to lament the fact that despite the radical change of perspectives regarding the concept of race by scientists, social scientists, and some governmental bodies, lay people continue to persist in the use of the concept and term "race":

> The practices of identifying selected *Homo Sapiens* by reference to their skin color, or other morphological features alleged to be indicative of significant, corresponding differences, remains endemic. As a consequence, various types of social interactions continue to be discussed under the rubric of "race relations," a frequently invoked social scientific term that seriously credits the notion of the existence of persons of different "races." On the basis of this paradigmatic, "common-sense" understanding, governments have in the past promulgated, and even today some continue to adopt, legislation aimed at the better regulation of such "relations." Thus, although the sanction of science has been fatefully withdrawn, the thoroughgoing triumph of the racialized conception of fluid social groups as unchangeably fixed closed entities continues to encode and preserve the notions of "race" and "race"-based hierarchy in law, literature and cultural praxis. (p. ix)

(For an informative discussion of the history of the concept of race, see Ashley Montagu, "The History of Idea" in his book *The Idea of Race*. Lincoln: University of Nebraska Press, 1965, pp. 3–41. Also instructive are two essays, "The Concept Popularised," pp. 13–42, and "The Concept Attacked," pp. 43–60. In Michael Banton and Jonathan Harwood, *The Race Concept*. New York: Praeger, 1975.)

The Nazis' Perspective on "Race" and the Jews

The doctrine of racism combines both the biologistic and the social views of "race." Racism maintains that the visible physical hereditary differences that certain peoples exhibit and which distinguish them from other peoples are inseparably linked with certain hereditarily determined behavioral traits. It is an essential tenet of this viewpoint that these hereditarily determined traits, especially with reference to behavior, differ significantly between these peoples, called "races," and are responsible for the differences in the learning capacities and achievements which distinguish one "race" from another.

This is the biologistic racist argument. From it the social racist argument follows. That argument is that since—and it is taken for granted that it is so—the behavioral differences between the "races" are for the most part biologically determined, it is desirable to make certain "racial" arrangements designed to achieve the following ends: (1) to prevent "homogenization" or "mongrelization," and thus deterioration of the superior "race." (Montagu, 1965, p. 44–45)

If there is no such entity as "race," then there certainly cannot be an "Aryan race" or a "Semitic race." Be that as it may, the Nazis based their beliefs, in large part, on the misguided conviction that there was an "Aryan race" and that *it* was *the superior race.*

As Berenbaum (1993) notes:

Racism was the central and pervasive theme of Nazi ideology. It shaped social policy in Germany between 1933 and 1939, was a major factor in Nazi conduct of World War II, motivated German policy in occupied countries and . . . resulted in the Holocaust.

Hitler's obsession with racial purity . . . his beliefs in German racial supremacy, and the notion of an Aryan master race that would take over the world should have come as no surprise when they became state policy after March 1933 [which is when the Nazis came to power in Germany]. He had stated them clearly not only in his speeches, but in his book, *Mein Kampf (My Struggle)*, which was first published in 1925. . . .

The Nazis regarded the Germans as racially superior, and considered Slavs, Gypsies, and blacks to be inferior. At the bottom of this scale were the Jews, the most dangerous of races. . . . In the racial struggle of history, the "master race" would dominate if it preserved its purity. Otherwise, it would be polluted, corrupted, and destroyed by inferior races. (pp. 20–21)

What inspired the fallacious concept of an "Aryan race" and the equally spurious notion that it was superior to all others? Holocaust scholar George L. Mosse (1995) writes that:

. . . [R]esearch seemed to confirm that Sanskrit, ancient Persian, and languages descended from them were related to many European languages, and that therefore there must have been an original "proto" language that had been imported from Asia into Europe by the migration of "Aryan" peoples—a language named by philologists "Indo-European" or "Aryo-European." It was in this context that the ominous term "Aryan" made its first appearance.

On the premise that a people's language is the expression of its accumulated experience over the ages, [certain] scholars claimed that the "Aryan" past reflected the superiority of contemporary Europe. . . . [W]ith the help of philology, they were able to establish a link with the "Aryan" prehistory of the Germanic peoples. The philologist described the "Aryans" as courageous and virile "tillers of the soil" who led a solid family life. A historical myth was created that gave legitimacy to pretensions of moral and national superiority—an element destined to be a part of the theory of racism throughout its development.

. . . Those opposed to the Jewish Emancipation asserted that the Jews were by nature incapable of speaking the language of their host nation, a trait that had historical roots and reflected the Jews' materialistic character.

. . . [T]he rise of racism, from the beginning of the nineteenth century, sought to establish a model for the "ideal type" of human being. . . . Anthropologists and the philologists had already paved the way for a school of thought which held that all "foreign" races were to be placed in between the human race and the apes.

. . . From the second half of the nineteenth century, it was not so much the existence of so-called black or yellow races but antisemitism that served as the breeding ground for racist views. . . . Jews were looked upon as the representative of a foreign culture in the heart of Europe; they dressed differently, prayed differently, and spoke a different language (Yiddish). As long as they lived in ghettos they had not aroused much interest, but this attitude changed in the wake of their emancipation [when they were free to leave the ghettos and live and work among others], at the beginning of the nineteenth century. (pp. 1207, 1208–1209)

The impact of this "research" and such ideas were not lost on the Nazis; indeed, they used the latter, in part, to construct and support their racist ideology. As Mosse (1995) points out:

Following World War I, an attempt was made to put theory into practice. Political movements used racism as a dynamic in order to wage war against their enemies. In that respect there was no difference between National Socialism in Germany, the Iron Guard in Romania, and the Ustasa in Croatia . . . Leaders of racist movements were no longer content with removing the Jews from economic or social life but called for their destruction.

Hitler declared that an inferior human specimen was closer to the apes than to the superior races of mankind. Heinrich Himmler, in order to reinforce his men's motivation for their part in the Holocaust, compared the Jews to fleas and mice—obnoxious forms of life that had to be destroyed.

Of decisive importance for the evolution of racism were the Nuremberg Laws (1935), which not only provided the legal basis for separating the Jews from the Christians, but also gave a precise definition of who was a Jew. (pp. 1214–1215, 1216)

Under the Nuremberg Laws, a person was considered a Jew if he or she had at least three Jewish grandparents. An individual who had only two Jewish grandparents was designated a *Mischling* or a person of mixed blood. *Mischlinge* were banned by law from having sexual relations with either Jews or Aryans; and thus, they were, in effect, destined to die out or become extinct. The Nuremberg Laws also defined for the first time who was and was not considered an "Aryan."

In regard to Hitler's obsession with the issue of "race," "blood," and the status and future of the "Aryan race," Holocaust historian Lucy Dawidowicz (1986) makes the following observation:

> The "Aryans" represented the perfection of human existence, whereas the Jews were the embodiment of evil. . . . The vileness of the Jew, he [Hitler] claimed, resided in the blood of the race and was evident in the Jew's physical, mental, cultural being. . . . Over and over again he kept describing the Jews in terms of filth and disease. . . . Jews, he asserted, were at the center of every abscess, were "germ-carriers," poisoning the blood of others, but preserving their own. The Jews were, Hitler said, "a ferment of decomposition". . . . The depiction of the Jews as the carriers of filth and disease and, hence, of death and destruction, goes back in the history of anti-Semitism to the Middle Ages, when Jews were accused of spreading the plague and poisoning the wells. . . .
>
> From the concept of the Jew as parasite, vampire, blood-sucker, contaminating the Aryan race, it was a small step to the Jew as figurative bloodsucker in the financial and economic spheres. (p. 19)

Since every single drop of "Jewish blood" was perceived as a contaminant by the Nazis, every single Jew—regardless of sex, age, beliefs, values, or even religious practices—was targeted for annihilation. In this regard, Holocaust scholar Michael R. Marrus (1987) notes that:

> Unlike the case with any other group, and unlike the massacres before or since, every single one of the millions of targeted Jews was to be murdered. Eradication was to be total. In principle, no Jew was to escape. . . . Consistent with the Nazis' biological racism, each and every Jew was a threat, including the old, the ill, women, children, and even tiny infants. (p. 24)

As obsessed as the Nazis were with the issue of "race," their designation of those who constituted a Jew or an Aryan was actually based on the religious background of an individual. As Holocaust historian Raul Hilberg (1985b) notes in his magisterial study, *The Destruction of the European Jews:*

> The term *non-Aryan descent* was defined in the regulation of April 11, 1933 [by the Nazis], as a designation for any person who had a Jewish parent or grandparent; the parent or grandparent was presumed to be Jewish if [he/she] belonged to the Jewish religion. . . . It should be noted that this definition is in no sense based on racial criteria, such as blood type, curvature of the nose, or other physical characteristics. Nazi commentators, for propagandistic reasons, called the decrees "racial laws." . . . But it is important to understand that the sole criterion for categorization

into the "Aryan or "non-Aryan" group was religion, not the religion of the person involved but the religion of his ancestors. After all, the Nazis were not interested in the "Jewish nose." They were concerned with the "Jewish influence." (pp. 66, 67, 68)

Still, as Holocaust scholar and survivor Henry Friedlander (1995) has observed, "Geneticists, anthropologists, and psychiatrists advanced a theory of human heredity that merged with the racist doctrine of ultra-nationalists to form a political ideology based on race. The Nazi movement both absorbed and advanced this ideology" (p. 1). Ultimately, this view of race became entwined with the Nazis' virulent and deadly strain of antisemitisim, its extreme nationalism, and its take on social Darwinism.

Friedlander (1995) further notes that, "After their assumption of power in 1933, the Nazis created the political framework that made it possible to translate this ideology of inequality [political ideology based on race] into a policy of exclusion. At the same time, the German bureaucratic, professional, and scientific elite provided the legitimacy the regime needed for the smooth implementation of this policy" (p. 1). As noted above, the apotheosis of this effort was the passage, in 1935, of the Nuremberg Laws (the Reich Citizenship Law and the Law for the Protection of German Blood and Honor). These laws "became the basis for the further legal exclusion of Jews from German life and the ensuing anti-Jewish policy" (Bankier, 1995, p. 1076). Referring to the Nuremberg Laws as "racial legislation" (p. 68), Yahil (1990) asserts that these two laws "established the inferior status of the Jewish community in two respects: (1) the civic equality granted the Jews by the emancipation was officially abolished and (2) the racial principle became law, segregating the Jews as individuals and as a community from the rest of the population" (p. 68).

(For a discussion of the genesis and evolution of the Nazis' use of the terms "Aryan," "non-Aryan," "full Jew," "Mischling of the first degree," and "Mischling of the second degree," see the section entitled "Definition by Decree," pp. 65–80. In Raul Hilberg, *The Destruction of the European Jews*. Volume 1. New York: Holmes & Meier, 1985b.)

(For an authoritative and relatively detailed discussion of the growth and spread of racist ideology, racism, and politics vis-à-vis the Nazi movement, see George L. Mosse, "Racism," pp. 1206–1217. In Israel Gutman [Ed.], *Encyclopedia of the Holocaust*. New York: Macmillan, 1995; and Robert Proctor, *Racial Hygiene: Medicine Under the Nazis*. Cambridge: Harvard University Press, 1988.)

Methods for Addressing the Issue of Race and Jews

An examination of the literature on teaching about the Holocaust reveals a serious dearth of attention on the issue of whether Jews constitute a race. In light of that, I shall highlight strategies I have found to be effective in raising and examining this issue with both secondary-level and university students.

Following the students' definition of the Holocaust, in which many refer to the concept of "race," I require the students to define the word "race," and to discuss why the concept of "race" has come to be a dubitable concept among biologists, geneticists, anthropologists, Holocaust historians, and others. They are required to use scholarly sources (examples of such are provided on a handout) for this assignment, and may not use standard dictionaries or encyclopedias. (Useful sources for such an assignment are: Nathaniel Gates. "Introduction," pp. vii–x 1997. In Nathaniel Gates [Ed.], *The Concept of "Race" in Natural and Social Science.* New York: Garland; Milton Kleg, *Hate Prejudice and Racism.* Albany: State University of New York Press, 1993; Ashley Montagu, *The Concept of Race.* New York: Free Press, 1967; Ashley Montagu, *The Idea of Race.* Lincoln: University of Nebraska Press, 1965; and George Mosse, "Racism" pp. 1206–1217. In Israel Gutman [Ed.], *Encyclopedia of the Holocaust.* New York: Macmillan, 1995.) Once the students have conducted their research, a general class discussion is held in which the students discuss their findings. The teacher must be ready to add to the discussion, deepen the discussion and correct, with concrete examples from the literature, any ongoing misconceptions or misunderstandings.

Another useful activity is to invite a rabbi from a local congregation to speak to the class about Judaism, including why Jews do not constitute a race. Prior to the visit, the students should be required to write out any and all questions they have regarding Judaism and the Nazis' views of the Jews.

An alternative to the above-mentioned activity is to arrange a panel discussion of experts around the fact that Jews do not constitute a race. Ideally, such a panel should be comprised of at least three to five individuals with an expertise in different areas such as Judaism, biology, genetics, anthropology, and history of the Holocaust. Such individuals might be located at the local or regional synagogue, community college, or university. Again, students should prepare before listening to the panel. At a minimum, they should be assigned to read and respond in writing to an article that is germane to the topic. Further, they should be required to write out the questions they want answered during the session. Finally, during the session with the panelists, it is imperative that ample time be allocated for the students to posit their questions to the panelists.

Another worthwhile activity is to engage the students in a study of the Nazis' racial policies, including how and why they latched onto the concept of an "Aryan race" and why and how such a concept is unscientific and racist. It is recommended that teachers provide their students with a detailed set of directions that clearly delineates the task as well as a rubric that establishes the criteria for the activity. Ideally, students should be required to use scholarly works for this task versus textbooks, basic encyclopedias, and other general works. (Two excellent sources, among many, for such an assignment are the above-mentioned George Mosse, "Racism." In Israel Gutman [Ed.], *Encyclopedia of the Holocaust*; and Michael Burleigh and Wolfgang Wipperman, *The Racial State: Germany 1933–1945.* New York: Cambridge University Press, 1991.)

For more advanced classes, and especially those that include students who are strong readers, a Jigsaw cooperative learning assignment could be devised around Chapter 4, "Definition by Decree," in Raul Hilberg's (1985) *The Destruction of the European Jews*. (Note: For information on the Jigsaw cooperative learning strategy, see Robert Slavin, "Jigsaw II," pp. 104–110. In *Cooperative Learning: Theory, Research, and Practice*. Englewood Cliffs, NJ: Prentice Hall, 1990; and Samuel Totten, "Jigsaw Synthesis: A Method for Incorporating a Study of Social Issues into the Extant Curriculum," pp. 389–424. In Jon E. Pedersen [Ed.], *Secondary Schools and Cooperative Learning*. New York: Garland, 1995.)

Conclusion

In order for students to understand the "why" behind the Holocaust, that is, to ascertain why the Nazis ostracized, discriminated against, degraded, isolated, brutalized, and murdered millions of Jews and others, they need to become conversant with the Nazis' racial policies. Without such knowledge, the study of the Holocaust simply becomes a study of mindless brutality and murder—indeed, just one more case of mass murder in a "century of genocide." At the heart of the Nazis' philosophy was the notion that Jews were not simply an *inferior* "race" but a *dangerous* "race"—a race so dangerous that it endangered not only the welfare but the very lifeblood of the mythological "Aryan race." For students to think and believe that Jews were a race plays directly into the hands of the Nazis' skewed philosophy, and that, to say the least, is monumentally counterproductive to a study of the Holocaust.

REFERENCES

Bankier, David. (1995). "Nuremberg Laws," pp. 1076–1077. In Israel Gutman (Ed.), *Encyclopedia of the Holocaust*. New York: Macmillan.

Banton, Michael, and Harwood, Jonathan. (1975). *The Race Concept*. New York: Praeger.

Berenbaum, Michael. (1993). *The World Must Know: The History of the Holocaust as Told in the United States Holocaust Memorial Museum*. Boston: Little, Brown.

Burleigh, Michael, and Wipperman, Wolfgang. (1991). *The Racial State: Germany 1933–1945*. New York: Cambridge University Press.

Dawidowicz, Lucy S. (1986). *The War Against the Jews 1933–1945*. New York: Bantam.

Friedlander, Henry. (1995). *The Origins of Nazi Genocide: From Euthanasia to The Final Solution*. Chapel Hill: University of North Carolina Press.

Gates, E. Nathaniel. (1997). "Introduction," pp. vii–x. In E. Nathaniel Gates (Ed.), *The Concept of "Race" in Natural and Social Science*, New York: Garland.

Hilberg, Raul. (1985a). *The Destruction of the European Jews*. Three Volumes. New York: Holmes & Meier.

Hilberg, Raul. (1985b). "Definition by Decree," pp. 65–80. In Raul Hilberg, *The Destruction of the European Jews*. Volume 1. New York: Holmes & Meier.

Kleg, Milton. (1993). *Hate Prejudice and Racism*. Albany: State University of New York Press.

Marrus, Michael. (1987). *The Holocaust in History*. Hanover, NH: Meridian.

Montagu, Ashley. (1941). "The Meaninglessness of the Anthropological Conception of Race." *The Journal of Heredity*, 23:243–247.

Montagu, Ashley. (1964). "Are the Jews a 'Race'?", pp. 317–338. In Ashley Montagu, *Man's Most Dangerous Myth: The Fallacy of Race*. Fourth Edition. Cleveland and New York: World.

Montagu, Ashley. (1965). *The Idea of Race*. Lincoln: University of Nebraska Press.

Montagu, Ashley (Ed.). (1967). *The Concept of Race*. New York: Free Press.

Mosse, George. (1995). "Racism," pp. 1206–1217. In Israel Gutman (Ed.), *Encyclopedia of the Holocaust*. New York: Macmillan.

Nicholls, William. (1995). *Christian Antisemitism: A History of Hate*. Northvale, NJ: Jason Aronson.

Parsons, William S., and Totten, Samuel. (1993). *Guidelines for Teaching About the Holocaust*. Washington, DC: United States Holocaust Memorial Museum.

Slavin, Robert. (1990). "Jigsaw II," pp. 104–110. In Robert Slavin, *Cooperative Learning: Theory, Research, and Practice*. Englewood Cliffs, NJ: Prentice Hall.

Totten, Samuel. (1995). "Jigsaw Synthesis: A Method for Incorporating a Study of Social Issues into the Extant Curriculum," pp. 389–424. In Jon E. Pedersen (Ed.), *Secondary Schools and Cooperative Learning*. New York: Garland.

Yahil, Leni. (1990). *The Holocaust: The Fate of European Jewry*. New York: Oxford University Press.

6 "Complicating" Students' Thinking Vis-à-Vis the History of the Holocaust

When teaching about the Holocaust (or any complex subject, for that matter), it is critical to "complicate" student thinking. In this context, "complicating students' thinking" means assisting students to appreciate the fact that historical situations and people's motives are generally complex and not easily explained or understood. Put another way, students need to understand that most of the policies, decisions, actions during the Holocaust period had multiple causes. Ultimately, students must appreciate the need to dig, search, analyze, and synthesize as they seek answers to questions regarding rationales, motives, and causes.

To complicate students' thinking, teachers need to help them: (1) contextualize the history, (2) "avoid simple answers to complex history" (Parsons and Totten, 1993, p. 3), (3) avoid stereotypical descriptions of individuals, their motives and their actions, and (4) carefully examine the purpose and intent of language, including its use to disguise, mislead, confuse, and obfuscate its real meaning.

In this chapter, suggestions are provided about how teachers can "complicate" students' thinking in order to assist them to gain a deeper understanding of various facets of Holocaust history. (Note: For the sake of brevity, examples that are applicable to more than one category will not be repeated.)

Contextualizing the History

In regard to the critical need to contextualize the historical events under study, the authors of the United States Holocaust Memorial Museum's *Guidelines for Teaching about the Holocaust* state:

> Events of the Holocaust . . . must be placed in a historical context so that students can begin to comprehend [specific and special] circumstances that [impacted events and actions]. [Teachers need to] frame [their] approach to specific events . . . by considering when and where an act took place; the impact of contemporaneous

events; the degree of control the Nazis had on a country or local population; [and] the cultural attitudes of particular native populations historically toward different victim groups. (Parsons and Totten, 1993, p. 5)

Not only events but various promulgations, decisions, actions, and reactions must be contextualized if students are to gain a thorough understanding of the history. Part and parcel of such an undertaking is the need to gain a clear understanding of the political and social climate of the period.

To even begin to understand the Holocaust period, for example, students need to learn about why and how the Nazis eventually gained power. Integral to such an understanding is comprehension of the impact of Germany's defeat in World War I, the humiliation Germany experienced as a result of the conditions set by the Versailles Treaty, the political and social upheaval Germany experienced between the end of World War I (1918) and 1933 when the Nazis assumed power, and the dire economic straits in which Germany found itself as a result of the worldwide depression. Indeed, no one can appreciate how the Nazis gained power without understanding these and other conditions and events as Germany moved from the period of the Weimar Republic into that of the Third Reich.

To begin to understand why and how the Nazis gained such a stranglehold on Germany once they were in power (as well as why and how people reacted to such power), students need a solid understanding of both the Nazis' propaganda efforts and the new state's totalitarian nature. Bereft of such knowledge, students are unable to appreciate why and how the Nazis sought to influence and control all facets of German life, from deciding who would and would not work to who would and would not be able to attend school. Eventually, such control led to decisions about those who would and would not be considered German citizens; and ultimately, to those who would and would not be deemed "worthy of life."

By learning about the totalitarian nature of Nazi Germany, students glean key insights into the evolution of Nazi policies as they related, for example, to the treatment of their "enemies," particularly the Jews. In doing so, they will learn that immediately after the Nazis took power in 1933, and throughout the rest of the 1930s, the Nazis' "enemies" were faced with ever expanding legislative decrees and laws that deprived them of their civil and human rights; and that this, in turn, slowly but inexorably limited their choices and actions as a free people.

As Kulka and Hildesheimer (1995) note:

On January 30, [1933,] President Paul von Hindenburg appointed Hitler Reich chancellor. As soon as Hitler was appointed, the National Socialist party and its paramilitary organizations—primarily the SA (*Sturmabteilung*: Storm Troopers) and the SS—launched a drive to seize, by violent means where necessary, all government and public institutions to transform Germany into a totalitarian state. In the ensuing terrorist actions (as early as February and March 1933) against opponents of National Socialism, especially members of the Left political parties, liberals, and intellectuals, the Jews were a major target. Many Jews were subjected to public humiliation and were arrested; others were forced to quit their posts, especially at the universities and law courts.

Before 1933, the Nazis had called for the plundering of Jewish property and for a boycott of Jewish businesses and services; this was now adopted as the official policy of the ruling party. A climax was reached with the anti-Jewish boycott of April 1, 1933, the first occasion on which the new regime openly took discriminatory action against a part of the country's citizens. The boycott was brought to a halt after a day had passed, but from April 7, anti-Jewish laws [400 in all] were enacted that in effect abolished the principle of equal rights for Jews, rights that had been established by the German constitution in 1871. The legal basis for these measures was the Enabling Law, passed on March 24, 1933, which gave the government dictatorial powers first for a four-year period and subsequently for the life span of the Third Reich.

. . . Anti-Jewish policy was put into effect on two parallel levels: by means of laws, decrees, and administrative terror; and by "spontaneous" acts of terror and incitement of the population to hostility against the Jews. The early anti-Jewish laws include the Law for the Restoration of the Professional Civil Service. The racist basis of that law was expressed by the "Aryan Paragraph," which became the foundation for all anti-Jewish legislation passed before the enactment of the Nuremberg Laws in the fall of 1935. Other laws passed at that stage restricted the practice of law and medicine by Jews; a special law mandated that the number of Jews in an educational institution must not exceed that proportional to their percentage of the population; and Jews were excluded from cultural life and journalism.

The methods employed in the regime's terror campaign against its opponents consisted mostly of arrest and imprisonment in concentration camps. The percentage of Jews among the detainees was quite high, and they were singled out for particularly cruel and humiliating treatment, which in many instances resulted in death. (pp. 561–562)

As Berenbaum (1993) notes, the four hundred pieces of legislation that were ultimately enacted between 1933 and 1939 *"defined, isolated, excluded, segregated, and impoverished" German Jewry* (italics added) (p. 22).

Contextually speaking, then, students must be taught that the Nazis did not simply appear out of nowhere and initiate their infamous killing process. Rather, the deprivation of civil and human rights of various individuals—but primarily the Jews—was, from the very outset of the Nazis' rise to power, steady and inexorable. Hand in hand with this, the process was "legitimized" every step of the way, via legislative decree. Students also need to realize that the legislative process was not hidden; and that the implementation of the various policies were—with the exception of the mass murder—out in the open for everyone to see. At a minimum, students need to appreciate that the average German above the age of fifteen was cognizant of the mistreatment meted out to the Jews on a daily basis by the Nazis.

On a different note, it is imperative that students come to understand and appreciate that different countries reacted in radically different ways to the Nazis' policies against the Jews. In large part, this was influenced by the nation's history, its form of governance, its ties with other nations, its strength as a sovereign nation, its economic situation, and its relationship to Jews through the years. The latter had a dramatic impact on how receptive various nations were to rescuing, hiding, and assisting Jews. Ultimately, these concerns and many others had a direct impact on how Nazi policies were implemented in the nations allied with and overrun by the Nazis. In this regard, Italy serves as a classic example. Even though Mussolini's Fascist Italy was an ally of Hitler's Germany and "there was [in Italy] a six-year span of increasingly violent antisemitism, beginning with racist propaganda and culminating in discrimination and persecution [between] 1937 and 1943" (Michaelis, 1995, p. 722), "[o]nly after his [Mussolini's] fall in 1943, and the subsequent German invasion and occupation of Italy, was there a serious attempt to round up and deport Italian Jews. Even then, most were rescued as a result of efforts by the Italian people to protect them" (Berenbaum, 1993, p. 167). As Michaelis (1995) reports:

> [In early 1933, following Hitler's rise to power,] Mussolini alternated declarations and acts in favor of the Jews with (strictly unofficial) antisemitic moves and expressions of sympathy for the German position. . . . After the German-Italian rapprochement of October 1936, the evolution of the Jewish question in Italy was determined by the exigencies of Axis policy, despite the fundamental conflict of interest between the Axis partners and the divergence of views on Hitler's doctrine of Nordic superiority. . . . In the fall of 1936 Mussolini launched an antisemitic press campaign that, unlike previous anti-Jewish polemics, was explicitly directed against Italian Jewry as a whole. The promulgation of discriminatory legislation was delayed because of the need to prepare Italian public opinion, the desire to avoid a premature clash with the Vatican, continued friction between Rome and Berlin, and a lingering fear of negative repercussions in the Western democracies.
>
> . . . With Italy's entry into World War II on June 10, 1940, new anti-Jewish measures were decreed and the anti-Jewish press campaign was intensified. However, though side by side, the two allies never marched in step, and this was . . . reflected in the field of Fascist Jewish policy. Given his military and economic dependence on the Germans, Mussolini could not back away from his anti-Jewish legislation, nor could he mitigate his racist ideology. On the other hand, the Jewish question outside Italy served the Fascists as a means of asserting what little freedom of action from their Axis partners they were able to maintain. Together with genuine expressions of spontaneous humanitarianism, this eminently political consideration explains why the Italian-occupied territories in France, Yugoslavia, and Greece became havens of refuge for persecuted Jews. It also explains why Mussolini, while approving of security measures against hostile Jewish elements, would never agree to the deportation of Italian citizens to the east. Hitler was determined to impose his anti-Jewish obsession on the whole of Europe, including Italy; but until Italy's surrender to the Allies, he was not prepared to jeopardize relations with Rome on a question of extending the "Final Solution" to the Italian sphere of influence. (p. 723)

In this case, students need to be assisted to understand that *even the allies of Nazis Germany* did not act in monolithic ways vis-à-vis the racial and antisemitic policies of Nazi Germany. Only through such contextualization and demonstrating to students the complexity of the situation will students begin to understand the ways in which various nations acted in the face of the Nazi juggernaut. (For a detailed discussion of Italy's relationship with the Jews and the Nazis, see Nicola Caracciolo, *Uncertain Refuge: Italy and the Jews During the Holocaust*. Urbana, IL: University of Illinois Press, 1995.)

As discussed in Chapter 4, many people (including students and teachers) are under the misconception that "concentration camps" and "death camps" were one and same. They were not. There were many different types of camps. They served different purposes that throughout the years were altered in accordance with changes in Nazi policies. Again, this is a critical issue of contextualization.

As Pingel (1995) notes, "Although the term 'concentration camp' is some-times used as a generic term for Nazi camps, not all the camps eventually estab-lished by the Nazis were designated as concentration camps proper. Their extensive camp system also included labor camps (Arbeitslager), transit camps (Durchgangslager), prisoner-of-war camps (Kriegsgefangenlager), and extermina-tion camps (Vernichtungslager)" (p. 308). In addition, there were police detention, private industrial, and work-education camps.

Pingel (1995) suggests that the history of the concentration camps can be divided into three distinct periods: 1933–1936, 1936–1942, and 1942–1944 or 1945 (p. 309). The following is an extremely truncated version of his detailed discussion:

> In the earliest period, the concentration camps were used primarily for incarcerat-ing internal political adversaries from the left and liberal circles, as well as mem-bers of the proscribed German labor movement organizations. Special places of detention for political prisoners came into being in the wake of the *Razzien* (raids) that were carried out after the Reichstag fire of February 28, 1933; . . .
>
> . . . From 1936 to 1942, the war preparations and the war itself led to an expansion of the concentration camp system. In addition to these detention instal-lations, which were officially designated as concentration camps, there were also hard-labor and "reeducation" camps. . . . Late in 1941 Chelmno began operation as an extermination camp, and in the spring of 1942 the extermination camps Treblinka, Sobibor and Belzec were established as part of Aktion Reinhard. Auschwitz-Birkenau (Auschwitz II) and Majdanek, which were existing concentra-tion camps, had extermination centers established in them as well. From 1942 to 1944–1945, concentration camp prisoners were systematically drafted for work in the armaments industry. The great losses suffered by the Germans in the fighting [of World War II], especially on the eastern front, forced the Nazi leadership to draft growing numbers of Germans from the labor force into the army. Their places were mostly taken by forced labor from the occupied territories, and to a lesser degree, by concentration camp prisoners. Previously, forced labor in the concentration camps had been a method of punishment and persecution intended to humiliate the prisoners and lead to their deaths through overwork. . . . In the meantime, the Auschwitz and Majdanek camps were integrated, in 1942, into the systematic exter-mination of Jews. (pp. 309–312)

As for the extermination centers, students need to understand that there were only six camps officially designated as killing centers where victims were gassed. All of these camps—Auschwitz-Birkenau (Auschwitz II), Chelmno, Belzec, Majdanek, Sobibor, and Treblinka—were located in Poland. Auschwitz-Birkenau and Majdanek also served as slave-labor and prison camps (Berenbaum, 1993, p. 119).

Students also need to learn about the evolution of the Nazis' policies as they moved from the practice of forced sterilization to the so-called euthanasia of the mentally and physically handicapped to the systematic mass murder of millions. Concomitantly, students need to appreciate how the Nazis perceived and, ultimately, treated the different victim groups such as the mentally and physically handicapped, the Gypsies, the Jews, and others.

Students need to understand that the Nazi policy against the Jews was altered as the Nazis faced obstacles in carrying out their ideological crusade to "solve" the "Jewish problem." The following passage succinctly delineates the evolutionary process of the Nazis' thought and actions vis-à-vis the Final Solution:

> The [September 1, 1939 German] occupation of Poland added two considerations to the previous Jewish policies of Nazi Germany. Two million Polish Jews were now under German control, and the German invasion "sanctioned" massive atrocities against the Polish elite and Jews. . . .
>
> On 21 September 1939 Reinhard Heydrich discussed the "Jewish question" with his aides. Topics included removal of the German Jews to Poland and possible evacuation of Polish Jews to Soviet-occupied Poland. [Ultimately,] Heydrich ordered the concentration of Polish Jews in ghettos. . . . Their final destination was not specified, but it is clear that Heydrich was aiming at [establishing] a reservation in eastern occupied Poland.
>
> The reservation was also intended to absorb all the Jews from greater Germany. Following the arrival in Nisko in October 1939 of the first transports of Jews . . . , this experiment was abandoned. *It proved that without careful planning, mass deportations in winter would result in an enormous death toll—not the intention at that time.* . . . (italics added)
>
> After the collapse of the Nisko plan, leading Nazis did not give up the idea of deporting all Jews under German control to the Generalgouvernement or to a special reservation. . . . [*The Nazis leaders'*] *statements betoken an intention to treat the deportees brutally even to the point of causing fatalities, but not (at this stage) to kill them all.* (italics added)
>
> The swift victory over France in the summer of 1940 appeared to give the Germans an opportunity to expel all the Jews from Europe. Under the [so-called] Madagascar Plan, four million Jews were to be transported to the island of Madagascar. . . . The plan contained an element of hostage-taking to keep the United States . . . in check. It envisaged Madagascar as an SS-controlled territory, so that the Jews [there] would remain at the mercy of the Nazis. . . .
>
> The decision to annihilate the whole of European Jewry was taken in response to the changed strategic and foreign policy situation of Nazi Germany from the end of 1940 to autumn 1941. Great Britain had mounted unexpectedly vigorous resistance to German air attacks and showed no sign of capitulation. American aid to the British was growing. . . . As American neutrality seemed to evaporate, Hitler believed that the value of the European Jews as hostages was fast disappearing.
>
> [P]lans for Operation Barbarossa—the invasion of the Soviet Union—[also] encouraged the indulgence in utopian idea of establishing an Aryan racial empire.

> The realization of such would justify and necessitate unprecedented measures: the destruction and enslavement of so-called inferior races. [This] entailed the first truly murderous "settlement" of the Jewish question in the occupied Soviet Union.
>
> ... In March 1941, according to a document recently found in Moscow, Heydrich submitted to Herman Göring a draft plan for the "Final Solution of the Jewish Question." The subsequent order was signed by Göring on 31 July 1941. ... The order gave Heydrich authority "to act so as to carry out all the necessary organizaton, substantive and material preparation for an overall solution of the Jewish question in the German area of influence in Europe." (Aronson and Longerich, 2001, pp. 188, 189)

(For a much more detailed and complete discussion of the evolution of the decision making vis-à-vis the Final Solution, see Shlomo Aronson and Peter Longerich, "Final Solution: Preparation and Implementation," pp. 184–198. In Walter Laqueur [Ed.], *The Holocaust Encyclopedia*. New Haven, CT: Yale University Press, 2001; Abraham J. Edelheit and Hershel Edelheit, *History of the Holocaust: A Handbook and Dictionary*. Boulder CO: Westview Press, 1994; and Henry Friedlander, *The Origins of Nazi Genocide; From Euthanasia to The Final Solution*. Chapel Hill: University of North Carolina Press, 1995.)

As Friedlander (1995) notes, on June 22, 1941,

> ... the German Wehrmacht invaded the Soviet Union, and the Nazi regime embarked on its second and, far more ambitious, killing operation [the first being the murder of the handicapped]. Mobile units of the SS, the Einsatzgruppen, crossed the Soviet border immediately after the battle troops. In the occupied territory of the Soviet Union, these units shot large numbers of civilians in mass executions. Their primary task was the murder of all Jews on Soviet soil. They also murdered all Gypsies and, whenever possible, the handicapped. (p. 284)
>
> In the first sweep through the Soviet Union in 1941 and early 1942, most Soviet Jews were shot; only those able to work for the Germans were permitted to live and relegated to ghettos and camps. But this primitive method of shooting the victims was too public. It also posed logistic problems for the killers, requiring a large killing staff and imposing a psychological burden on the shooters. The SS and police, therefore, soon began to search for a better killing method. They soon turned to the euthanasia programs as a model. But carbon monoxide [canisters] were too expensive, and a dependable supply from distant factories could not be assured. The RSHA [Central Office for Reich Security] motor pool ... developed a gas van, which, like a perpetual motion machine, recycled exhaust fumes to kill its human cargo.
>
> Himmler's men eventually realized, just as the T4 killers [those who were in charge of the so-called "euthanasia" program] had discovered several years earlier, that it was more efficient to bring the victims to a central killing place. ... But the killers had also learned from the public response to euthanasia that such installations could not be established inside Germany. Therefore, the first killing center of the final solution began functioning in December 1941 at Chelmno (in the Wartheland).
>
> At the same time, Himmler commissioned Odilo Globocnik, the SSPF [SS and police leader) in Lublin, to kill the Jews of Poland. ... To accomplish his mission,

Globocnik established three killing centers in the Lublin region—the Belzec, Sobibor, and Treblinka extermination camps—which started to operate, one after the other, in the spring and summer of 1942. Unlike Chelmno, [these camps] used stationary gas chambers, in which a diesel motor propelled gas fumes into the chambers.

Because the killing task was so massive, Himmler also selected some of his concentration camps to serve as killing centers. He chose the newly established camp at Auschwitz in Upper Silesia and the so-called POW camp at Majdanek, a suburb of Lublin, to perform the killing function. . . . Auschwitz and Majdanek remained concentration camps while also running the killing centers as part of their operation. At Auschwitz, the killing center was located at Birkenau, also known as Auschwitz II. The agent used to kill the victims differed slighty at Auschwitz, where the SS replaced carbon monoxide with hydrogen cyanide, known under the trade name Zyklon B, which was already in use as a pesticide in all concentration camps to fumigate barracks. (pp. 286, 287)

It is also important to mention the Wannsee Conference that was held at a villa in Wannsee, Berlin, on January 20, 1942, to discuss and coordinate the implementation of the "final solution." This was where Reinhard Heydrich, head of the Reich Security Main Office, met with the secretaries of the most important German government ministers *to discuss Hitler's "decision to solve the so-called Jewish question, through systematic mass murder"* (Browning, 1995, p. 1591). *It was at this meeting where the latter decision was "officially transmitted to the leaders of the Nazi bureaucracy"* (Browning, 1995, p. 1591) *and at which time they were informed that their "participation was deemed necessary"* (italics added) (Browning, 1995, p. 1591). It is vitally significant to realize that the Wannsee Conference "was not a meeting at which the decision [about the Final Solution was made] or debated, but rather one at which the participants discussed the implementation of a decision already taken" (Browning, 1995, p. 1591).

Avoiding Simplifying Complex Situations

Avoiding simplifying complex situations complements the need to contextualize the history. In certain cases, they are synonymous. Again, as the authors of *Guidelines for Teaching About the Holocaust* state:

A study of the Holocaust raises difficult questions about human behavior, and it often involves complicated answers as to why events occurred. Be wary of oversimplifications. Allow students to contemplate the various factors which contributed to the Holocaust; do not attempt to reduce Holocaust history to one or two catalysts in isolation from the other factors which came into play. (Parsons and Totten, 1993, p. 3)

For students to even begin to attempt to understand the "why" behind the Holocaust, they need to be conversant with the various historical trends that ultimately merged and culminated in the Final Solution. Far too many educators, however, neglect to address such critical issues. In 1992, Holocaust scholar Lucy Dawidowicz noted that many Holocaust curricula were "better at giving pupils basic information, and better at describing what happened than explaining why it happened" (p. 69). *Unfortunately, this assertion is as true today as it was the day she made it.*

As mentioned in earlier chapters, Holocaust historian Donald Niewyk (1995), for one, argues that the historical trends that "combined to make the Holocaust possible [were]: anti-Semitism,* racism, social Darwinism, extreme nationalism, totalitarianism, industrialism, and the nature of modern war. The absence of any one of these trends would have made the genocide of the Jews unlikely" (p. 175). (Note: Different scholars place different emphases on various trends, and teachers interested in such perspectives need to examine the work of various scholars to ascertain their positions. In this regard, the examination of historiographical essays vis-à-vis Holocaust history are extremely useful. A good starting point is Saul Friedländer's "The Extermination of the European Jews in Historiography.")

Corroborating Niewyk's point about the synergistic nature of the various historical trends and other key factors that combined to make the Holocaust possible, the authors of *Guidelines for Teaching About the Holocaust* observe that:

> [T]he Holocaust . . . was not simply the logical and inevitable consequence of unbridled racism. Rather, racism, combined with centuries-old bigotry, renewed by a nationalistic fervor which emerged in Europe in the latter half of the 19th century, fueled by Germany's defeat in World War I and its national humiliation following the Treaty of Versailles, exacerbated by worldwide economic hard times, the ineffectiveness of the Weimar Republic, and international indifference, and catalyzed by the political charisma, militaristic inclusiveness, and manipulative propaganda of Adolf Hitler's Nazi regime, contributed to the eventuality of the Holocaust. (Parsons and Totten, 1993, p. 3)

Only by addressing the "why" behind the whats, whens, hows, and wheres of this history *and* avoiding simplistic explanations, such as the "single cause" view, for complex phenomena will teachers and students begin to gain a deeper understanding of the various factors that resulted in the Holocaust. To that end, teachers should ask themselves, "Why teach this history if students do not begin to understand why and how such an event came about?"

Students need to learn that there were varied and complex reasons as to why people acted the way they did during the Holocaust years. The ways in which they acted depended on a complex set of circumstances, including but not limited to the following: their personality makeup; their belief systems (i.e., cultural, religious,

---

*Dawidowicz (1992) further observed that "Though all curricula [that she examined] discuss Nazi anti-Semitism, preferring generic terms like "racism" and "prejudice" instead of the specific "anti-Semitism," fifteen of the twenty-five never even suggest that anti-Semitism had a history before Hitler. Of those that do, barely a handful present coherent historical accounts, however brief (p. 69).

political); the political climate; those for whom they were responsible or not responsible (e.g., children, elderly parents, extended family members); the actual and perceived possible consequences of acting or not acting in a certain manner; peer pressure; propaganda; one's health; one's financial situation, and so forth. *No situation was black or white;* this is true regarding why and how the potential victims of the Nazis acted and responded, as well as why and how the perpetrators, collaborators, and bystanders acted.

As for the Nazis' victims, Holocaust scholar Lawrence Langer (1982) asserts that many "were plunged into a crisis of what we might call 'choiceless choice,' where crucial decisions did not reflect options between life and death, but between one form of abnormal response and another, both imposed by a situation that was in no way of the victim's own choosing" (p. 72). Elaborating on this definition, Langer (1982) observes that "In the absence of humanly significant alternatives— that is, alternatives enabling an individual to make a decision, act on it, and accept the consequences, all within a framework that supports personal integrity and self-esteem—one is plunged into a moral turmoil that may silence judgment, . . . but cannot paralyze all action if one still wishes to remain alive" (pp. 73–74).

Berenbaum (1997) asserts that, "In the universe of choiceless choices, one could not choose between good and bad or even a lesser of two evils, but between the impossible and the unacceptable. In the morally denuded atmosphere of the death camps, [for example,] a system of meaning evaporated and we have no means by which to judge the behavior of the victim. . . . [As Langer has argued,] in the concentration camps, the Nazis so dominated the victim that we cannot speak of moral choice" (p. 202).

In a similar vein, Langer (1995) argues that

> . . . [T]he most notorious example of this dilemma [making a choiceless choice] is the "Give Me Your Children" speech delivered by Elder of the Jews Chaim Rumkowski in the Lodz ghetto on September 4, 1942. Evidently convinced . . . that by surrendering the few he could preserve the many, Rumkowski conceded, "I must cut off limbs in order to save the body itself." But those "limbs" were all the children in the ghetto under the age of ten (as well as the ill and the elderly over sixty-five).
>
> "A grievous blow has struck the ghetto," Rumkowski began. "They are asking us to give up the best we possess—the children and the elderly. . . . So which is better?" he asks. "What do you want: that eighty to ninety thousand Jews remain, or, God forbid, that the whole population be annihilated? . . . Put yourself in my place, think logically, and you'll reach the conclusion that I cannot proceed any other way. The part that can be saved is much larger than the part that must be given away."
>
> The mystery we will never solve is how the Germans managed to persuade Rumkowski—and through him, many of the Jews he addressed—to delude himself into believing that he was acting within a framework of choice, thus preserving the faculty that endowed both him and his audience that measure of freedom. (pp. 46–47, 48)

For many years after the Holocaust, Jews were often perceived (and/or accused) of having been passive in the face of the Nazi onslaught. Indeed, many made the now largely disavowed assertion that the Jews acted like sheep going to their slaughter. Again, such an assertion presents an utterly simplistic view of the situation faced by the Jews. Be that as it may, today's students are apt to ask, and understandably: "When threatened, why didn't the Jews just pack up and leave?" What students need to understand is that for the first eight years of Nazi rule tens of thousands of Jews *did* emigrate from Germany. However, not everyone was able to leave due to personal circumstances; and as time went on, geopolitics made it more and more difficult to leave. And ultimately, the Nazis themselves prevented the Jews from leaving. Specifically:

> According to the census taken in June 1933, the Jewish population in Germany was 502,799 (by religion) or 540,000 (by race); these figures show that since January of that year about 26,000 Jews "by race" had left the country. By the end of 1933, 63,000 Jews had emigrated. . . . As far as official antisemitic policy was concerned, 1934 was a relatively uneventful year, and some of the Jewish émigrés living in difficult circumstances as temporary refugees in neighboring countries even decided to return to Germany. . . . Hitler's secret memorandum on the Four-year Plan, which he wrote in August 1936, contained an ideological and political section in which he called for an all-out war against Judaism as a driving motive in Germany's future foreign policy. . . . The interim goals for the "solution of the Jewish question" were to include an intensified drive to eliminate Jews from the economy, and increased pressure for their emigration by such means as the "people's fury," that is, officially organized terror. . . . In 1938 and 1939, emigration of Jews ("by race") from Germany reached new heights—49,000 in 1938 and 68,000 in 1939— *despite the many difficulties that stood in the way, such as new restrictive entry regulations in the target countries, restrictions on immigration to Palestine, and the failure of the Evian Conference. . . . [And then, all] Jewish emigration was prohibited . . . [in] October 1941* (italics added). (Kulka and Hildesheimer, 1995, pp. 562, 566, 567, 570)

As for those individuals and families who stayed behind in Germany between 1933 and October 1941, there were many factors that prevented them from leaving or induced them to remain in a hostile environment. Many were poor and did not have the means to pick up and leave. Others were old and infirm. Many had justifiable doubts about the feasibility of making a living abroad. That is, some did not have the skills, including a second language, needed for living and working in a different country. Some people's allegiance, patriotism, and overidentification with Germany blinded them to the reality of the situation under the Nazis. Concomitantly, those who fought in World War I believed—understandably so— that the country owed them for their own sacrifices, and possibly believed that in the end they would be left alone. Some, undoubtedly, hoped against hope that the situation would change for the better. And, significantly, many were not accepted into the countries to which they applied.

Addressing such issues, Holocaust survivor and author Primo Levi (1988) perspicaciously observed:

> They ask: Why didn't you run away before? Before the borders were closed? Before the trap snapped shut? . . . To emigrate one needed not only a lot of money but also

a "bridgehead" in the country of destination, relatives or friends willing to offer sponsorship and/or hospitality. . . . The frontiers of Europe were practically closed, and England and the Americas had extremely reduced immigration quotas. Yet, greater than this difficulty was another of an inner, psychological nature. This village or town or region or nation is mine, I was born here, my ancestors are buried here. I speak its language, have adopted its customs and culture . . . I paid its [taxes], observed its laws. I fought its battles . . . I risked my life for its borders, some of my friends or relations lie in the war cemeteries. . . . I do not want to nor can I leave it: if I die I will die "in patria" [the fatherland]." (pp. 161, 162, 163, 164)

Again, there are no simple answers to such a complex situation.

As for what Jews knew and did not know in regard to the Nazis' plans, Holocaust scholar Yehuda Bauer (1989) asserts that:

Jewish reaction to Nazi policies was radically influenced by the lack of comprehension of the Nazi policies. Rational arguments and rational reasons were sought to explain policies that were essentially based on the practical application of a myth. It was therefore only after the mass murder of the Jews had already gone a long way that the Jews realized the fact of the total Nazi design of murder. Paradoxically, the Nazi themselves had no systematic extermination plans before 1941; until that time, extrusion by emigration or forced deportation abroad was the prevalent policy. Mass murder was inherent in Nazi ideology, but did not emerge into consciousness or practical policies until a situation arose in 1940–41 when extrusion could no longer serve as a practical means to make the Jews disappear, to use Himmler's phrase. *If the Nazis were not aware, until 1941, of their intent to murder the Jews, it is difficult retroactively to ask of their victims to be so aware.* (italics added). (p. 236)

The key here, again, is that students need to understand that how the Jews reacted—or any other group, for that matter—was due to a wide variety of reasons. Again, their reasons, actions, and reactions were not monolithic. Obviously, it did not come down to a simple choice of wanting to leave or not, as many entangled issues and barriers came into play vis-à-vis such a decision and/or desire.

An excruciating choiceless choice made by many potential victims was whether to remain at home with one's family (assuming they had decided not to flee or to go into hiding, for whatever reasons) or to join a partisan group to actively fight against the Nazis. Many of today's students, particularly males, are apt to assert that if they and their loved ones were faced with something similar to the Nazi onslaught they would surely choose to fight. Such bravado is easy to understand from adolescents in a free society weaned on television shows—from cartoons to cowboy movies to cop-and-robber shows and other outlandish fare—studded with "heroics" and "violence that wins out"; but in a society where one's family was in constant peril due to a lack of adequate wages, adequate food, and potential retribution visited on the whole family for the action of one member, to assume such options were a given is a simplistic and ludicrous notion. Students need to appreciate this by studying the history of the period and contemplating the words of the victims and the primary documents of the perpetrators. Only in this way will the students begin to understand the trauma that was involved in making such potentially life-shattering decisions—and not only for a single individual but for his or her entire family, and in certain cases, one's entire community.

Throughout the Holocaust period, from 1933 through 1945, the Jews and other targeted populations were caught between the Scylla and Charybdis of such choices. Historical accounts by historians (Dawidowicz, 1986; Gilbert, 1987; Hilberg, 1985; Yahil, 1990); first-person accounts by survivors, bystanders, and others; and documentaries and videos of survivor accounts about the period include example after example of the extremely difficult and numerous choiceless choices that they faced. For students to even begin to gain a modicum of understanding regarding the thoughts, reasons, and motives as to why and how the potential and actual victims acted, they must become conversant with the concept of "choiceless choices." By doing so, students may begin to appreciate *the critical need to avoid settling for a simplistic view of a complex situation.* And if they do, they are bound to gain a deeper and truer understanding of this history.

(See Chapter 15, "Choiceless Choices" in Michael Berenbaum, *Witness to the Holocaust: An Illustrated Documentary History of the Holocaust in the Words of Its Victims, Perpetrators and Bystanders,* New York: HarperCollins, 1997, for other examples of choiceless choices that could be incorporated into a study of the Holocaust.)

Students also need to begin to understand that there were various and complex reasons as to why people ended up as bystanders. For brevity's sake, the following discussion about bystanders shall be limited to those individuals and groups who lived in Nazi-occupied Europe, as opposed to the governments of other nations or international organizations. Many people were antisemitic (either overtly or passively) and either did not care what happened to Jews (and/or other victimized groups) or may have actually reveled in the victimization of the Jews. Still others were indifferent and/or apathetic and simply did not want to get involved. The latter situation was likely due to a variety of reasons: from people genuinely not caring about the fate of others or others "different" from themselves to being consumed with their own problems. Such problems may have run the gamut, from suffering economic distress during the early years in Germany, living in a country (during the later years) that was engaged in war, or—in the case of those living in a Nazi-occupied country—being under a state of siege. Many who were suffering various hardships and indignities themselves may simply not have had the reserves to worry about the fate of others. Still other reasons for the inaction of various individuals may have involved believing, at least to a certain extent, the Nazis' propaganda about the ills caused by the Jews. Other individuals may have lacked the empathy needed to place themselves in others' shoes. And undoubtedly, there were many who feared the consequences, whatever they might be, if they spoke out or attempted to help the victims. Each of these positions, as well as others, could have, and often were, contingent upon a host of related issues: the country in which one lived, what he or she actually witnessed personally, peer pressure by one's family members or acquaintances, whether one had dependents who relied on him or her, the threats imposed by the authorities, the extent of terror one had actually experienced, and so forth.

Over the past several decades it has been somewhat "fashionable" among educators to revile the stance of *all* bystanders. In many ways, that is understandable. It is extremely difficult to fathom how anyone can stand by when another is maligned, threatened, or injured. However, teachers need to assist students to reflect upon and ponder several key issues germane to the bystander issue—*and this is not, it must be clearly understood, to make excuses for the bystanders*—before they can attempt to begin to understand what it meant to be a bystander during the Nazi years. First, students need to ponder just how easy or difficult it is *in a free society such as their own* to stand up for someone they do not know or care about or who is "different" from them. Second, students need to ponder just how easy or difficult it would be to speak out in order to protect someone if the individual or group assaulting the victim was armed. Third, students need to consider what it truly means to live in a totalitarian society, where everything and everybody is controlled by those in power. The latter, of course, means that *those in power control everything* from the legislature to the courts to the media; have the power to arrest anyone at will; can imprison an individual for as long as they wish without filing a charge; dictate whether one is able to work or not, and so on. It also means that those in power control the police and the armed forces and can use any amount of force against a group or individual, including but not limited to beatings, torture, or murder, anytime and anyplace, without fear of adverse consequences.

Even though, for the most part, he is speaking about the international community's lack of action during the Holocaust period, the following point by Holocust scholar Michael Marrus (1987) is germane to the observations made above:

> In assessing [the] work [on the issue of the bystanders], we should note that many of [the current] analyses center explicitly on what did not happen—an awkward approach for the historian. . . . Jews were not admitted, Jewish communities failed to unite, Allied governments spurned rescue suggestions, and access to Auschwitz was not bombed. It is, essentially, a negative report—the history of inaction, indifference, and insensitivity. It should be obvious that there is a pitfall here: in any such assessment, there is great danger that the historian will apply to subjects the standards, value systems, and vantage points of the present, rather than those of the period being discussed. We believe that people should have acted otherwise, and we set out to describe how they did not. Occasionally the thrust of such work is an extended lament that the people being written about did not live up to our standards. This temptation is the historian's form of hubris: to yield fully to it is to denounce the characters we describe for not being like ourselves.
>
> Put more simply, there is a strong tendency in historical writing on bystanders to the Holocaust to condemn, rather than to explain. . . . I suggest that we shall go much further in the attempt to comprehend the behavior and activity (or inactivity) of bystanders by making a painstaking effort to enter into their minds and sensibilities. . . . If the Holocaust was indeed unprecedented . . . then it is also true that people had no experience upon which to base their understanding at the time, and no reliable guides for action. To a degree, everyone was in the dark. (pp. 156, 157)

Marrus's points are as pertinent to educators and students as they are to historians. The only caveat is that in the latter part of his statement, in which he asserts that "to a degree, everyone was in the dark" (p. 157), he is essentially talking about the early mass killing of the victims, and not about the early and middle years of the Holocaust, when anyone who was conscious was certainly cognizant of the ever increasing discrimination against the Jews, at least in their own areas when it took place.

(Note: At some point, it is vitally significant for students to learn about those who stepped up and refused to be bystanders during the Holocaust years. Though relatively few in number, their actions are extremely worthy of note.)

Finally, when all is said and done, it is imperative for students to realize that a person who was a bystander in the early years of the Nazi reign may have ended up becoming, at a later point, a collaborator, perpetrator, or rescuer.

> Students should be reminded that individuals and groups do not always fit neatly into the same categories of behavior. The very same people did not always act consistently as "bystanders," "collaborators," "perpetrators," or "rescuers." Individuals and groups often behaved differently depending upon changing events and circumstances. The same person who in 1933 might have stood by and remained uninvolved while witnessing social discrimination of Jews, might later have joined up with the SA and become a collaborator or have been moved to dissent vocally or act in defense of Jewish friends and neighbors. (Parsons and Totten, 1993, p. 5)

(For additional insights into the bystander concept during the Holocaust period, see "Part III: Bystanders" [pp. 195–268]. In Raul Hilberg, *Perpetrators, Victims, Bystanders: The Jewish Catastrophe 1933–1945*. New York: HarperCollins, 1992; and Hans Mommsen, "The Reaction of the German Population to the Anti-Jewish Persecution and the Holocaust" [pp. 141–154]. In Peter Hayes [Ed.], *Lessons and Legacies: The Meaning of the Holocaust in a Changing World*. Evanston, IL: Northwestern University Press, 1996.)

Avoiding Stereotypical Descriptions of Individuals, Their Motives, and Their Actions

Teachers and students must assiduously avoid accepting stereotypical views regarding the motives and actions of individuals and groups. This concern, of course, complements the need to contextualize the history and avoid simplistic answers to complex situations:

> Stereotyping takes place when groups of people are viewed as monolithic in attitudes and actions. . . . [Teachers need to] remind [their] students that although members of a group may share common experiences and beliefs, generalizations about them, without benefit of modifying or qualifying terms (e.g., "sometimes," "usually," "in many cases but not all") tend to stereotype group behavior and distort historical reality. Thus, all Germans cannot be characterized as Nazis, nor

should any nationality be reduced to a singular or one "dimensional description."
(Parsons and Totten, 1993, p. 4)

As mentioned earlier, not all German Jews reacted in the same way to the decrees, actions, and threat posed by the Nazis in the early, mid-, and late 1930s. Each responded based on his or her position in life, past and current experiences, belief systems, personality makeup, responsibilities, and so on.

> That the degree of antisemitic violence can serve as a barometer of emigration is beyond question. In the years 1933–35, 20–25 percent of the Jewish population left Germany. What effect did the legal harassment, particularly the Nuremberg Laws [passed and implemented in 1935], have on the will to leave? The answer is equivocal. The sources speak of various, sometimes contradictory reactions among different portions of the Jewish population and in different localities. In some cases, the desire to remain in Germany became stronger; in others, the wish to leave predominated.
>
> . . . By retaining their traditional values, liberal German Jews may have wished to escape reality, immersing themselves in a world of nostalgia. Equally strong was their wish to demonstrate that the Jews were not abandoning their German cultural heritage. The concerted influence of these efforts, the sense of attachment to the past and of self-perception as an inseparable link in the chain of Jewish history, acted as a barrier against despair, a compensation for the humiliation and degradation to which Germany was subjecting Jews.
>
> . . . As a direct consequence of the Nazi ascension to power, there was a remarkable enlargement of the Zionist movement and increase in its influence in Jewish society. The Zionist movement had always given precedence to winning over the younger generation to the Jewish national idea. It now redoubled its efforts concentrating on education aimed to reorient Jewish youth toward emigration to Palestine.
>
> . . . From its inception in February 1919, the Jewish war veterans' union, the *Reichsbund Jüdischer Frontsoldaten* (RJF), avowed its desire for full integration into German society, blurring the differences generated by the historical antagonism between Jews and Germans. Its members wished to counteract the belief prevalent in Germany after World War I that Jews did not share the war experience. The RJF reiterated that the Jews had fulfilled their duty to Germany and made the same sacrifices as their Gentile comrades, 12,000 Jewish soldiers having given their lives in the war. By 1933, the RJF comprised 30,000 members in 360 local branches.
>
> When Hitler assumed power, the RJF decided to defend the interest of its rank and file, who had been shattered morally and economically by the antisemitic policy, and attempted to obtain preferential treatment for its members through intercession with President Paul von Hindenburg. From 1933 on, the RJF strove to achieve two objectives: as regards the state, to vindicate the rights of Jewish veterans and protect their interest by preventing the extension of the segregation policy; and within the Jewish community, to prove the validity of its ideals and reiterate its immutable German patriotism.
>
> . . . After the racial legislation [in 1935], the RJF subordinated its principles to a more realistic practical unity, understanding that in the Nazi state a dogmatic response could not meet German Jews' demands. Consequently, in practice it had to yield and support emigration. (Bankier, 2001, p. 245–250)

It must also be noted that, sadly, throughout (and due to) the Nazi reign of terror, many German Jews also committed suicide.

Also, as mentioned earlier, not all of Nazi Germany's allies acted in a monolithic manner against the Jews—Italy being the classic case. Japan, too, provides another excellent example along these lines:

> Japan's policy toward the Jews during the Hitler era was anomalous. A full partner in the Berlin-Rome Axis, and greatly influenced by Nazi propaganda, Japan had its own influential "experts on Jewish affairs" who wrote as well as translated anti-semitic works and sponsored antisemitic fairs that were subsidized by the German Ministry of Foreign Affairs. Yet the fifteen thousand or so stateless Russian Jews living in eight communities of northern China and Manchuria under Japanese control were granted legal status. Within this status, the Jewish refugees were recognized as one of the Manchurian nationalities and were enabled to carry out their autonomous community affairs within the laws of the country. As part of this, the Japanese government officially recognized their Zionist organization. Moreover, during this period, Japan provided a haven from Hitler's clutches for about seventeen thousand Jewish refugees from Germany, Austria, and Poland, in Shanghai.
>
> With the beginning of the war in the Pacific, the Japanese became more susceptible to Nazi influence. . . . By February 18, 1943, the Japanese finally gave in to German demands to set up a ghetto for the Jews. (Kranzler, 1995, pp. 735, 737)

Among the many other issues and questions that could be raised and examined in the classroom vis-à-vis the need to avoid stereotypical descriptions of individuals, groups, organizations and/or their motives and actions are: the economic status of the Jews in pre-Nazi and Nazi Germany; the ways in which different non-Jewish Germans acted towards the Jews; the Jewish response in the "free world" to the plight of the Jews under the Nazis; Christian religious leaders' responses to the plight of the Jews at the hands of the Nazis; and the various motivations of the rescuers of Jews, and so on.

The Need to Carefully Examine the Purpose and Intent of Language

An examination of an individual's or a particular group's use of language is likely to provide a unique glimpse into their belief systems, motives, and actions. Thus, for students to develop as deep an understanding as possible about the Nazis' mentality, policies, and deviousnesses, they need to reflect upon the Nazis' use of language. Likewise, in order to begin to appreciate the profoundly dire, almost "otherworldly" circumstances in which the victims found themselves, students must consider how "normal" language or words were profoundly inadequate to describe the horrific experiences that were forced upon them by their tormentors.

The Nazis used language to dehumanize those they considered inferior and/or subhuman. They also used language to obfuscate their real intentions, particularly when it came to their plans for mass murder.

A simple listing of the terms used by Hitler and other Nazis in their writings and speeches provide clear evidence of their intent to dehumanize their victims and to create images of inferiority and "otherness." Hitler himself described the Jews as "germ carriers," "a ferment of decomposition," and "blood-suckers" (Dawidowicz, 1986, pp. 19–20). Hitler and other Nazis referred to the Jews as bacillus (Edelheit and Edelheit, 1994, p. 8), cancer (Edelheit and Edelheit, 1994, p. 8), parasites and pests (Doneson, 1995, pp. 484–485), and fleas (Mosse, 1995, p. 1215).

The Nazis made a practice of hiding their true intentions with euphemistic language. Some of the more classic examples of the Nazis' use of euphemisms are the following terms: *aktions,* euthanasia, *Einsatzkommando* (Levi, 1988, p. 31), "preventive custody" (Berenbaum, 1993, p. 51), resettlement "to the east" (Langer, 1995, pp. 31–32), selections, and Final Solution (Edelheit and Edelheit, 1994, pp. 225, 424–425). As Primo Levi (1988) observed, most of the aforementioned words, as well as others, "were not only used to deceive the victims and prevent defensive reactions on their part; they were also meant, within the limits of the possible, to prevent public opinion, and those sections of the army not directly involved, from finding out what was happening in all the territories occupied by the Third Reich" (p. 31).

Aktions were procedures of any length conducted for political, racial, or eugenic ends—many of which included the murder of targeted groups of people. "Euthanasia" is the term the Nazis used to describe the Nazis' murder of the physically and mentally handicapped (Gallagher, 1995, p. 265). Gallagher notes that: "The officially sanctioned killing program [to systematically kill the severely disabled and chronically mentally ill patients], begun in 1939, was called 'Euthanasie' although most of its victims were neither terminally ill nor in unbearable pain, nor were they anxious to die" (p. 265). *Einsatzkommando*, which literally means "prompt-employment unit" (Levi, 1988, p. 31), were the individuals who belonged to the Einsatzgruppen or the mobile killing squads of the SS during World War II. The latter were responsible for the murder of approximately "1.25 million Jews [in the Soviet Union] and hundreds of thousands of other Soviet nationals" (Spector, 1995, p. 438). "Preventive custody" actually referred to incarceration in a concentration camp. "Resettlement" was the term the Nazis used to attempt to deceive those who were being sent, for example, from a ghetto to a death camp where they were to be murdered en masse. "To the east" was a euphemism for shipping victims to the death camps located in Poland. "Selections" was a seemingly innocuous term that referred to those individuals who were either being sent to the gas chambers or being allowed to live a little longer in order to perform brutal slave labor. And "Final Solution" was the code term for the mass extermination or total annihilation of every last Jew in Europe. As one can readily ascertain, the Nazis stringently avoided using the words "murder" or "killing."

To assist students in understanding how these words were used as well as what they really meant for the victims, the terms need to be placed in context. A powerful way of doing this is to use excerpts from first-person accounts that not only use the terms but illustrate the reality behind their facade. The use of the word "selection" provides a case in point in the following passage, describing the day (October 28, 1941) in which twenty-seven thousand Jews from the Kovno ghetto were ordered to appear at a "roll call" from which ten thousand were to be selected for execution:

> The square was surrounded by machine-gun emplacements. Rauca [a Gestapo official] positioned himself on top of a little mound from which he could watch the great crowd that waited in the square in tense and anxious anticipation. His glance ranged briefly over the column of the Council members and the Jewish Ghetto police, and by a movement of his hand he motioned them to the left, which, as it became clear later, was the "good" side. Then he signaled with the baton he held in his hand and ordered the remaining columns: "Forward!" The selection had begun.
>
> The columns of employees of the Ghetto institutions and their families passed before Rauca, followed by other columns, one after another. The Gestapo man fixed his gaze on each pair of eyes and with a flick of the finger of his right hand passed sentence on individual families, or even whole groups. (Tory, 1990, p. 51)

In yet another example, Levi (1988) describes the daily "roll calls" the prisoners faced in the camps:

> It is well known that a roll call took place in all camps once or twice a day. . . . It was *Zahlappell,* a complicated and laborious counting-call because it had to take into consideration prisoners transferred to other camps or to the infirmary the evening before and those who had died during the night, and because the present number must square exactly with the figures of the preceding day, and counting by fives took place as the squads headed for work filed by. [It is reported] that in Buchenwald also the dead and dying had to show up for the evening roll call; stretched out on the ground rather . . . they too had to be aligned by fives, to facilitate the count.
>
> This roll call took place (in the open, naturally) in all weather and lasted at least an hour, or even two or three if the count did not balance out—and even twenty-four hours or longer if an escape was suspected. When it rained or snowed, or the cold was intense, it became a torture . . . it was perceived as an empty and ritual ceremony, but probably it was not. . . . [N]either hunger nor exhausting labor were useless, and not even . . . the death by gas of adults and children. All these sufferings were the development of a theme, that of the presumed right of a superior people to subjugate or eliminate an inferior people. . . . The suffering it caused, and which in the winter led every day to some breakdowns or some deaths, fit into the system. . . . (pp. 114–116)

The extreme nature of what the victims were subjected to twisted the meaning of words into something that is difficult to fathom. And even though Holocaust survivors attempt, time and again, one after another, to try to describe what they experienced, many end up claiming that what they experienced was "beyond words," or that they "have no words to express it." As one survivor has written:

I don't think the human tongue can describe the horror we went through in the ghetto. In the streets, if you can call them that, for nothing was left of the street, we had to step over heaps of corpses. There was no room to get around them. Besides fighting the Germans, we fought hunger, and thirst. We had no contact with the outside world; we were completely isolated, cut off from the world. We were in such a state that we could no longer understand the very meaning of why we went on fighting. (quoted in Lanzmann, 1985, pp. 197–198)

Thus, while a survivor or scholar can certainly delineate in words what the victims experienced, a *true understanding* of the nature of the horror approaches the ineffable. Ultimately, students must comprehend that the contemporary world's understanding of certain words meant something entirely different to the victims who lived through the horror of the Holocaust. For example, such words as "cold," "hunger," "fear," and "tired" had a profoundly different meaning in the ghettos and the slave labor, concentration, and death camps than they do for those of us residing in the United States today. Levi (1985) asserts that:

We fought with all our strength to prevent the arrival of winter. We clung to all the warm hours, at every dusk we tried to keep the sun in the sky for a little longer, but it was all in vain. . . . [T]oday is winter. . . . It means that in the course of these months, from October till April, seven out of ten of us will die. Whoever does not die will suffer minute by minute, all day, every day: from the morning before dawn until the distribution of the evening sup we will have to keep our muscles continuously tensed, dance from foot to foot, beat our arms under our shoulders against the cold. . . . Wounds will open on everyone's hands, and to be given a bandage will mean waiting every evening for hours on one's feet in the snow and wind.

Just as our hunger is not that feeling of missing a meal, so our way of being cold has need of a new word. [Today, years later,] we say "hunger," we say "tiredness," "fear," "pain," we say "winter" and they are different things. They are free words, created and used by free men who live in comfort and suffering in their homes. If the Lagers had lasted longer a new, harsh language would have been born; only this language could express what it means to toil the whole day in the wind, with the temperature below freezing, wearing only a shirt, underpants, cloth jacket and trousers, and in one's body nothing but weakness, hunger and knowledge of the end drawing nearer. (p. 91)

Another example of this phenomenon is provided by Lawrence Langer (1995), who has written extensively about the "language of extremity": "[E]ven 'deaths' is not an exact term for the doom of Hitler's victims, who lacked our retrospective vision of what awaited them at the end of their boxcar journey. . . . [The term] did not anticipate gas chambers and the genocide of European Jewry" (p. 55).

Langer also warns that those who think about and study the Holocaust must be careful in how they use language:

The role of language . . . illustrates how easy it is to change the impact of a disastrous event simply by renaming it. When we speak of the survivor instead of the victim and of martyrdom instead of murder . . . or evoke the redemptive rather than the grievous power of memory, we draw on an arsenal of words that urges us to build verbal fences between the atrocities of the camps and ghettos and what we are mentally willing—or able—to face. When we greet "liberation" with relief and celebrate it as a victory for endurance, we block out the images of the emaciated bodies that Allied troops found as they entered places like Buchenwald and Bergen-Belsen, as if a single honorific term could erase the paradoxical possibility that survival might also be a lifelong sentence to the memory of loss. (p. 6)

Conclusion

As teachers teach about the Holocaust, they will undoubtedly come across many other aspects of the history that merit the "complication" of their students' thinking. Such opportunities constitute "teachable moments," and they need to be capitalized on and addressed in a good amount of detail.

Throughout a study of the Holocaust teachers continually need to raise penetrating questions about significant and thorny issues for the students to wrestle with as they attempt to gain a modicum of understanding about the events that unfolded during this period. When positing a question, teachers need to challenge the students not to answer the questions off the top of their heads but to keep the questions in mind and to mull them over as they read and study about this tragic event. In attempting to answer the questions, students must come to understand that it is imperative to support their answers by citing key aspects of the history and/or points made by scholars. And finally, *all must come to understand and appreciate that there are no simple answers when studying this, or any other, period of history.*

Note: For a somewhat different discussion of the issues examined here, see William S. Parsons and Samuel Totten, *Guidelines for Teaching about the Holocaust.* Washington, DC: United States Holocaust Memorial Museum, 1993.

REFERENCES

Aronson, Shlomo, and Longerich, Peter. (2001). "Final Solution: Preparation and Implementation," pp. 184–198. In Walter Laqueur (Ed.), *The Holocaust Encyclopedia*. New Haven, CT: Yale University Press.

Bankier, David. (2001). "German Jewry," pp. 241–251. In Walter Laqueur (Ed.), *The Holocaust Encyclopedia*. New Haven, CT: Yale University Press.

Bauer, Yehuda. (1989). "Jewish Resistance and Passivity in the Face of the Holocaust," pp. 235–251. In François Furet (Ed.), *Unanswered Questions: Nazi Germany and the Genocide of the Jews*. New York: Schocken.

Berenbaum, Michael. (1993). *The World Must Know: The History of the Holocaust as Told in the United States Holocaust Memorial Museum*. Boston: Little, Brown.

Berenbaum, Michael. (1997). "Introduction—XV. Choiceless Choices," pp. 202–204. In Michael Berenbaum (Ed.), *Witness to the Holocaust: An Illustrated Documentary History of the Holocaust in the Words of Its Victims, Perpetrators and Bystanders*. New York: HarperCollins.

Browning, Christopher. (1995). "Wannsee Conference," pp. 1591–1594. In Israel Gutman (Ed.), *Encyclopedia of the Holocaust*. New York: Macmillan.

Caracciolo, Nicola. (1995). *Uncertain Refuge: Italy and the Jews During the Holocaust*. Urbana: University of Illinois Press.

Dawidowicz, Lucy S. (1986). *The War Against the Jews 1933–1945*. New York: Bantam.

Dawidowicz, Lucy S. (1992). "How They Teach the Holocaust," pp. 65–83. In Lucy S. Dawidowicz (Ed.), *What Is the Use of Jewish History?* New York: Schocken.

Doneson, Judith E. (1995). "Films, Nazi Antisemitic," pp. 484–485. In Israel Gutman (Ed.), *Encyclopedia of the Holocaust*. New York: Macmillan.

Edelheit, Abraham J., and Edelheit, Hershel. (1994). *History of the Holocaust: A Handbook and Dictionary*. Boulder, CO: Westview Press.

Friedlander, Henry. (1995). *The Origins of Nazi Genocide: From Euthanasia to The Final Solution*. Chapel Hill: University of North Carolina Press.

Friedländer, Saul. (1998). "The Extermination of the European Jews in Historiography: Fifty Years Later," pp. 3–17. In Alvin H. Rosenfeld (Ed.), *Thinking About the Holocaust After a Half Century*. Bloomington and Indianapolis: Indiana University Press.

Gallagher, Hugh Gregory. (1995). "Holocaust: The Genocide of Disabled People," pp. 265–298. In Samuel Totten, William S. Parsons, and Israel W. Charny (Ed.), *Genocide in the Twentieth Century: Critical Essays and Eyewitness Accounts*. New York: Garland.

Gilbert, Martin. (1987). *The Holocaust: A History of the Jews of Europe During the Second World War*. New York: Henry Holt.

Hilberg, Raul. (1985). *The Destruction of the European Jews*. 3 Volumes. New York: Holmes & Meier.

Kranzler, David. (1995). "Japan," pp. 735–738. In Israel Gutman (Ed.), *Encyclopedia of the Holocaust*. New York: Macmillan.

Kulka, Otto Dov, and Hildesheimer, Esriel. (1995). "Germany," pp. 557–575. In Israel Gutman (Ed.), *Encyclopedia of the Holocaust*. New York: Macmillan.

Landau, Ronnie S. (1994). *The Nazi Holocaust*. Chicago: Ivan R. Dees.

Langer, Lawrence L. (1982). *Versions of Survival: The Holocaust and the Human Spirit*. Albany: State University of New York Press.

Langer, Lawrence L. (1995). *Admitting the Holocaust: Collected Essays*. New York: Oxford University Press.

Lanzmann, Claude. (1985). *Shoah: An Oral History of the Holocaust*. New York: Pantheon.

Levi, Primo. (1985). "Survival in Auschwitz," pp. 5–132. In *If This Is a Man: Remembering Auschwitz*. New York: Summit Books.

Levi, Primo. (1988). *The Drowned and the Saved*. New York: Summit.

Marrus, Michael R. (1987). *The Holocaust in History*. New York: Meridian.

Michaelis, Meir. (1995). "Italy—General Survey," pp. 720–726. In Israel Gutman (Ed.), *Encyclopedia of the Holocaust*. New York: Macmillan.

Mosse, George. (1995). "Racism," pp. 1206–1217. In Israel Gutman (Ed.), *Encyclopedia of the Holocaust*. New York: Macmillan.

Niewyk, Donald. (1995). "Holocaust: The Genocide of the Jews," pp. 167–207. In Samuel Totten, William S. Parsons, and Israel W. Charny (Eds.), *Genocide in the Twentieth Century: Critical Essays and Eyewitness Accounts*. New York: Garland.

Parsons, William S., and Totten, Samuel. (1993). *Guidelines for Teaching about the Holocaust*. Washington, DC: United States Holocaust Memorial Museum.

Pingel, Faith. (1995). "Concentration Camps," pp. 308–317. In Israel Gutman (Ed.), *Encyclopedia of the Holocaust*. New York: Macmillan.

Spector, Shmuel. (1995). "Einsatzgruppen," pp. 433–439. In Israel Gutman (Ed.), *Encyclopedia of the Holocaust*. New York: Macmillan.

Tory, Avraham. (1990). *Surviving the Holocaust: The Kovno Ghetto Diary*. Cambridge: Harvard University Press.

Yahil, Leni. (1990). *The Holocaust: The Fate of European Jewry*. New York: Oxford University Press.

7

Diminishing the Complexity and Horror of the Holocaust: Using Simulations in an Attempt to Convey Personal and Historical Experiences

In an effort to provide students with a "real sense" of what Jews suffered during the Holocaust, some teachers (including university professors) latch onto the use of simulations. Others, including many longtime Holocaust educators and concerned Holocaust survivors, however, look askance at the use of such simulations,[1] arguing that they provide a simplistic and unrealistic view of tortuously complex and horrific situations and serve to minimize the significance of what the victims experienced.

The focus of this chapter is twofold: first, it delineates why and how some educators have used simulations to teach their students about various aspects of the Holocaust; and second, it argues that the use of such simulations constitutes poor pedagogy as a result of its drastic oversimplification of Holocaust history.

The Problematic Use of Simulations to Teach about the Holocaust

"The truth of the matter is that we need to use anything we can find to allow students to make connections between their lessons and their life" (a teacher on the Holocaust.listserve, July 26, 1995). This sentiment expressed by one teacher in regard to Holocaust education is, unfortunately, shared by many others at the elementary through university levels. Some teachers believe that simulations are an extremely desirable pedagogical device for capturing student interest. First, they argue that simulations are a powerful way to provide students with a sense of what people have experienced in different historical situations. Second, they insist that through simulations, students are able to glean insights into aspects of history that they would not necessarily gain via more traditional methods such as reading the history of the period. Third, they argue that because simulations tap into the affective domain *and* are so radically different from other classroom activities, they thoroughly engage student interest and are capable of leaving lasting impressions on students.

None of these arguments stand up under close scrutiny when applied to teaching about the Holocaust. As for the first point, to suggest that one can approximate even a scintilla of what the victims went through is sheer folly. Addressing the second and third points, there are ample resources available—such as primary documents, first-person accounts of survivors and liberators, secondary sources, and powerful and accurate documentaries—that are informative, highly engaging, thought-provoking, and memorable. If none of these materials engage students, then it is incumbent upon teachers to examine the resources, pedagogical strategies, and learning activities they are using and/or to reevaluate whether their students are mature enough to study this history.

Commenting on the use of simulations to attempt to convey to students what the victims lived through (e.g., in the ghettos, during the deportations, and in the concentration and death camps), Stephen Feinberg, a noted Holocaust educator who taught history at Wayland (MA) Middle School for eighteen years and is now employed by the United States Holocaust Memorial Museum, states:

> I am very leery about using simulations to teach *any* aspect of the Holocaust. While it may be appealing to some educators to use simulations when addressing certain issues raised by the Holocaust, I believe the result would be more negative than positive. According to William A. Nesbitt (1971), the author of *Simulation Games for the Social Studies Classroom,* "the reality represented [in a simulation] is reduced in size so that it is manageable. Only selected aspects of the real situation are included in a simulation. Developers of simulations reduce and simplify reality so students can focus on selected aspects of reality." This simplification of reality can, when applied to a study of the Holocaust, lead to a facile understanding of complex issues and, worse, still, a trivialization of the Holocaust. (personal correspondence, July 17, 1991)

I am in total agreement with Feinberg's position.

Examples of Typical Simulations
Used by Teachers to Teach about the Holocaust

Highlighted below are examples of simulations that some teachers use to "recreate" aspects of Holocaust history in order to "place students in the shoes of the victims." They were gleaned from various sources: Holocaust curricula, articles in which teachers describe their use of simulations, descriptions of simulations that teachers have shared over the Internet on the Holocaust.listserve, and examples that teachers shared with my colleagues and me as we presented sessions at conferences on Holocaust education.

1. Prior to class, a seventh-grade social studies teacher clears all the desks from the middle of the room and draws a long, broad rectangle in chalk on the floor. After the students enter, she explains that today they are going to gain an understanding of what it was like for the Jews to be deported to concentration camps in cattle cars. After lining the kids up, she swiftly marches them into the imaginary boxcar. As the space becomes increasingly crowded, she urges them to squeeze tighter together; and as they do so, she keeps feeding more students into the space. When the last student is in, she pretends to slam the imaginary door closed. Then, as they stand there, giggling, complaining about their feet being stepped on, gently pushing and shoving each other, she orders them quiet and then reads them a selection from a first-person account that describes the cattle cars. At the end of the "simulation," she announces, "Now you have some idea as to what the Jews went through. You should *never* forget it!" (Shared by a teacher at a workshop on on Holocaust education, July 1995, Washington, DC)

2. "My students and I [Hilve Fierek] spent . . . two weeks exploring Hitler's war against the Jews and other 'undesirables': the historical events, the facts and figures, the personal accounts. We watched videos and read poem after poem, story after story. I was certain my students were learning. I mean, I had brought in all this *stuff*; surely now my ninth graders recognized the importance of our study.

"To test my theory, I . . . asked my students to . . . 'Imagine this is Germany during World War II. . . . 'Decide whether you'd rather be a Nazi soldier or a Jew and explain why.' Most started writing, but one young man raised his hand. With sincere curiosity, he asked, 'Now which ones got beaten up again?'

"My first impulse was to run from the room crying . . . I had failed, and failed miserably. . . . Thinking quickly, I told students to clear their desk and give me their absolute, undivided attention. 'This mobile unit is now Germany in 1943,' I told them with every bit of total authority I could muster. 'I am Adolf Eichmann, a chief administrator for the Final Solution. Decide now whether you are a Nazi or a Jew. If you choose to be a Nazi, line up along the right wall. If you choose to be a Jew, assemble in the left corner. You may not choose to be an 'innocent' bystander . . .

"I was surprised at how quickly and easily I assumed the role of dictator. I was equally surprised at how quickly and easily my students assumed their chosen roles. . . . I took the five students who had elected to be Nazis outside. I assigned each one a rank, naming one young woman my second-in-command. They were to follow my orders to the letter, with no questions asked. They readily agreed.

"Back in the room, I told one Nazi commander to select three Jews for immediate extermination. 'But how . . . ,' he began. 'Do it,' I commanded. He chose three students randomly. . . . I told the selected students they were now dead and could not participate in the rest of the activities. There were a few giggles, giggles that I immediately stifled with my newly found dictator glare.

"For the next 15 minutes my mobile unit was, for us, World War II Germany. The tension became so thick that several times I considered stopping the activity. For instance, when I told one girl who had elected to be a Jew to select two of her classmates for medical experimentation, she at first refused. 'Choose now, or I take six,' I barked. The girl, a Jehovah's Witness, replied with tears in her eyes, 'Take me.'" (Fierek, 1996, pp. 10–11)

3. "When I [Ginger Moore] was a sophomore in college, in a three-week Winter term course on the Holocaust, the professors wanted us to understand at least a little bit what trips in cattle cars were like (most of us never having been inside a cattle car in our lives!). So they had us squeeze into the approximate space on the floor, try sitting (not possible), try moving (not possible), and then try to imagine having to go to the bathroom (horrifying!). They also gave us other qualifiers; we were indoors, not out with the weather and temperature, it was light, we had had breakfast, and so forth. I know *I* came away from it with a much clearer idea than words or even pictures could have provided. While I'm sure it didn't even come close to what the victims experienced, it did make a connection with most of the students which we otherwise would not have had. It was a way to avoid numbing. So we came away not with the feeling that we really felt what the victims had felt, but with a much clearer idea than we had had before" (Ginger K. Moore, July 26, 1995, Holocaust.listserve).

4. "The Auschwitz Platform: to allow students to consider the arbitrary decisions made at Auschwitz and the effects on the survivors who are aware that death has only been postponed:

    a. The teacher should prepare a supply of blue cards and white cards;

    b. As each student enters the class, give him or her a white card or a blue card;

    c. All students holding blue cards should sit on the teacher's left; all those holding white cards should sit on the teacher's right;

    d. After all of the students have been seated, inform those with blue cards that they are to be exterminated and their bodies burned in the gas chambers. Those holding white cards will be allowed to live one more day at least;

    e. Explain what happened on the notorious platform at Auschwitz when the railroad cars delivered the prisoners to the camp and life-and-death decisions were made, depending on sex, age, strength, and the intended use of the prisoners; and

    f. Allow the students to express their feelings about the Auschwitz platform through classroom discussion and/or writings.

(Brewer, Bijwaard, and Payne, 1987, pp. 46–47).

5. "You are a member of the Judenrat [Jewish council] in the Warsaw Ghetto. With the other members of that Council, you must select five of your people in the ghetto to be removed from the transport to a death camp. The Judenrat has been called into session to discuss the people who are listed below as 'possible candidates' for removal and eventual extermination. . . . In your Council, decide on five people who you as the Judenrat will remove from the ghetto and send to the extermination camp tomorrow morning" (New Jersey Commission on Holocaust Education, 1995, Unit IV, p. 49).

On the surface, such simulations may seem interesting and engaging. Certainly, as mentioned above, they are vastly different from the typical classroom fare that most students in the United States face in their courses on a daily basis (Goodlad, 1985, pp. 229–232). That is, such simulations move students from passive to active, literally involve student movement, and are interactive. Yet, are such activities pedagogically sound? Do they truly involve the students in a solid study of the history? Do they really provide students with accurate and deep insights into the what the victims experienced? Are the students left with anything more than a sense that they have had fun for a period? And, do such simulations possibly add insult to the horrific injury already suffered by the survivors of the Holocaust?

In response to the first four questions, some teachers would answer with a resounding "Yes!" One such person would likely be Hilve Fierek, a professor of education at the University of North Carolina at Charlotte, who implemented one of the aforementioned simulations. Concerning the impact of the simulation on her students, she writes:

> [I]n some small way, I had engaged my students in actual learning. . . . For a brief second, [I] helped my ninth graders find relevance in historical material they considered as removed from them as the Trojan War. If nothing else, I had them search their souls to consider if, given a choice, they would rather kill than be killed. . . . Without an understanding of humanity, the Holocaust becomes just another footnote in history to be memorized and regurgitated on some standardized test. I chose instead to explore, with my students, why we, as human beings, make the decisions we do. (pp. 11, 12)

Such arguments are common, but naive. They set up straw men in their unspoken assumption that the only way to engage students in an exploration of what it means to be human and personally and socially responsible is through jejune activities. This is not only anti-intellectual but disingenuous. As Sidney Bolkosky, a historian and coauthor of the Holocaust curriculum entitled *Life Unworthy of Life,* asserts: "Nothing about the Holocaust needs dramatization" (Holocaust.listserve, July 27, 1995).

The Problems Posed by Holocaust Simulations

For many scholars, educators, and survivors, there are a host of problems inherent in the use of simulations to teach about the Holocaust. These include, but are not limited to, the following: They are invariably simplistic; they frequently convey both skewed and incorrect information vis-à-vis the Holocaust; and more often than not, they are ahistorical. The simple fact is, no matter what a teacher and his or her students do in a simulation, *they will never ever even begin to approximate or simulate the horror that the victims suffered at the hands of the Nazis*. What is of critical importance here is that the use of such simulations often result in students believing that—at least to some extent—they do.

As for the problematic nature of using simulation activities to study complex human behavior for the purpose of helping students to "experience" unfamiliar situations, Totten and Feinberg (1995) argue that:

> It needs to be understood that helping students in the course of a discussion or in a writing activity to explore a different perspective or to "walk in someone else's shoes" is different from involving a class in a simulation game. Likewise, conducting a simulation in order to thoroughly engage students in the study of a concept is vastly different from conducting a simulation in order to have students "experience" what it was like for a victim to be jammed into a boxcar en route to a concentration camp or killing center or to experience what it was like to live day-in- and day-out under the threat of abject brutality and death.
>
> . . . By their very nature, simulations are purposely toned down in order to make them easier for students to grasp. As a result, students who use simulations only end up being exposed to an [absurdly] watered-down version of the actual situation. When applied to a study of the Holocaust, this inevitably leads to a facile oversimplification. It presents a skewed view of the history, and often serves to reinforce negative stereotypes. Indeed, in more cases than not, such simulations lead to a trivialization of the Holocaust. Such situations can also degenerate into a time of "play" that is bereft of real thinking. In the end, students often remember the excitement of the game to the exclusion of the intended meaning of the exercises or its relationship to the history under examination. (pp. 331–332)

In a related line of criticism about the use of simulations in teaching about the Holocaust, the authors (including this writer) of *Guidelines for Teaching about the Holocaust*, developed under the auspices of the United States Holocaust Memorial Museum, note:

> Holocaust survivors and eyewitnesses are among the first to indicate the grave difficulty of finding words to describe their experiences. Even more revealing, they argue the virtual impossibility of trying to simulate accurately what it was like to live on a daily basis with fear, hunger, disease, unfathomable loss, and the unrelenting threat of abject brutality and death.
>
> . . . *Since there are numerous primary source accounts, both written and visual, as well as survivors and eyewitnesses who can describe actual choices faced and made by individuals, groups, and nations during this period, teachers should draw upon these resources*

and refrain from simulations that lead to a trivialization of the subject matter (italics added). (Parsons and Totten, 1993, pp. 7–8)

In her discussion of classroom simulations to teach about the Holocaust, historian and Holocaust scholar Lucy Dawidowicz (1992) asserts that:

> Besides lectures, readings, films, and discussions, most of the curricula [on the Holocaust which she discusses in her essay "How They Teach the Holocaust"] use simulation games or role-playing to teach their moral lessons. Students play Gestapo, Concentration Camp, and Nuremberg Trial. They act out the roles of murderers, victims, judges (p. 71). . . . The Jews who lived under Hitler's rule were confronted with cruel dilemmas, forced to make difficult, even impossible, choices about matters of life and death for which conscience could offer no direction and the past could give no guidance. Yet many high-school curricula frivolously suggest role-playing exercises in which students imagine how they would behave if confronted with such dilemmas. What kind of answers can come from American children who think of the Gestapo as the name of a game? (p. 80)

Curriculum developers and teachers at all levels need to face the simple but profound fact that there is absolutely no way *anyone,* let alone secondary level students, will ever be able to experience the terror, horror, stench, and butchery of what millions went through as they were humiliated and brutalized by the Nazis. Indeed, no one but no one can even begin to approximate through simulations or role plays what it was like for people to be forced from their homes, crammed into ghettos under the most horrific circumstances where people were literally dying in the street from disease and starvation, or to be forced to undress at the lip of a ditch full of dead and wounded people and stand and wait until they, too, were shot and killed. Likewise, no one can experience, let alone truly fathom, the horror of being crammed into a boxcar that was either suffocatingly hot or literally freezing cold for days on end without food or water in which people were urinating, defecating, going mad, and dying. As horrible as these images are, *they* do not even begin to approximate what the victims experienced. To illustrate this stark fact, it is worth going to the victims themselves for descriptions of what they, their loved ones, and others were subjected to during the Holocaust period.

Yitskhok Rudashevski, a fourteen-year-old Lithuanian Jew, who kept a diary while incarcerated in the Vilna Ghetto from June 1941–April 1943, recorded the following on April 6, 1943:

> The situation is an oppressive one. We now know all the horrible details. Instead of Kovno, 5,000 Jews were taken to Ponar where they were shot to death. Like wild animals before dying, the people began in mortal despair to break the railroad cars, they broke the little windows reinforced by strong wire. Hundreds were shot to death while running away. The railroad line over a great distance is covered with corpses. (Holliday, 1995, p. 183)

In early October 1943, Rudashevski and some family members were discovered in their hideout by the Nazis and taken to Ponar, where they were all murdered.

Survivor Elie Wiesel (1990) tells this heartrending story of a mother and her two children:

> And in the city, the grand, ancient city of Kiev, that mother and her two children in front of some German soldiers who are laughing. . . . [T]hey take one child from her and kill it before her eyes. . . . then, they seize the second and kill it too. . . . She wants to die; the killers prefer her to remain alive but inhabited by death. . . . Then, she takes the two little bodies, hugs them against their chest and begins to dance . . . how can one describe that mother? How can one tell of her dance? In this tragedy, there is something that hurts beyond hurting—and I do not know what it is. (p. 186)

Speaking about the nature and impact of the deportations on people, Sonja Fritz, a survivor of Auschwitz, relates the following:

> I remember very well the transports that came from Greece. Some of the staff of Block 10 had to go to the ramp to shave the hair of the new arrivals. The poor Greek girls had spent a long time in cattle cars and their hair was full of lice and so infested that we got blisters on our hands. (quoted in Shelley, 1991, p. 24)

In this recollection of arrival at a camp, a young girl speaks of her shock, horror, and dismay:

> A fat S.S. woman said, "Take off everything." I think of my mother and all these strange people naked, and the German soldiers watching, and I cry. I had long, black, beautiful hair and they cut it, not even. Then into the shower, many under one shower, very little water, and so cold. Everything happened so fast, no dress, no hair, nothing, wet and cold like an animal. (Lewin, 1990, p. 46)

Upon his arrival at Auschwitz as a thirteen-year-old boy and prisoner, Elie Wiesel was confronted with this scene:

> Not far from us, flames were leaping up from a ditch, gigantic flames. They were burning something. A lorry drew up at the pit and delivered its load—little children. Babies! Yes, I saw it—saw it with my own eyes . . . those children in the flames. (Wiesel, 1969, p. 42)

Speaking about a death march, Reska Weiss, a survivor, recalls that:

> Urine and excreta poured down the prisoners' legs, and by nightfall the excrement, which had frozen to our limbs, gave off its stench. We were really no longer human beings in the accepted sense. Not even animals, but putrefying corpses moving on two legs. (1961, p. 211)

To take something so horrific, so profoundly disturbing, so overwhelming to those who lived through it, and to turn it into something that becomes, for many, though certainly not all, "fun and games," is to make a mockery of what the victims lived through. No matter what teachers say in regard to the supposed efficacy of such simulations, students know full well that the simulation is simply a classroom activity that will last approximately twenty-five to forty-five minutes before it is over. Throughout the activity they, of course, know that they are in no real danger, and that, ultimately, what they are experiencing is not much more than a "game." *And yet, again, at the end of the activity some teachers and, who knows how many students, actually think the class has experienced something that approximates what the victims experienced.*

For students to walk away thinking that they have either experienced what a victim went through or have a greater understanding of what the victims suffered is shocking in its naiveté. *Even more galling is for teachers to think that they have provided their students with a true sense of what the victims lived through—and/or to think they have at least approximated the horror and terror that the victims experienced.*

When one really thinks about it, Holocaust simulations are a waste of precious classroom time. This is especially true since so little time anyhow is given over to this history in our nation's classrooms. In light of the fact that teachers at all levels are constantly battling the clock and calendar to teach an overpacked curriculum, it is imperative that they use their time as wisely as possible. Thus, to attempt to teach the Holocaust over several days (which is all the time most teachers dedicate to this history) and then to do so with such simplistic devices as simulations, which leave students with a skewed view of this history, simply does not make sense.

A Need to Show Sensitivity to the Memory of the Victims and the Feelings of the Survivors

Over and above the pedagogical inappropriateness of using simulations to teach this history, there is the issue of being respectful and sensitive to both the victims who perished at the hands of the Nazis and the survivors of the Holocaust who are still haunted by what they lived through. More specifically, those who exploit the subject of the Holocaust to "engage" their students, to "get them *really* interested in history," are, despite their best intentions, guilty of nothing less than mindless vulgarity. Many survivors have said as much.

Although the following comments by Elie Wiesel (1990) are directed at certain films of the Holocaust, they are equally apropos vis-à-vis the use of simulations to teach about it:

> How can one "stage" a convoy of uprooted deportees being sent into the unknown, or the liquidation of thousands of men, women, and children? How can one "produce" the machine-gunned, the gassed, the mutilated corpses, when the viewer knows that they are all actors, and that after the filming they will return to the hotel

for a well-deserved bath and a meal? Sure, this is true of all subjects and of all films, but that is also the point: the Holocaust is not a subject like all the others. It imposes certain limits. . . . In order not to betray the dead and humiliate the living, this particular subject demands a special sensibility, a different approach, a rigor, strengthened by respect and reverence and, above all, faithfulness to memory. (pp. 167–168)

Continuing to address the production of films on the Holocaust, Wiesel asks, "How can one explain such obscenity? How can anyone justify such insensitivity?" (Wiesel, 1990, p. 170). He further states that: "Newcomers to this history appoint themselves experts. . . . They give the impression of knowing better than the victims or the survivors how to name what Samuel Beckett called the unnameable. . . . [T]he temptation is generally reductionist, shrinking personalities to stereotypes and dialogue to clichés. All is trivial and superficial, even death itself" (p. 171).

He concludes by asserting:

But then, the "experts" will ask, how do we transmit the message? There are other ways to do it, better ways to keep the memory alive. Today the question is not what to transmit but how. Study the texts—such as the diaries of Emanuel Ringelblum and Chaim Kaplan; the works by the historians Raul Hilberg, Lucy Dawidowicz, Martin Gilbert, Michael Marrus. Watch the documentaries, such as . . . Claude Lanzmann's *Shoah,* and Haim Gouri's *81st Blow*. Listen to the survivors and respect their wounded sensibility. Open yourselves to their scarred memories, and mingle your tears with theirs. And stop insulting the dead. (pp. 171, 172)

Conclusion

Whether teachers like to admit it or not, by using simulations to try to provide students with a sense of what the victims of the Nazis were subjected to, they are minimizing, simplifying, distorting, and possibly even denying the horror of the Holocaust. These are strong words and accusations, but they are carefully chosen. By leaving students with even a minimal notion that they possess a real sense as to what the victims went through, teachers may be inadvertently playing into the hands of Holocaust deniers—people who absurdly and falsely assert that "things were not as bad as the Jews and other victims purport them to have been."

The best advice in regard to simulations intended to provide students with a sense of Holocaust history, including what the victims lived through and/or the choices that both perpetrators and victims made, is to avoid them. Instead, as previously mentioned, teachers and students should focus on examining the primary documents, the first-person accounts, the accurate and well-written histories, and the best films on this subject.

Also, at this juncture in time, when survivors of the Holocaust and liberators of the concentration and death camps are still living, a teacher could hardly do better than to provide his or her students with an opportunity to listen to and engage in discussion with one of these people—one who was there and saw the degradation, the horror, and the injustice up close. The next best avenue is to view videotapes in which the survivors and liberators tell about their experiences and/or to read their accounts available in print. Such accounts, if carefully chosen, *will* leave students with something they will never forget.

REFERENCES

Brewer, B. J., Bijwaard, Patricia A., and Payne, Lynn P. (1987). *Teaching the Past Describes Today . . . Tomorrow—Human Rights Education. Focus: The Holocaust.* Richmond: Virginia Department of Education.

Dawidowicz, Lucy. (1992). "How They Teach the Holocaust," pp. 65–83. In Lucy Dawidowicz, *What Is the Use of Jewish History?* New York: Schocken.

Fierek, Hilve. (1996). "By Fifth Bell, There Were No Nazis." *Inquiry in Social Studies: Curriculum, Research, and Instruction. The Journal of the North Carolina Council for the Social Studies*, pp. 10–12.

Goodlad, John. (1985). *A Place Called School: Prospects for the Future.* New York: McGraw-Hill.

Holliday, Laurel (Ed.). (1995). "Yitskhok Rudashevski," pp.137–183. *Children in the Holocaust and World War II: Their Secret Diaries.* New York: Pocket Books.

Lewin, Rhoda G. (Ed.). (1990). *Witnesses to the Holocaust: An Oral History.* Boston: Twayne.

New Jersey Commission on Holocaust Education. (1995). *The Holocaust and Genocide: Curriculum Guide 7–12.* Trenton: New Jersey Department of Education.

Parsons, William S., and Totten, Samuel. (1993). *Guidelines for Teaching About the Holocaust.* Washington, DC: United States Holocaust Memorial Museum.

Shelley, Lore. (1991). *Criminal Experiments on Human Beings in Auschwitz and War Research Laboratories: Twenty Women Prisoners' Accounts.* San Francisco: Mellen Research University Press.

Totten, Samuel, and Feinberg, Stephen. (1995). "Teaching About the Holocaust: Rationale, Context, Methodology, and Resources." Special Issue (Teaching the Holocaust) *Social Education*, 59 (6): 323–327, 329, 331–333.

Weiss, Reska (1961). *Journey Through Hell.* London: Vallentine, Mitchell.

Wiesel, Elie. (1969). *Night.* New York: Avon Books.

Wiesel, Elie (1990). "Trivializing Memory." In Elie Wiesel, *From the Kingdom of Memory: Reminiscences.* New York: Schocken.

NOTES

1. This is not to say that all simulations should be banned from use during a study of the Holocaust but, rather, only those that purport to provide students with a sense of the actual experiences that victims lived through at the hands of the Nazis. There is a distinct difference between the two, and that needs to be understood. Some of the more innocuous and, in certain cases, more effective simulations, when conducted with care and intelligence, deal with attitudes of people and such subjects as prejudice, bias, and the use and abuse of power. Such simulations are not about the history of the Holocaust per se, but rather factors that come into play in students' everyday lives. Feinberg (personal correspondence, February 17, 1991), for one, cogently argues that "a simulation such as *Star Power*, which can effectively deal with the issue of powerlessness, is preferable to a simulation that attempts to 'put students back into an historical reality.'" Continuing, Feinberg asserts that:

If such simulations [as *Star Power*] are employed, then it is imperative that there be intensive discussion *before* the simulation. The students need to be helped to see how the simulation relates to the Holocaust. *This should be done in a very explicit manner.* The students should also be assisted in identifying the major intended outcomes of the simulation. There should also be intensive discussion *after* the simulation in which students clearly summarize and evaluate the simulation. They should be expected to relate the simulation to that part of the Holocaust that originally warranted the inclusion of the simulation.

8 Closing a Lesson or a Unit on the Holocaust: Assisting Students to Synthesize and Reflect upon What They Have Learned

The test for a modern curriculum is whether it enables students, at any level, to see how knowledge grows out of, resolves and produces questions.
—Grant Wiggins

All aspects of a study of the Holocaust should be carefully crafted to encourage, guide, and even prod students to think about the history in an in-depth and reflective manner. Nothing in such a study should be perfunctory. This is as true for the close of a lesson as it is for the introduction or the body of the lesson or unit itself. In closing lessons and units on the Holocaust, many teachers are satisfied to conclude the study by giving a traditional quiz or examination. More often than not, however, such quizzes and examinations are less than adequate in assisting students truly to synthesize, let alone reflect on, what they have learned. They also tend to leave students with the notion that they "know" the history. As a result, many students walk away thinking they "know" *the answers* when, in reality, there are innumerable profound questions and issues worthy of consideration long after a study has concluded.

It is true, of course, that quizzes and examinations *can be* designed in a way that challenge students thoroughly to synthesize, ponder, and wrestle with what they have learned; but, again, more often than not, they are not designed in that way or for such a purpose. As Wiggins (1989) notes: "[C]ompetence [or mastery of a subject] can be shown in various, sometime idiosyncratic ways. Why must all students show what they know and can do in the same standardized way?" (p. 208). It seems as if this is a question that all teachers should contemplate and then act upon.

There are, in fact, numerous concluding activities that can be used to complete a study of the Holocaust. Some are ideal for use prior to and/or in conjunction with traditional or authentic assessments, while others are capable of standing on their own. Teachers need to use their own judgment in selecting the type of closing activities that will guide their students in accomplishing one or more of the following three goals: (1) synthesize what they have learned, (2) reflect on what they have learned, especially as it pertains to their own lives and the world in which they reside, and (3) plant seeds for ongoing rumination about their newfound knowledge. In this chapter, I discuss various closing activities that I have implemented during a study of the Holocaust or which I have been informed about by colleagues whose specialty is Holocaust education.

Preparing for the Conclusion of a Study

An interesting way to set the stage for a final discussion (which could last one or more class sessions) and/or for student-designed extension projects is to have the students address any and/or all of the following issues in writing: Is there anything about which you are still perplexed in regard to this history; and if so, what is it and why? What issues and concerns still elude you in your effort to gain a clear understanding of the whats, whys, hows, wheres, and whens of the Holocaust? What issues, events, and concerns do you feel you need to learn about in more detail, and why? Are there any issues and/or concerns that you would personally be interested in researching on your own, and why? What are the most significant insights, concepts, or pieces of information you have gleaned from your study of the Holocaust and why?

Closing Discussion Based on Probing/Philosophical Questions

In addition to addressing the questions broached above, a final discussion around such questions as the following is also useful: Can any lessons at all be learned from the Holocaust? If so, what are they and why? If not, why not? Can it be said that the history of humanity has been a history of progress in human relations? Why or why not? Does the idea of technical progress correlate to human behavior? Why should we, humanity living after the fact, even care about the Holocaust? Now that you know about the Holocaust, do you think or feel you have a responsibility to be more aware and/or concerned about human rights abuses and genocide perpetrated in your own lifetime? Why or why not? And if so, what will that look like in regard to your own actions? These and other open-ended questions can serve as a means for the students to reflect on what they have learned from their study of the Holocaust. A discussion of issues such as these moves the study from one that may be solely fact and concept oriented to one that is immersed in the personal. It is also one that is likely to prod students to be more reflective about what they've learned as well as how what they have learned is relevant to their own lives and society.

Having Students Note What They Never Want to Forget about the Holocaust

A simple but powerful closing activity is to have the students, individually, write down those facts, concepts, events, issues, and images that they *never want to forget* about the Holocaust. Taking part in such an activity encourages students to articulate that which is most meaningful to them as a result of their study. It also has the potential of planting the seeds for ongoing concern about the ubiquitous deprivation of human rights around the world, including that of genocide.

This activity also provides a teacher with a sense of those facts, ideas, concepts, issues, events, discussions, films, and so on, that most powerfully impacted students. In turn, such information can provide invaluable insights for the teacher as he or she revises and hones lessons for students in future classes.

Writing a Letter to a Parent, Guardian, or Oneself

A more structured and more in-depth approach than the above activity is to have the students write a letter to their parents or guardians about what they have learned during their study of the Holocaust, including those aspects of the lesson that they will never forget and why they will never forget them.

Alternatively, a student can write a letter to himself or herself and then seal it. Some time in the future—after he or she turns twenty-one, graduates from college, or has his or her first child—the student could open it and reflect on his or her earlier thoughts. This encourages the student to think of himself or herself in a different context or role; and hopefully, it will also nudge the student to seriously consider those ideas that he or she deems most worthy of remembering, and why. If such an assignment is taken seriously, this concluding activity becomes something more than simply another assignment to get through.

Those students who wish to do so should be allowed to share their letters with the class. Initially, this could be done in small groups of three to four students, which is often a more comfortable setting for students to share personal insights than is a whole class setting. Following the small group activity, a whole-class session can be held. *The sharing of letters in both the small and the large groups should be on a voluntary basis only. This avoids embarrassing anyone who has written something close to the heart that he or she does not want to air with his or her peers.*

An Alternative Letter Assignment: A Missive to a Wider Audience

Another thought-provoking exercise involves each student in writing a letter to a larger audience about what he or she has gleaned as a result of studying the Holocaust. At the outset of this activity, the teacher might wish to share the following letter with his or her students:

> Dear Teacher, I am a survivor of a concentration camp. My eyes saw what no man should witness. Gas chambers built by learned engineers. Children poisoned by educated physicians. Infants killed by trained nurses. Women and babies shot and burned by high school and college graduates. So, I am suspicious of education. My request is: Help your students become human. Your efforts must never produce learned monsters, skilled psychopaths, educated Eichmanns. Reading, writing, arithmetic are important only if they serve to make our children more humane.

Once the above letter has been read and discussed, students should reflect on what they ardently wish to share with others in regard to what they gleaned from their study. After reflecting on what they have learned, the students should jot down key words, phrases, and thoughts that come to mind. Next, students should pair up and discuss their insights. Then, each student should write a letter to whomever they want (a letter to the editor of a local, regional, or national newspaper; the congregation of a church, synagogue, or mosque; the local school board; younger students in their school) in which they succinctly but powerfully convey the thoughts and ideas they would like others to ponder, and/or warnings that they feel people should heed.

Note that the danger in sharing the above letter with the students is that they may latch onto the format and thoughts presented therein, and then simply present a rough facsimile as their own. Thus, teachers who share such a letter with their students must urge them to create their own formats, and incorporate their own thoughts and voices into their respective letters.

Webbing or Clustering as a Postassessment Activity

As discussed in Chapter 2, an effective way to provide students with an opportunity to depict the depth of their knowledge vis-à-vis the Holocaust (or for that matter, any topic) is through the development of a cluster (alternatively referred to as a mind-map, web, or conceptual map) around the "target" word and event "Holocaust." A cluster is "a nonlinear brainstorming process that generates ideas, images, and feelings around a stimulus word until a pattern becomes discernible" (Rico, 1987, p. 17).

To develop a cluster, simply have the students place the term "Holocaust" in the center of a piece of paper (a minimum of 8½" by 11"), circle it, and then draw spokes out from the circle on which they attach related terms or ideas. Each time a term is added, they should circle the term and connect it, with a simple line, to those other terms and/or concepts that are related to it. Each new or related idea should lead to a new clustering of ideas. As Rico (1987) points out: "A cluster is an expanding universe, and each word is a potential galaxy; each galaxy, in turn, may throw out its own universes. As students cluster around a stimulus word, the encircled words rapidly radiate outward until a sudden shift takes place, a sort of 'Aha!' that signals a sudden awareness of that tentative whole" (p. 17). Furthermore, "[s]ince a cluster draws on primary impressions—yet simultaneously on a sense of the overall design—clustering actually generates structure, shaping one thought into a starburst of other thoughts, each somehow related to the whole" (Rico, 1987, p. 18).

Clustering (or mind-mapping or webbing) is a more graphic and, generally, easier and more engaging method to delineate what one knows about a topic than, say, outlining a topic. (For some excellent and thought-provoking discussions by classroom teachers on clustering, see Carol Booth Olson, *Practical Ideas for Teaching Writing as a Process*. Sacramento: California State Department of Education, 1996).

To help students understand the concept of clustering (as well as to provide a comparison and contrast between that which constitutes a complex versus a simplistic cluster), the teacher should first create a very simple cluster of a topic (other than that of the Holocaust; e.g., the school's sports program), and then a more complex cluster on the same topic. In doing so, the teacher can explain the process as he or she develops the clusters. He or she can also use the two clusters as a nonexemplar (e.g., the simplistic cluster) and as an exemplar (the more complex cluster). *It is important for teachers to develop a cluster on a topic other than the Holocaust because many students may be tempted to simply copy the information and/or make the same connections the teacher has made in his or her cluster. (Ideally, if a teacher uses a cluster as a concluding activity, he or she should also use it as an opening activity at the start of the lesson or unit. In this way, the initial cluster is used as a preassessment activity of the students' knowledge base, and the concluding activity is used as a postassessment activity. For a more a detailed discussion of such introductory activities, see Chapter 2.)*

In giving directions for the development of the cluster, the teacher should encourage the students to develop the most detailed, comprehensive, and accurate cluster they possibly can. At the same time, students should be encouraged to strive to delineate the connections, when appropriate, between and amongst the various and separate items, concepts, events, and ideas.

Having each student develop his or her own cluster could constitute the first step in such a postassessment activity. Next, students could be placed in groups of three to four, and directed as follows: "In quiet voices, each person in the group should explain his or her cluster to the other members. In doing so, each student should succinctly (in one to three minutes) discuss his or her cluster by doing the following: providing a succinct overview of key points, noting the rationale as to why he or she included certain ideas, and providing a brief explanation regarding the connections between and amongst various ideas. Next, the job of each group is to design a group cluster." Students should be informed that they cannot simply copy what each person has on his or her personal cluster, as that would be a waste of time; rather, *their job is to develop a new cluster that uses the correct ideas and connections on each map to develop a final map that is, ideally, much stronger, more accurate, and more sophisticated in its depiction of key ideas and connections than any of the single maps in their group. To accomplish that goal, they need to discuss thoroughly the accuracy of the information and connections on each map and then plot how they are going to develop the most sophisticated single map possible. As they proceed with the development of their cluster they need to discuss the breadth, depth, and accuracy of their collective body of information as well as their final design.* At the end of this session, everyone should sign his or her name on the cluster.

If a class has the time, this activity can be carried at least one step further. Each group should share its cluster with the other class members. In doing so, the group members should note why they included various items and why they made the connections they did. At the conclusion of a brief presentation, the large group should posit questions about the cluster and, when appropriate, challenge the students' inclusion of information, connections, and so forth.

Having students develop clusters serves a number of purposes. First, it is an excellent way to get students to synthesize their knowledge and the connections they are making between various concepts, facts, events, antecedents, relationships, and causes and effects. Second, it provides the teacher with a vivid illustration of both the students' depth of knowledge and the sophistication of their conceptual framework of a subject. Third—and this is obviously related to the second point—a teacher is able to ascertain the accuracy of his/her students' knowledge as well as any inaccuracies, misconceptions, and/or myths they may still hold about the subject. Fourth, clustering provides students with a unique method to express their ideas; and in doing so, it allows them to tap into an "intelligence," to borrow a term from Howard Gardner (1983; 1993), (e.g., spatial intelligence) other than the typical concept of writing (linguistic intelligence). In that regard, this method also constitutes a unique form of assessment.

Developing Projects That Assist Students in Synthesizing Their Newfound Knowledge

A Multiple Intelligences-based Activity

Another powerful way to assist students to synthesize their newfound knowledge about the Holocaust is an activity that requires students to use multiple intelligences (i.e., linguistic, logical-mathematical, spatial, bodily kinesthetic, musical, interpersonal, and intrapersonal). Such activities can serve as powerful precursors to a final exam, and are capable not only of providing students with an opportunity to review what they've learned but to synthesize that knowledge. (For a theoretical discussion of multiple intelligences, see Howard Gardner, *Frames of Mind: The Theory of Multiple Intelligences.* New York: Basic Books, 1983. For a detailed discussion of multiple intelligences and how to incorporate them into the instructional process, see Howard Gardner, *Multiple Intelligences: The Theory in Practice.* New York: Basic Books, 1993; and Thomas Armstrong, *Multiple Intelligences in the Classroom.* Alexandria, VA: Association for Supervision and Curriculum Development, 1994.)

As with any project, the directions for such an activity must be clear and specific and the criteria should be clearly spelled out. If the criteria are not adequately addressed, then teachers can almost be assured of receiving projects that are not as historically accurate, in-depth, sophisticated, or as carefully constructed as they could or should be. Obviously, during the study of any piece of history, it is pointless to have the students engage in learning activities that are historically inaccurate and not much more than "fun and games."

Once the directions and criteria (or rubrics) for the project are designed, the teacher should encourage the students to work individually, in pairs, or in medium-sized groups (three to five students) in order to bring to bear various "intelligences" for the purpose of synthesizing their ideas. The activities in which the students might participate could include creating a poster, creating a collage, creating and conducting a choral reading, developing and then delivering a speech on the Holocaust to another class or a community organization, or completing a series of paintings or drawings. Again—and this cannot be overstated—*prior to undertaking such activities, it is imperative that the students have a deep knowledge of the Holocaust as well as a strong sense of the sort of seriousness, rigor, depth of thought, and commitment that is needed to complete such a project.*

Steve Feinberg, a former social studies teacher at Wayland (MA) Middle School and currently an employee of the Education Department at the United States Holocaust Memorial Museum, has developed and used the following variation of the above assignment:

> Concluding activities can serve to show students that the history of the Holocaust is relevant to the world they live in today. By examining the implications of this history, students can learn to better analyze events in their neighborhoods, community, and the larger world. While it is essential that students realize the particularity of this history, it is also important for them to relate this history to today's world. This can be done by asking students to consider the implications of this history within the context of today's world. One way of accomplishing this goal is to have students create works (posters and collages, for example) that address these implications. Connecting the history of the Holocaust to the world in which they live today encourages students to continue to explore this remarkable history. (personal correspondence, 1992)

Developing an Encyclopedia Article

Another synthesizing activity is to form groups of three to five students for the purpose of developing encyclopedia-like articles that thoroughly and accurately summarize what they have learned about the Holocaust. Prior to assigning the task, the teacher should select and xerox a rather lengthy entry from a respected encyclopedia, and assist the students in examining how a solid encyclopedic entry is constructed. Ideally, the entry should be a topic that the students have studied earlier in the semester (one other than the Holocaust), thus enabling them to work from a solid knowledge base in order to critique the thoroughness and accuracy of the entry. During the examination of the entry, the teacher should also direct the students' attention to the following: the succinctness of the writing; how the article is composed of and packed with key information, versus superfluous information; how the role of key personages is delineated; and how the chronology of events is interwoven into the fabric of the article.

Next, under the guidance of the teacher, the entire class should design a rubric presenting the type of information that should be included in the summary. This can be generated in various ways: individual students developing lists and then coming together as a class to finalize the rubric; small groups of three to four students developing a rubric over which there is a consensus and then coming together as a class to develop a class rubric; or having the class, from the outset, develop the rubric.

In developing the rubric, students need to take into consideration such issues as:

- the historical trends that combined to make the Holocaust possible (anti-semitism, racism, social Darwinism, extreme nationalism, totalitarianism, industrialism, and others);
- the various groups involved and/or impacted by the events, including the victims, perpetrators, collaborators, and bystanders;
- the chronology of the Holocaust;
- the different stages of the Holocaust period, including but not limited to the Nazis' rise to power and various events and incidents that influenced such a rise (e.g., Germany's loss in World War I, the ramifications of the Versailles Treaty, the Depression, etc.); the ever increasing discrimination against the Jews and others; the laws passed to enforce the discriminatory practices and isolation and ostracism of the Jews; the ghettoization of the Jews; the deportations; the first systematic killing by the Nazis (e.g., the so-called euthanasia of the mentally and physically handicapped); the evolution of the mass murder/genocide of the Jews, beginning with the actions of the Einsatzgruppen in the Soviet Union;
- the plight of the "other victims" such as the Gypsies, Poles, other Slavs, Soviet prisoners of war, the handicapped, homosexuals;
- the discussion of the decision to systematically kill the Jews at the Wannsee Conference;
- the establishment and running of the death camps;
- the plight of the children;
- the world's response to the mass killings;

- liberation of the concentration and death camps;
- the Nuremberg Trials, and so forth.

Ultimately, each and every entry needs to address the whys, hows, whens, wheres, and whos of the Holocaust, otherwise the entry is bound to be incomplete and inaccurate.

Once the rubric is agreed on by the entire class, pairs or trios of students should team up to write the encyclopedic entry. After the students complete their entries, any number of things could be done with them: They could be exchanged with other groups for the purpose of critiquing them, and subsequently the critiques could be revised; the teacher could read each, make suggestions for revisions, and upon revision, each could be placed in a booklet for use by future classes; or the pieces generated by the students could be compared and contrasted to similar entries found in various encyclopedias.

Having a Concluding Speaker

Bringing in a knowledgeable guest speaker (a survivor of the Holocaust, or a liberator of one of the concentration or death camps) toward the conclusion of a study adds a special dimension to the concluding activities. Survivors and liberators provide unique, firsthand insights to the history that students are not likely to find anywhere else. If neither a survivor nor a liberator is available, then it is worthwhile to bring in a history professor from a local college or university.

Such guest speakers can set the stage for the final assessment or, conversely, conclude the study by speaking after the final assessment has been conducted. Either way, several days prior to the speaker's presentation, students should be informed of the speaker's background and be required to prepare questions for him or her to address. (For a detailed discussion of issues related to guest speakers, see Samuel Totten, "Incorporating First-Person Accounts into a Study of the Holocaust," pp. 107–138. In Samuel Totten and Stephen Feinberg [Eds.], *Teaching and Studying the Holocaust*. Boston: Allyn & Bacon, 2001).

Addressing a Key Quote for the Purpose of Synthesizing and Reflecting on One's New Knowledge of the Holocaust

Both Steve Feinberg, a noted Holocaust educator, and I are strong advocates of concluding exercises that are reflective in nature. Two ways in which Feinberg has prompted students both to synthesize their new knowledge about the Holocaust and to reflect on its meaning for them is through reflective journal entries and final essays. More specifically, he states that:

Concluding activities should encourage students to reflect upon the history and/or literature studied in the unit. Students need to be encouraged to combine the various elements of their study of the Holocaust into a coherent whole. One activity that can assist students in this synthesis of information is a reflective journal-writing assignment or a reflective essay. This activity permits students to blend and unify their thoughts about this particular history into an integrated whole.

Providing students with an evocative quote and asking them to respond to the quote is a good way to accomplish the above. For example, Gerda Lerner has said that "It is not the function of history to drum ethical lessons into our brains. The only thing one can learn from history is that actions have consequences and that certain choices once made are irretrievable" (1997). Students can be asked to respond to this quote (or others like it) in either essay or journal form, using the information they have examined in their Holocaust unit. Hopefully, the general historical nature of such quotes will serve as a catalyst for thinking reflectively about the history of the Holocaust. (personal correspondence, 1998)

Student-Developed Questions for the Final Examination

For those teachers who wish to use a final essay examination at the completion of a study of the Holocaust, one engaging activity is to have each student develop a minimum of two essay questions, with the understanding that *they might be used on the final exam.* Students need to be given directions as to what constitutes a sound question: a question that truly addresses what the class has studied rather than something so far afield that a fellow student wouldn't have the knowledge to answer the question; one that is not so narrow or so broad that an individual would have a torturous time addressing it; one that is thought-provoking and requires the writer to bring to bear both a broad and deep knowledge base about the subject; a question that does not call for rote recitation of facts but an analysis and/or synthesis of facts, concepts, ideas, and issues; and one that is crystal clear about what the respondent needs to address in his or her paper. If such criteria is not provided, then many students are likely to write questions that are of little value or use.

Students should be informed that the teacher will select those questions that are well written, comprehensive, and most thought-provoking. They should also be told that the teacher reserves the right to refine and/or combine questions for use on the exam. When selecting the final set of questions (a total of six to eight from which the students select a single question to answer), a teacher needs to make sure that he or she includes a wide variety of questions so that students have ample choice in regard to what they choose to write about.

Having the students design their own questions is a good synthesizing activity in and of itself. The very act of creating solid questions forces students to wrestle with what they have studied. In order to emphasize the seriousness of developing these questions, a grade can be given for the students' efforts.

Designing such questions also provides students with an opportunity to have a real say about the exam. Most students find this refreshing.

Finally, nothing, of course, precludes a student from answering his or her own question on the exam. This, too, is enticing to students.

A Challenging Essay Examination

When well-thought-out and carefully crafted, open-book essay examinations (whether take-home or in-class) are an excellent means for students to synthesize their newfound knowledge. William Fernekes, a high school social studies supervisor and teacher at Hunterdon Central High School in New Jersey, finds that such essays are an extremely useful method for assessing his students' knowledge in an elective course entitled The Holocaust and Human Behavior. Speaking of such an exam, he states that:

> Students are assigned a take-home essay constituting 50 percent of their final exam grade in the course. The essay topic integrates learning from the entire course while permitting flexibility in the choice of sources to support the student arguments. A critical requirement for the essay is the application of key course concepts regarding human behavior: prejudice, stereotyping, discrimination, in-group/out-group relationships, psychological distancing and compensating behaviors, and the creation of "the other" (dehumanization). Students must employ evidence from their two outside reading books (survivor memoirs) as well as a selection of three or more additional eyewitness accounts by participants in the Holocaust (perpetrators, victims, rescuers or bystanders). (personal correspondence, 1998)

The following question is one that Fernekes has required his students to answer:

> The Holocaust can be viewed as the outgrowth of choices made by individuals and groups in a wide variety of situations. Drawing primarily upon personal eyewitness accounts, explain what you consider to be (1) the key factors which significantly influenced the choices made by perpetrators and victim groups, and (2) the most important insight for understanding human behavior in today's world based upon your analysis of these factors and the choices that were made. (personal correspondence, 1998)

Performance-Based Assessment

Noted educator Theodore Sizer observes that performances and exhibitions "serve at once as evaluative agent and expressive tool: We expect people to show us and explain to us how they use content—it's more than mere memory. It's the first real step towards coming up with some ideas of their own. . . . In its original form, the exhibition was the public expression by a student of real command over what she'd learned" (quoted in Coalition of Essential Schools, 1990, p. 1). And, as Grant Wiggins (1989) has pointed out in a thought-provoking article entitled "The

Futility of Trying to Teach Everything of Importance," a good way of assisting students to ultimately develop such demonstrations of mastery is to frame the study of a subject and the assessment of the study around key or "essential" questions such as: "'What must my students actually demonstrate to reveal whether they have a thoughtful as opposed to thoughtless grasp of the essentials?' and 'What will 'successful' student understanding (with limited experience and background) actually look like?'" (p. 208). (Teachers who are interested in developing a project- or performance-based assessment may wish to contact the Coalition of Essential Schools project at Brown University, Box 1938, Providence, RI 02912, and request their materials on "demonstrations [performances and exhibitions] of mastery." The coalition has developed numerous outstanding and detailed models for the development of rigorous performances that, when implemented with care can truly tap students' critical and creative faculties.)

Such performances or exhibitions may take any form whatsoever (e.g., an individual project, a group project, a preparation of a portfolio, an oral presentation and "defense"). No matter what form it takes, however, "the performance must engage the student in real intellectual work, not just memorization or recall. The 'content' the students master in the process is the means to an end, not the end itself" (Coalition of Essentials Schools, 1990, pp. 3–4).

Even an abbreviated list of some of the coalition's "qualities of 'authentic performances'" provides a good sense of the uniqueness and rigor factored into well-structured performances and exhibitions of mastery. More specifically, each should: "require some collaboration with others; [be] constructed to point the student towards more sophisticated use of his/her skills or knowledge; [consist of] contextualized, complex intellectual challenges, not 'atomized' tasks corresponding to isolated 'outcomes'; involve the student's own research or use of knowledge, for which 'content' is a means; assess student habits and repertoires, not mere recall or plug-in skills; [constitute] representative challenges—designed to emphasize depth more than breadth; [be] engaging and educational; involve criteria that assesses essentials, not easily counted but relatively unimportant errors; [be] graded not on a curve but in reference to performance standards (criterion-referenced, not norm-referenced); make self-assessment a part of the assessment; use a multifaceted scoring system instead of one aggregate grade; ferret out and identify (perhaps hidden) strengths; minimize needless, unfair, and demoralizing comparisons; allow appropriate room for student learning styles, aptitudes, and interests; [be] attempted by all students, with the test 'scaffolded up,' not 'dumbed down,' as necessary; and reverse typical test-design procedures. A model task is first specified; then, a fair and reliable plan for scoring is devised" (Coalition of Essential Schools, 1990, p. 2).

(For a description of a unique and powerful example of performance assessment, see Cathy Greeley, "Making Plays, Making Meaning, Making Change," pp. 80–103. In Samuel Totten and Jon E. Pedersen [Eds.], *Social Issues and Service at the Middle Level.* Boston: Allyn & Bacon, 1997. This essay describes a fascinating unit that resulted in the development and production of a play informed in part by the history of the Holocaust.)

Conclusion

One of my key goals in teaching about the Holocaust is to plant seeds in students' minds and hearts—seeds that germinate and bloom and grow over a lifetime. What kind of seeds? Seeds of concern. Seeds that result in lingering questions about what happened during the Holocaust and why. Seeds that sprout into questions about prejudice, bias, antisemitism, racism, hate, fairness, and justice. Seeds that eventually spawn vines that wrap around one's mind, soul, and heart that tug and pull at one to consider what one knows and does not know, what one hears and does not hear, what one sees and does not see concerning contemporary human rights infractions, including genocide. And finally, seeds that produce ideas that bloom into ongoing consideration about one's own place in the world, and what it means to be a citizen in a democracy.

Ultimately, then, my goal in developing a strong ending to a lesson or unit on the Holocaust is twofold: first, to assist the students in synthesizing all of their newfound knowledge; and second, to plant seeds (including questions) that will remain within their minds and hearts long after the study of the Holocaust has concluded. If these two goals are accomplished, then it is more likely to insure that the study of the Holocaust is not just one more of the many thousands of lessons "learned" today and forgotten tomorrow.

REFERENCES

Armstrong, Thomas. (1994). *Multiple Intelligences in the Classroom.* Alexandria, VA: Association for Supervision and Curriculum Development.

Coalition of Essential Schools. (1990, March). "Performances and Exhibitions: The Demonstration of Mastery." *Horace,* 6(3):1–12.

Gardner, Howard. (1983). *Frames of Mind: The Theory of Multiple Intelligences.* New York: Basic Books.

Gardner, Howard. (1993). *Multiple Intelligences: The Theory in Practice.* New York: Basic Books.

Lerner, Gerda. (1997). *Why History Matters: Life and Thought.* New York: Oxford University Press.

Niewyk, Donald L. (1995). "Holocaust: The Genocide of the Jews," pp. 167–207. In Samuel Totten, William S. Parsons, and Israel W. Charny (Eds.), *Genocide in the Twentieth Century: Critical Essays and Eyewitness Accounts.* New York: Garland.

Rico, Gabrielle. (1987). "Clustering: A Prewriting Process," pp. 17–20. In Carol Booth Olson (Ed.), *Practical Ideas for Teaching Writing as a Process.* Sacramento: California State Department of Education.

Totten, Samuel. (1998). "The Start is as Important as the Finish: Establishing a Foundation for Study of the Holocaust." *Social Education,* 62(2):70–76.

Totten, Samuel, and Pedersen, Jon E. (1997). *Social Issues and Service at the Middle Level.* Boston: Allyn & Bacon.

Wiggins, Grant. (Winter 1987). "Creating a Thought-Provoking Curriculum." *American Educator,* 11:4.

Wiggins, Grant. (1989). "The Futility of Trying to Teach Everything of Importance." *Educational Leadership,* pp. 44–48, 57–59.

Wiggins, Grant. (May 1989). "A True Test: Toward Authentic and Equitable Assessment." *Phi Delta Kappan,* 70:9.

9 The Imperative to Avoid Clichés

"Never again!"

"Remember."

"Those who do not remember the past are condemned to repeat it."

Over the past two decades, an ever increasing number of teachers at the secondary level have taught their students, in varying depth and with varying success, about the Holocaust. Not unexpectedly, there are pros and cons to the popularity and proliferation of this subject in upper elementary and secondary school classrooms. It is, of course, heartening that so many educators care about the history of the Holocaust and perceive the need to teach it to their students. Unlike much history that is taught and studied in schools, the history of the Holocaust seems to resonate with teachers in that they perceive this history as having a special message for those of us living today, more than fifty years after the conclusion of World War II. Ample evidence of this is seen in the great number of teachers (an estimated sixty-five thousand social studies teachers alone) who develop and teach lessons and units on this history, many of them voluntarily (Sobol, 1995).

Yet, as Holocaust scholar and survivor Henry Friedlander (1979) remarked over twenty years ago in his landmark essay "Toward a Methodology of Teaching About the Holocaust," "too much is being taught by too many without focus [and] this poses the danger of destroying the subject matter through dilettantism" (p. 520). This observation is as true today as it was when written. There is ample evidence of this in the many lessons and units of study developed by teachers, curriculum coordinators, and state departments of education that are rife with incorrect facts, significant gaps in the portrayal of the history, and lack of attention to the critical historical antecedents that contributed to and ultimately culminated in the killing process (Dawidowicz, 1992; Lipstadt, 1995; Totten and Parsons, 1992;

and Totten (n.d.). Friedlander's (1979) subsequent assertion that "[t]he problem of popularization and proliferation should make us careful about how we introduce the Holocaust into the curriculum" (p. 522) is also as relevant today as it was when he first posited it.

This chapter focuses on one crucial problem in Holocaust education—the perfunctory use of phrases such as "Never again!", "Remember", and "Those who do not remember the past are condemned to repeat it" by many who address the Holocaust in speeches, publications, and classrooms. Due to their overuse, these phrases, which were once imbued with profound meaning by the victims and survivors, have become clichés. Often used as the titles of Holocaust education conferences, at the conclusion of speeches, pedagogical pieces, and student essays, and as rationales and goals for teaching Holocaust history, the impact and significance of such phrases is gradually but inexorably being minimized. That, of course, is the fate of most sayings that devolve into clichés.

The aforementioned phrases are not inappropriate in and of themselves; however, their use in a perfunctory manner diminishes their profound import. Indeed, the facile use of such phrases leads to simplistic and vacuous thinking. As Holocaust scholar John Roth (1996) has observed, "Words used in an automatic, unreflective manner are problematic in that they are likely to 'distract and detract from the needs that deserve concern and care'" (p. 108).*

Latching onto Clichés

Many of those who latch onto sayings such as "Remember" and "Never again!" do not seem to make much effort to ascertain what these phrases meant to the victims and/or survivors of the Holocaust, nor do they make a genuine attempt to come to grips with what the words and phrases could and should mean for us today. *That is particularly true when the words are simply stated and not expounded upon to acknowledge the fact that genocide has been perpetrated time and again since 1945.* Indeed, when the terms are used in talks at Holocaust conferences, political speeches, classroom lectures, and/or in Holocaust curricula, it is rare for the speakers or authors even to mention the numerous genocides perpetrated since 1945. Rarer yet is the speaker or curriculum that addresses how and why society failed to prevent post-World War II genocides. And still rarer is the speaker or a curriculum that broaches and seriously examines what society needs to do to prevent future genocides. To exclaim "Never again!" and not to mention even one of the numerous genocides perpetrated since 1945 does not make much sense—not when genocide has been perpetrated in every single decade since 1945 in various places around the world, including but not limited to Bangladesh, East Timor, Paraguay, Cambodia, Burundi, Rwanda, and Bosnia.

Granted, the use of the phrase "Never again!" is normative; however, when

---

*In "What is the Value of Teaching the Holocaust?" James F. Farnham (1992) addresses some of these same concerns, but in a somewhat different context.

the phrase is used as the final "punctuation mark" in a speech or a curriculum because it sounds or feels good to say, or because it rolls off one's tongue easily, or it is the expected thing to say, its use is rather mindless. In many cases, it seems as if some of those who use the phrase are uncomfortable even in acknowledging the fact that genocide has been, is, and will likely continue to be a problem that plagues contemporary society.

As for evidence supporting these assertions, one need only listen to or read the words, speeches, and writings of certain politicians, world leaders, educators, and students. It is almost pointless to cite examples where the aforementioned phrases are used in a perfunctory manner, for one needs to experience them within their context. This is necessary since tone and nuance are of the utmost significance. Likewise, by citing a limited number of examples some may be apt to think, "That's the exception, not the rule." Evaluating the validity of these claims is most effective on an individual basis, and by weighing words and phrases as they are encountered. By carefully listening to what a speaker says or how a curricular resource uses such admonitions, one can ascertain for oneself whether the terms are being used in a meaningful and genuine as opposed to a perfunctory manner.

Notwithstanding the above caveat, several examples will be provided here as to how the terms "Never again!" and "Remember" or variants thereof are commonly used. In an article entitled "Using Literature to Teach About the Holocaust," a classroom teacher from Wyoming states: "Hopefully, by remembering the past through books, events such as the Holocaust will be remembered, but never repeated" (Palmer, 1993, p. 2). This is a classic use of the variant of "Remember," where there is absolutely no acknowledgment of just how common the perpetration of genocide has been since 1945.

The heading of another article, "Lest We Forget: The Importance of Holocaust Education," by a teacher in Watertown, Connecticut, reads "We Must All Remember" (Holroyd, 1994, p. 16). Ostensibly, the latter was inserted as a header by the editor or publisher. In the body of the paper, the author notes that: "By suggesting civic or national commemorations, the Holocaust Memorial Council provides opportunities to renew our pledge to the victims and to our children: Never Again!" (p. 16). Again, no mention is made of the fact that genocide has been a constant in the post-World War II world. In his conclusion, the author uses a variant of "Remember" by exhorting: "The Holocaust happened within the lifetime of many of us. For the sake of the victims . . . for the sake of our children, for the sake of children yet unborn, such events must not happen again. Humankind must learn the lessons of the Holocaust. We must not forget" (p. 25). Although this is a worthy appeal, the author does not seem to be aware of the fact that genocide has been perpetrated many times over since the Holocaust.

Not surprisingly, variations of the need to remember and not to forget show up repeatedly in the essays of secondary school students who have studied the Holocaust—both in essays written for class assignments and essays entered in Holocaust essay contests. One such example appears in an article entitled "Teaching the Unteachable: Public Schools Teach the Holocaust": "Many students emphasize the need to study the subject and the cautionary message it offers for the future. Jared Stern, a Long Island eighth grader, warned, "It could happen again if we don't learn about it" (Weiner, 1992, p. 39). Again, there is no acknowledgment or recognition that *"it" has happened again.*

On a different but related note, in an article entitled "And Then There Were None: A Requiem for the Hutu Refugees," Holocaust and genocide scholar Henry R. Huttenbach (1997b) makes this trenchant comment:

> Yom HaShoah [Holocaust Day of Remembrance] has come and gone; sufferings past of yesteryear's victims were duly acknowledged and reverently observed; . . . in the United States "distinguished" speakers repeated worn-out Holocaust litanies ["Remember" and "Never again"] and profundities. And watching them all from afar, speakers and their audiences, were the hollow eyes of the dying and dead Hutu refugees rotting away in east Zaire's jungles.
>
> As the annual Holocaust Day came and went (now a predictable routine), the vivid images of emaciated Hutu refugees passed before us unnoticed by the throngs of Holocaust Day participants, unmentioned by "concerned" guest speakers. The faces of the deliberately starved Hutus, the maimed bodies—hacked by machetes—are there for us to see and . . . ? To ignore? To forget? To push aside? To do what? Something? Nothing? To mention piously in passing? To place on the back burner? . . . Why not heed the *only* message of the Six Million? "Do Something!" "Help Them!" "Do not abandon them as we were!" (p. 2)

In a somewhat similar and yet different vein, Peter Novick (1999), in his provocative and controversial book *The Holocaust in American Life,* argues that:

> Only the most starry-eyed can believe that the universal version of "Never again"—never again will the United States tolerate genocidal atrocities—is a lesson American political leaders are willing to put into practice. Henceforth, wrote Leonard Fein, founding editor of the Jewish magazine *Moment,* "let us have the decency to refrain from ever saying 'Never again.'" "Never again," said another disillusioned advocate of intervention in Bosnia, appeared to mean "Never again would Germans kill Jews in Europe in the 1940s." One might as well say, he added, referring to the thirteenth-century Crusades, "Never again the slaughter of the Albigensians." Those people who continued to say "Never again" did so the way secular Jews, at the conclusion of a Seder, say "Next year in Jerusalem": not an expectation, not even an aspiration; rather, a ritualized reminder of expectations and aspirations now tacitly abandoned. It was not that events in Bosnia constituted "a Holocaust," which was clearly hyperbolic; rather, it was that the way in which American policy evolved, in this and other crises, revealed the hollowness of high-sounding phrases mouthed by political leaders—the ongoing reign of *Realpolitik.* There seems not the slightest likelihood that this will change in the foreseeable future." (p. 257)

Ultimately, the overuse and misuse of such terms and phrases as "Remember" and "Never again!" prods one to question whether those who use the terms are truly committed to seeing to and acting upon the implied intent of the phrases.

Remembrance Vis-à-Vis the Holocaust

What would man be without his capacity to remember? Memory is a passion no less powerful or pervasive than love. What does it mean to remember? It is to live in more than one world, to prevent the past from fading and to call upon the future to illuminate it. It is to revive fragments of existence, to rescue lost beings, to cast harsh light on faces and events, to drive back the sands that cover the surface of things, to combat oblivion and to reject death.

—Elie Wiesel

As the horror of the Holocaust unfolded—especially in the ghettos, during the deportations, and in the concentration and death camps—many of the Jewish victims responded by beseeching all who might survive to remember and never to forget—never to allow the *world* to forget what they were forced to suffer and endure. Never to forget the evil that was perpetrated as the result of a racist ideology. Never to forget that the world, for the most part, stood by and allowed it to happen.

The admonition to "remember" has a long and significant history in Judaism (Wieviorka, 1994, p. 32). Traditionally, Jews are obligated to remember their exile, their enslavement, their deliverance to freedom, the destruction of their two temples, and the giving of the law at Sinai. Historically, remembrance for the Jews has been a sacred responsibility.

That said, there is a distinct difference between the way Holocaust survivors use memory and the way in which many of their ancestors used it. In the shadow of the Holocaust, remembrance, for many, no longer focuses solely on the Jews' covenant with God but on one of the most horrific evils perpetrated by humanity—the genocide of a people. Thus, for some, and particularly for survivors of the Holocaust, "forgetting [about what happened during the Holocaust] is collaboration with evil" (Alterman, quoted in Friedlander, 1994, p. 240). For many, then, not only must the historical facts of the myriad injustices and slaughter be remembered, but those who deny the facts must be countered.

It is noteworthy that one curriculum in particular, the New Jersey Commission on Holocaust Education's *The Betrayal of Mankind: Holocaust & Genocide*, makes a valiant effort to address what Hitler's victims meant by remembrance. The inclusion of the following "oath," originally spoken by Elie Wiesel in 1981, may assist teachers and students to gain a clearer understanding of the almost sacred sense the phrases "Remember" and "Never again!" had for the survivors of the Holocaust:

> We take this oath! We take it in the shadow of flames whose tongues scar the soul of our people. We vow in the name of dead parents and children; . . . We vow, we shall never let the sacred memory of our perished six million be scorned or erased.
>
> We saw them hungry, in fear, we saw them rush to battle, we saw them in the loneliness of night—true to their faith. At the threshold of death, we saw them. We received their silence in silence, merged their tears with ours.

Deportations, executions, mass graves, death camps; mute prayers, cries of revolt, desperation, torn scrolls; cities and towns, villages and hamlets; the young, the old, the rich, the poor, ghetto fighters and partisans, scholars and messianic dreamers, ravaged faces, fists raised. Like clouds of fire, all have vanished.

We take this oath! Vision become WORD . . . to be handed down from father to son, from mother to daughter, from generation to generation.

Remember what the German killers and their accomplices did to our people. Remember them with rage and contempt. Remember what an indifferent world did to us and to itself. Remember the victims with pride and with sorrow. Remember also the deeds of the righteous Gentiles. (Wiesel, 1995b, p. 55)

"Remember" and "Never again!" have been and still are uttered by Jewish victims and survivors in a manner that is categorically different from their facile and commonplace usage today by many politicians, speech writers, educators, students, and others. For survivors, the phrases describe the rupture in history that constitutes the Holocaust—a rupture in the sense that "[n]ever in history has a state attempted to make a whole country—indeed, in this case, a whole continent—*rein* [rid] of every single member of a whole people, man, woman, and child" (Fackenheim, 1996, p. 384). *It is this rupture that must be understood by all of us.*

For many survivors, Jews and others, who penetrate to the core of these admonitions, such remembrance also constitutes a battle against the evil in today's world—the perpetrators of contemporaneous massive human rights violations. For them, remembering and not forgetting are dual in nature—an eye cast to the past with an eye trained on the present. Inherent in remembrance and not forgetting, then, is the imperative not only to remember the evil perpetrated during the Holocaust but to act to try to prevent present-day genocides not only against Jews but against anyone and everyone around the world.

At one and the same time, inherent in these admonitions is a call not to be a bystander during such tragic moments. In that regard, it is a call to action. *When such phrases are solely used because of the "nice ring they have" and are bereft of any real intention or commitment to act when such injustices erupt, the phrases ring hollow and hypocritical.*

Holocaust scholar Henry Huttenbach addresses this very issue in an article entitled "J'Accuse! An Open Letter: Remembering the Past: Forgetting the Present." More specifically, commenting on the focus of the Twenty-Seventh Annual Scholars' Conference on the Holocaust and Churches, Huttenbach states:

At the very end of the Conference, a single panel on "Other Genocides" is appended, as if the topic were an afterthought, a gesture of tokenism. It is there as if not to disturb the atmosphere of total devotion to the Holocaust. Yet it gives rise to the question 'Why Study the Holocaust at all, if not to deter genocide in the future?' . . . We seem to be remembering for the sake of the past, for the sake of remembering, itself a form of amnesia. (p. 2)

Santayana's Injunction

Santayana's injunction that "Those who do not remember the past are condemned to repeat it" is also extremely popular with many curriculum developers and teachers of the Holocaust. When they use this injunction, many teachers (and students) seem to be implying, "Let there be no other genocide, period." More often than not, however, no acknowledgment is made by those who speak these words that the latter half of the twentieth century was plagued by one genocidal act after another. In this respect, then, the use of Santayana's injunction is similar to the repeated use of "Never again!" To parrot Santayana's statement and not acknowledge that genocide is a very real and serious problem facing the post-Holocaust world illustrates one's blindness and/or insensitivity to the many victims of genocide since 1945.

The simple point is, it is incumbent upon all of us to remain vigilant and proactive in staving it off "the next time." Words are not enough. Elie Wiesel (1990), for one, has recognized this fact:

> After the war we reassured ourselves that it would be enough to relate a single night in Auschwitz, to tell of the cruelty, the senselessness of murder, and the outrage born of apathy; it would be enough to find the right word and the propitious moment to say it, to shake humanity out of its indifference and keep the torturer from torturing ever again. . . . It would be enough to describe a death camp "selection" to prevent the human right to dignity from being violated ever again.
>
> We thought it would be enough to tell of the tidal wave of hatred which broke over the Jewish people for men everywhere to decide once and for all to put an end to hatred of anyone who is "different"—whether black or white, Jew or Arab, Christian or Moslem—anyone whose orientation differs politically, philosophically, sexually. A naive undertaking? Of course. But not without a certain logic. (pp. 244–245)

Pondering the Significance of Such Terms and Conveying That in Both Curricula and the Classroom

Based upon the discussion thus far, it is obvious that curriculum developers and teachers, among others, must ponder the various nuances and meanings carried by phrases like "Never again!" "Remember," and "Those who do not remember the past are condemned to repeat it." They also need to consider the reasons and rationales for using such terms. If their use is deemed appropriate, students must be helped to understand their meaning. Likewise, it is imperative to assist students to examine how the perfunctory use of such phrases results in clichés.

The following suggestions might be useful to curriculum developers and teachers who wish to incorporate such terms and phrases into a study of the Holocaust:

1. Become conversant with the various genocides that have been perpetrated since 1945, and ascertain the reasons for the passivity of the post-Holocaust world in the face of such ongoing horrors.

2. Invite a Holocaust survivor to speak to the class about his or her experiences and to specifically address the significance of what "Remember" and "Never again!" meant to him or her and other victims prior to, during, and following the Holocaust. The teacher can build on the foundation established by the survivor.

3. Assist students to examine first-person accounts (diary entries, letters, speeches, or oral histories) of the Holocaust, paying particular attention to those instances where the victims and survivors speak of the imperative to "Remember" and say, "Never again!" The students should analyze the pieces in regard to when, where, and why the statement was made (e.g., the conditions and situation in which the person found himself or herself). Each statement and an accompanying analysis could be discussed in small and large groups. The gist of the analyses and discussions could be depicted on posterboards and mounted on the walls for the duration of the study of the Holocaust.

4. Have students research the roots, original meaning, and evolution of the phrases "Remember" and "Never again!", thus placing them in their proper context.

5. Have students examine what the words and phrases "Remember" and "Never again!" really mean for those of us living today vis-à-vis the Holocaust and contemporary acts of genocide—in our personal lives, in our lives as citizens of a democracy, and in a world where genocide and the deprivation of human rights are regular occurrences.

6. As for Santayana's quote, "Those who do not remember the past are condemned to repeat it," have students:

  a. Examine how people today interpret the saying, and determine the significance it has for humanity now;

  b. Examine the history of genocide in the latter part of the twentieth century in order to ascertain the frequency with which genocide has been perpetrated since 1945 and, in doing so, attempt to ascertain whether any part of humanity has attempted to abide by Santayana's injunction (and if so, which part of humanity);

  c. Analyze the issue of realpolitik and its impact on how and why nations react to genocide being perpetrated within the boundaries of another nation;

  d. Analyze and discuss the question: "Has humanity really learned anything from the tragedy of the Holocaust in regard to stanching genocide; and if so, what? If not, how so and why? In either case, provide concrete evidence."

(Note: In addressing the above issues and questions, students should be encouraged to examine the role[s] of the perpetrators, collaborators, rescuers, and bystanders—especially nations and organizations outside of the area in which the genocide was perpetrated.)

7. As an extension project at the conclusion of a study of the Holocaust, students alone or in groups of two or three can examine an act of genocide that has occurred since 1945. To avoid mere regurgitation from encyclopedias or other sources, teachers need to provide students with research guidelines, such as the following:

- Students must use at least three sources written by noted genocide scholars.
- Students must use a minimum of three newspaper articles from one or more major newspapers (such as the *Christian Science Monitor,* the *Globe & Mail,* the *London Times,* the *Los Angeles Times,* the *New York Times,* the *Toronto Star,* the *Washington Post*).
- Each report must incorporate at least three first-person accounts by eye-witnesses to the genocide (e.g., correspondents, relief workers, survivors).
- A solid discussion of the historical antecedents leading up to and culminating in the genocide must be included in the report.
- A thorough description of the actual genocide should be included in the report. This should include the role of the perpetrators, the collaborators, the victims, and rescuers, if any.
- Each report should present and analyze world reaction to the genocide (including the statements and actions of world leaders, the United Nations, and leading human rights organizations). The success (or lack thereof) of these reactions in halting the crimes should also be examined.

Once the study has been completed, students can transfer their most significant findings to a posterboard. Finally, a posterboard session could be conducted for one's own class, as well as others. To conduct the posterboard session, the class should be divided in half. As one-half of the class circulates to look at the various posterboards, those whose posters are being examined should stand next to their work to explain and discuss their ideas. This process should be repeated, reversing the roles of the students.

Addressing the Issue of the Intervention and Prevention of Genocide in Today's World

Various options exist for students and teachers who wish to move beyond the confines of the classroom and into the world at large in order to address the notions inherent in the phrases examined in this chapter. For example:

1. Whenever the phrases "Never again!", "Remember," and "Those who do not remember the past are condemned to repeat it" are uttered, particularly with reference to the Holocaust, make a point of acknowledging that genocide has been a dismal fact of life in the world since 1945, and indicate where and when such acts have taken place.

2. Establish Amnesty International (A.I.) adoption groups in which students and others work on various human rights issues (including human rights infractions that sometimes constitute preconditions leading up to genocide) and either "adopt" prisoners of conscience in order to work for their release from prison or take part in one of A.I.'s other ongoing campaigns.

3. Become conversant with the theory and practical application of genocide early warning systems (systems that detect early warning signs of possible genocide), and advocate their use by encouraging legislators, national leaders, and the United Nations to support the development and implementation of such systems. (For information on general early warning systems, see Kumar Rupesinghe and Michiko Kuroda, *Early Warning and Conflict Resolution*. New York: St. Martin's Press, 1992; and for information on genocide early warning systems, see Israel W. Charny, "Intervention and Prevention of Genocide," pp. 20–38. In Israel W. Charny (Ed.), *Genocide: A Critical Bibliographic Review*. New York: Facts On File, 1988; and Neil Reimer, *Protection Against Genocide: Mission Impossible?* Westport, CT: Praeger, 2000.)

Conclusion

> *Forgetfulness leads to indifference; indifference to complicity and thus to dishonor.*
>
> —Elie Wiesel

The past must be remembered, but humanity must go beyond remembrance. Inherent in the call for remembrance is a challenge to be vigilant. At the same time, it is a call to action. Ultimately, authentic remembrance is an imperative not to forget, to remember accurately, to remember because there is a moral imperative to do everything in one's power to assist those facing genocide. As scholar James E. Young (1994) asserts: "We [need to] ask to what ends we have remembered. That is, how do we respond to the current moment in light of our remembered past? This is to recognize that the shape of memory cannot be divorced from the actions taken in its behalf, and that memory without consequences contains the seeds of its own destruction" (p. 230).

The history of the Holocaust is too important to be treated with clichés. It is the responsibility of all those who teach it to teach it with accuracy and great sensitivity. To do otherwise harms the memory of the victims and the survivors, and mars the significance that this history has for humanity—those of us living today and in the future.

Finally, as Elie Wiesel has eloquently and powerfully stated: "Memory can be a graveyard, but it also can be the true kingdom of man." The choice is before every teacher and every student who either teaches or studies the Holocaust. Only through the nurturance of *authentic remembrance,* one imbued with the need to act when others are treated unjustly, will we, humanity, forge the possibility of stanching potential genocides.

REFERENCES

Dawidowicz, Lucy. (1992). "How They Teach the Holocaust," pp. 65–83. In Lucy Dawidowicz (Ed.), *What Is the Use of Jewish History?* New York: Schocken.

Fackenheim, Emil L. (1996). pp. 381–391. "The Holocaust: A Summing Up After Two Decades of Reflection." In Steven Jacobs (Ed.), *The Holocaust Now: Contemporary Christian and Jewish Thought.* East Rockaway, NY: Cummings & Hathaway.

Farnham, James F. (1992). "What is the Value of Teaching the Holocaust?" *Journal of General Education,* 41:18–22.

Friedlander, Albert H. (1994). *Riders Toward the Dawn: From Holocaust to Hope.* New York: Continuum.

Friedlander, Henry. (1979). "Toward a Methodology of Teaching About the Holocaust." *Teacher's College Record,* 18(3):519–542.

Holroyd, Peter R. (March 1994). "Lest We Forget: The Importance of Holocaust Education." *NASSP Bulletin,* 79(569):16–25.

Huttenbach, Henry R. (April 1997a). "J'Accuse! An Open Letter: Remembering the Past: Forgetting the Present." *The Genocide Forum,* 3(8):2–3.

Huttenbach, Henry R. (September 1997b). "And Then There Were None: A Requiem for the Hutu Refugees." *The Genocide Forum,* 4(1):2–4.

Lipstadt, Deborah. (March 6, 1995). "Not Facing History," *The New Republic,* 16-17, 19.

New Jersey Commission on Holocaust Education. (1995). *The Betrayal of Mankind: Holocaust & Genocide.* Trenton: New Jersey Department of Education.

Novick, Peter. (1999). *The Holocaust in American Life.* Boston: Houghton Mifflin.

Palmer, Rosemary G. (August/September 1993). "Using Literature to Teach About the Holocaust. *Reading Today,* pp. 1–2.

Reagan, Ronald. (April-June 1981). "The President's Remarks for Yom Hashoa." *Martyrdom and Resistance,* 7:9.

Roth, John K. (1996). "Asking and Listening, Understanding and Doing: Some Conditions for Responding to the Shoah Religiously," pp. 97–115. In Steven Jacobs (Ed.), *The Holocaust Now: Contemporary Christian and Jewish Thought.* East Rockaway, NY: Cummings & Hathaway.

Sobol, Marcia. (1995). "The Status of Holocaust Education in the United States." Unpublished speech delivered at the European Conference on Holocaust Education on the behalf of the United States Holocaust Memorial Museum, London.

Totten, Samuel, and Parsons, William S. (Spring 1992). "State Developed/Sponsored Holocaust and Genocide Curricula and Teacher Guides: A Succinct Review and Critique." *Inquiry in Social Studies: Curriculum, Research and Instruction: The Journal of the North Carolina Council for the Social Studies,* 28(1):27–47.

Totten, Samuel, and Riley, Karen. (n.d.) *The Problem of Inaccurate History in State Developed/Sponsored Holocaust and Genocide Curricula and Teacher Guides: A Challenge to Scholars of the Holocaust and Genocide.*

Totten, Samuel, Parsons, William S., and Charny, Israel W. (Eds.) (1995). *Genocide in the Twentieth Century: Critical Essays and Eyewitness Accounts.* New York: Garland. [Revised and republished in 1997 as *Century of Genocide: Eyewitness Accounts and Critical Essays.*]

Weiner, Staacy. (April 1992). "Teaching the Unteachable: Public Schools Teach the Holocaust." *The Jewish Monthly*, 35–39.

Wiesel, Elie. (June 1981). *The Legacy.* Unpublished paper.

Wiesel, Elie. (1990). *From the Kingdom of Memory: Reminiscences.* New York: Schocken.

Wiesel, Elie. (1995a). *All Rivers Run to the Sea: Memoirs.* New York: Schocken.

Wiesel, Elie. (1995b). "We Take This Oath," p. 55. In the New Jersey Commission on Holocaust Education. *The Betrayal of Mankind: Holocaust & Genocide.* Trenton: New Jersey Department of Education.

Wieviorka, Annette. (1994). "On Testimony," pp. 21–32. In Geoffrey H. Hartman (Ed.), *Holocaust Remembrance: The Shapes of Memory.* Cambridge, MA: Blackwell.

Yerushalmi, Yosef Hayim. (1983). *Zakhor: Jewish History and Jewish Memory.* Seattle: University of Washington Press.

Young, James E. (1994). "Jewish Memory in Poland," pp. 215–231. In Geoffrey H. Hartman (Ed.), *Holocaust Remembrance: The Shapes of Memory.* Cambridge, MA: Blackwell.

CHAPTER

10   What's Next?

The twentieth century has been deemed "the century of genocide" (Smith, 1987; Charny, 1988; Totten, Parsons, and Charny, 1997), and with good reason. Since the conclusion of World War II, decade after decade, one genocide after another has been perpetrated somewhere in the world: Tibet, mid- to late 1950s; Indonesia, 1965; Equatorial Guinea, 1968–1979; Bangladesh, 1971; Burundi, 1972; East Timor, mid-1970s; Cambodia, 1975–1979; Chittagong Hill Tracts in Bangladesh, mid-1980s; Rwanda 1994; former Yugoslavia, various points in the 1990s. And that is true despite the fact that the shock of the devastating horror of the Holocaust "provided the impetus for the formal recognition of genocide as a crime in international law, thus laying the basis for intervention by judicial process" (Kuper, 1981, p. 20). As genocide scholar Leo Kuper (1981) noted, the "declared purpose of the [United Nations Genocide] Convention, in terms of the original resolution of the General Assembly of the United Nations, was to prevent and punish the crime of genocide" (p. 36). Thus far, the prevention of genocide has been a false hope. As for the issue of punishment, it has been erratic at best.

Evidence of such failure is rife. Among the most moving are the many first-person accounts and journalistic reports of the atrocities. Cited below are three first-person testimonies and one secondary account (the one by Gourevitch) about four of the genocides that have been perpetrated since 1945:

> **Bangladesh, 1971:** [H]undreds of non-Bengalis had assembled near the Pump house. . . . The Bengalis who had been brought in were tied up. They were huddled by the side of the lake. . . . Many of the Biharis were carrying knives, swords and other sharp instruments. The Biharis were first kicking and beating up the Bengalis brutally and then were shoving their victims towards those carrying weapons. These other group of armed Biharis were then [stabbing] their victims in the stomach and then severing their heads with the swords. I witnessed several groups of Bengalis being killed in such a manner. . . .
>
>   The massacre went on till about two o'clock in the afternoon. After they had disposed of the last Bengal victim, the Biharis brought in a group of ten to twelve Bengali men. It was evident from their gestures that they were asking the Bengalis to dig a grave for the bodies lying about. I also understood from their gestures that the Biharis were promising the group that if they completed the task they would be

allowed to go free. The group complied to their wish. After the group had finished burying the bodies, they were also killed, and the Biharis went away rejoicing. (quoted in Jahan, 1997, pp. 315–316)

Burundi, 1972: There was a manner of cutting the stomach (of pregnant women). Everything that was found in the interior was lifted out without cutting the cord. The cadaver of the mama, the cadaver of the baby, of the future, they rotted on the road. Not even burial. . . . My older brother, he was roped, and then he was made to roll, slide on the asphalted road behind a car. The Tutsis' intention was to equalize the population, up to 50 percent. It was a plan. My brother's body was left in the forest. If it had been left on the road, the foreigners would have seen it, and they would have written about it. . . . The girls [Tutsi] in secondary schools . . . killed the Hutu [girls].

The Tutsi girls were given bamboos. They were made to kill by pushing the bamboo from below (from the vagina) to the mouth. It is a thing against the law of God . . . God must help us. During the Genocide every Tutsi had to make an action [to kill]. In the hospital, in the Churches. . . . Even the sick were killed in the beds of the hospitals. The Genocide lasted three months, from the twenty-ninth of April to the end of August. . . . [O]ther women and children, they were put inside a house, like 200, and the house was burned. Everything inside was burned. . . . But the killing was started again in 1973. (quoted in Lemarchand, 1997, p. 330)

Cambodia, 1975–1979: On April 17, 1975, when I was fourteen years old, the Khmer Rouge army came into Phnom Penh with tanks. . . . The soldiers came to our house and ordered us to leave. . . . It was the dry season and it was very hot. There was no water. People began to get heat-stroke and fall down on the road. The soldiers wouldn't let us stop to help those who were sick. . . . We walked for days, then weeks. Pregnant women gave birth under trees by the road. Old people died from exhaustion and lack of water. Everywhere was the sound of babies screaming and people crying for loved ones who had died and had to be left on the road. There was no time for funerals. . . .

[Months later, out in the countryside,] if someone was suspected of having an education or being an intellectual, the soldiers would pull him out of his hut at night and shoot him or cut his throat. . . . I remember one soldier saying to the other, "We will save our bullets." Then they took big bamboo shoots and beat my brothers again and again until they were dead. Their bodies were kicked into the hole. The grave was not far from where my grandfather was killed. . . . Those who were not murdered by the soldiers were dying a slow death. We were always hungry. We were always sick. . . . So many had been buried around the village that it was impossible to keep track of the burial places. (Pran, 1997, pp. 21, 22–23)

Rwanda, 1994: "You cockroaches must know you are made of flesh," a broadcaster gloated over RTLM [a radio station in Kigali]. "We won't let you kill. We will kill you." With the encouragement of such messages and of leaders at every level of society, the slaughter of Tutsis and the assassination of Hutu oppositionists spread from region to region. Following the militias' example, Hutus young and old rose to the task. Neighbors hacked neighbors to death in their homes, and colleagues hacked colleagues to death in their workplaces. Doctors killed their patients and schoolteachers killed their pupils. Within days, the Tutsi populations of many villages were all but eliminated. . . . Throughout Rwanda, mass rape and looting accompanied the slaughter. . . . Radio announcers reminded listeners not to take pity on women and children. . . . A council woman in one Kigali neighborhood was reported to have offered fifty Rwandan francs apiece (about thirty cents at the time) for severed Tutsi heads, a practice known as "selling cabbages." (Gourevitch, 1998, p. 115)

What (and Who and Where) Is Next (2000 . . .)?

The sad fact is, the implementation of the United Nations Convention on Genocide has been sorely ineffective. Millions have been brutally murdered in the various genocides perpetrated since 1945. More often than not, the international community has failed to intervene or prevent the genocide; and, for the most part, the perpetrators have not been held accountable for their actions.

That said, as of late, there has been important improvement in regard to trying the perpetrators of some of the more recent genocides—those in former Yugoslavia and Rwanda. Still, for the most part, the actual accomplishments of such efforts have been rather dismal. Telling evidence of this is that relatively few individuals have been tried, let alone found guilty, and many of the major perpetrators—the key decision makers and leaders—are still at large.

Hopefully, students who are interested in the Holocaust will be interested in and concerned about at least some of the genocides that have taken place during the latter half of the twentieth century and beyond. First, however, they need to be made aware of the fact that such genocides have been perpetrated. That is where individual teachers and curriculum developers come into to play.

Numerous Rationales for Teaching the Holocaust Suggest the Need to Teach about "Other Genocides" *and* Major Human Rights Violations

As mentioned in Chapter 1, over the past thirty years or so, educators have developed numerous rationales for teaching about the Holocaust. Among some of the more notable are the following:

- to study human behavior;
- to teach students why, how, what, when, and where the Holocaust took place, including the key historical trends/antecedents that led up to and culminated in the Final Solution;
- to explore concepts such as prejudice, discrimination, stereotyping, racism, antisemitism, obedience to authority, the bystander syndrome, conflict resolution, decision making, and justice;
- to illustrate "the effects of peer pressure, individual responsibility, and the process of decision-making under the most extreme conditions" (Schwartz, 1990, p. 101);

- to become "cognizant that 'little' prejudices can easily be transformed into far more serious ones" (Lipstadt, 1995, p. 29);
- to "make students more sensitive to ethnic and religious hatred" (Lipstadt, 1995, p. 29);
- to develop in students an awareness of the value of pluralism and diversity in a pluralistic society;
- to reflect on the roles and responsibilities of individuals, groups, and nations when confronting life in an information age, including the abuse of power, civil and human rights violations, and genocidal acts;
- "to develop a deeper appreciation of the relationship of rights and duties, and to realize that human rights and the corresponding duties they entail are not the birthright of the few but the birthright of all—every man, woman, and child in the world today" (Branson and Torney-Purta, 1982, p. 5);
- to "become sensitized to inhumanity and suffering whenever they occur" (Fleischner, quoted in Strom and Parsons, 1982, p. 6);
- to provide a context for exploring the dangers of remaining silent, apathetic, and indifferent in the face of others' oppression;
- "to teach civic virtue . . . [which is related to] the importance of responsible citizenship and mature iconoclasm" (Friedlander, 1979, pp. 532–533);
- to understand that the Holocaust was *not* an accident in history (Parsons and Totten, 1993, p. 1); and
- to illustrate that the Holocaust resulted from a cumulative progression of numerous historical events and deeds, *and* that it was not an event in history that was inevitable (Parsons and Totten, 1993, p. 3).*

Even a quick perusal of such statements suggests the "future-oriented" nature of many of them. Understandably, over and above the merits of teaching the history of the Holocaust itself, many teachers teach about this event to encourage their students to consider seriously what it means to be living—as a citizen in a free country that is a global power—in a world rife with ongoing human rights violations and genocide.

On completion of their study of the Holocaust, it behooves teachers and students to undertake a study of contemporary genocides and/or human rights infractions. Not to do so leaves the students with an incipient understanding about one of the most horrendous human rights crimes of this or any other century (the Holocaust), *but not a real sense as to the status of human rights violations during their own lifetimes.* Nor does it provide them with a sense as to what they, as individuals and as members of concerned groups, can do to help to extend and protect the human rights of all people, at all times, around the world.

It is my belief that it does little to no good to decry one horrendous human catastrophe (e.g., the Holocaust) if one is ignorant of or uninterested in those that follow in its murderous wake.

---

*For a detailed discussion of issues of rationale, see Samuel Totten, Stephen Feinberg, and William Fernekes's essay (Chapter 1).

Studying Other Acts of Genocide and/or Major Human Rights Violations

Ignorance may be bliss for some, but students need to understand that ignorance on the world's part about genocide is hardly bliss for those suffering the horrors of genocidal atrocities. It seems incumbent upon teachers and students to question, at least in part, the validity of studying the Holocaust if they are not going to use their newfound knowledge to keep themselves informed about future mass human rights interactions. Likewise, it seems incumbent upon them to question the value of their study of the Holocaust if they are more apt to look away than to speak out when future genocidal situations rear their ugly faces.

If, on the other hand, students are not interested in maintaining an awareness about contemporary genocidal actions, then one must ask: Has much of anything, *at least of real value*, been learned during their study of the Holocaust? Especially in regard to the ramifications that the Holocaust has for those living in its aftermath?

Although great strides have been made in recognizing the need to protect the basic civil and human rights of individual citizens and groups—and this includes the development and ratification of numerous international human rights covenants—it is a sad fact that horrifying human rights violations around the world are still ubiquitous. Such violations as torture, mass rape, extrajudicial killings, suppression of free speech and the press, and unfair trials are some of the many violations that are perpetrated somewhere in the world on a daily basis. Even slavery, which the international community thought had been eradicated, has reappeared in parts of the world. With only certain exceptions—most notably, human rights activists all over the world, concerned journalists, and a small number of scholars and politicians—much of this activity goes unnoticed, much less decried. And, shamefully, the culprits are not the sole perpetrators; indeed, those nations which have political ties to the perpetrators, which provide foreign aid and/or weaponry to the perpetrators, train and arm the perpetrators' security forces, and trade with such perpetrator states are, in their own inimical way, contributing to such violations, whether they wish to face the truth of it or not. In a world of realpolitik, the hands of many—including those of the United States—are stained with the blood of millions.

What are teachers to do if they are, in fact, interested in addressing genocidal acts other than the Holocaust? Following are some ideas:

- The first thing one needs to do is seek out key works on genocide, in general, and become familiar with the major genocidal events. Useful sources are: Leo Kuper, *Genocide: Its Political Use in the Twentieth Century.* New Haven: Yale University Press, 1981; Samuel Totten, William S. Parsons, and Israel W. Charny, (Eds.). *Century of Genocide: Eyewitness Accounts and Critical Essays.* New York: Garland, 1997; Israel W. Charny, Rouben Adalian, Steven Jacobs, Eric Markusen, and Samuel Totten, (Eds.). *The Encyclopedia of Genocide.* Santa Barbara, CA: ABC-CLIO Press, 1999.

At one and the same time, teachers need to become conversant with key issues germane to the field of genocide studies (e.g., the debate over definitions, key theories of genocide, the preconditions that can lead up to and culminate in genocide).

- Second, if possible, it is helpful to obtain a few key texts for classroom use that provide insights into the theory of genocide and an overview of genocide, if not through the ages, then certainly in the twentieth century.
- Third, instead of focusing on the same genocidal act every semester or year, teachers can engage students in a study of different ones from time to time.
- Fourth, students should be encouraged/required to conduct individual and/or small group studies about a given genocide. This can be done in lieu of a class study of a single genocide; or, it can be conducted as a follow-up or extension activity once the class has concluded its study of a particular genocide. Once the students have conducted their study, they could present a report on it in a unique and powerful way to the rest of the class. One way, for example, might be to hold a session in which the students highlight their key findings on posterboards. Half the class could circulate while the other half of the students stand by the exhibit of their posterboards in order to discuss their findings with interested peers. Once the initial session is completed, the students could switch roles.

There are now available ample materials on many other genocides perpetrated in the twentieth century. Among these are books, monographs, essays and articles, primary documents, first-person accounts, photographs, and even some teaching guides. The same is true of key issues pertaining to international human rights violations. *So, a lack of teaching materials is not a legitimate excuse for not addressing such issues.*

On a different note, an instructive activity is for teachers and students to co-found a student-led Amnesty International Adoption Group. In such groups, students work on the behalf of prisoners of conscience all over the world. Although the main focus of such groups is a wide range of human rights violations and not genocide per se, such work provides students with unique insights into problems faced by nations and individuals everywhere in the world, some of which periodically result in smaller scale genocidal massacres, if not outright genocide. (For information about student A. I. Adoption Groups, contact Amnesty International USA at 322 8th Avenue, New York, NY 10001; e-mail: aimember @aiusa.org; or phone 212–807–8400.)

Conclusion

It is estimated that thousands upon thousands of students in the United States are being introduced to and taught, at various levels of depth and sophistication, about the Holocaust (personal correspondence, 2000; Sabol, 1995). The number of students that learn about other genocides in the classroom is an infinitesimal percentage of the latter.

It is a simple but profound fact that while many students are knowledgeable—at least to some extent—about the Holocaust, most students are unlikely to be aware of the fact that one genocidal act after another was perpetrated in just about every decade of the twentieth century. That is a significant "oversight." *And, it is one that needs to be changed.*

As noted earlier, with the development and ratification of the United Nations Convention on Genocide in 1948, there was widespread hope that the crime of genocide would become a thing of the past. As it has turned out, that was a naïve hope. Sadly, and ironically, the latter part of the twentieth century was as murderous, if not more so, than the first half.

Many scholars and human rights activists fear that the twenty-first century could be as violent as the twentieth vis-à-vis genocidal actions. Indeed, few scholars or human rights activists are hopeful about the possibility of eradicating genocide in this new century, even though the world does seem to be focusing more attention on massive human rights violations and, in turn, is more vocal about the need to address how genocide can be prevented or at least stanched in its early stages. *But "vocal" is the operative term here, for sadly, there are more good intentions along these lines among politicians and nations than real movement to implement safeguards or an early warning system that is truly efficacious in saving lives from the maw of genocide.* Thus, the need for a concerned, vigilant, and outspoken general populace regarding massive violations of human rights and genocide is more critical than ever.

As beings with a moral conscience, it is imperative that each and every individual do his or her utmost to stave off any and all major human rights violations. To ignore or, worse yet, to reject this moral imperative, results in one becoming a bystander to a process that demeans and destroys the "civilized" in each and every one of us.

It is easy to point one's finger at bystanders of past genocides, but it is difficult to look in the mirror and admit to oneself that one's country and oneself is a bystander when either and/or both say or do nothing while major human rights violations occur. Concomitantly, it far too easy to assume that one's own nation or the United Nations will act on one's behalf when a genocidal situation rears its ugly head. However, for an individual to assume that one's government or the United Nations will automatically act to ameliorate human rights violations and/or genocide is naïve, at best. Indeed, in this day and age of realpolitik it is disingenuous to the nth degree. If nothing else, recent events clearly indicate that, more likely than not, neither independent nations nor the United Nations will necessarily do the right thing; and even if they do, they will neglect to do so in a timely fashion. Thus, if and when they decide to do something, hundreds of thousands, if not millions, of innocent people will already have been tortured, raped, and/or brutally murdered. It is imperative, then, that *each and every individual* be as proactive as possible in protecting the rights of others. By not speaking up, by not acting, by not insisting that the world wake up and do the right thing, an individual, for all intents and purposes, ultimately capitulates to the murderous deeds of the perpetrator and is left with blood on his or her conscience.

At a minimum, then, it seems that anyone who studies about the Holocaust must be availed of the fact that massive human rights violations are an ongoing horror in the world today and that genocide has been perpetrated time and again throughout the ages, and right up to today. For a student to "complete" a study of the Holocaust and not be cognizant of that fact is unconscionable.

REFERENCES

Branson, Margaret S., and Torney-Purta, Judith (Eds.). (1982). *International Human Rights, Society, and the Schools.* Washington, DC: National Council for the Social Studies.

Charny, Israel W. (Ed.). (1988). *Genocide: A Critical Bibliographic Review.* New York: Facts On File.

Charny, Israel W. (Ed.). (1991). *Genocide: A Critical Bibliographic Review.* Volume II. New York: Facts On File.

Charny, Israel W. (Ed.). (1994). *The Widening Circle of Genocide: Genocide. Volume III of A Critical Bibliographic Review.* New Brunswick, NJ: Transaction.

Friedlander, Henry. (1979). "Toward a Methodology of Teaching About the Holocaust." *Teachers College Record,* 80(5):519–542.

Gourevitch, Philip. (1998). *We wish to inform you that tomorrow we will be killed with our families: Stories From Rwanda.* New York: Farrar, Straus & Giroux.

Jahan, Rounaq. (1997). "Genocide in Bangladesh," pp. 291–316. In Samuel Totten, William S. Parsons, and Israel W. Charny (Eds.). *Century of Genocide: Eyewitness Accounts and Critical Views.* New York: Garland.

Kuper, Leo. (1981). *Genocide: Its Political Use in the Twentieth Century.* New Haven, CT: Yale University Press.

Lemarchand, René. (1997). "The Burundi Genocide," pp. 317–333. In Samuel Totten, William S. Parsons, and Israel W. Charny (Eds.), *Century of Genocide: Eyewitness Accounts and Critical Views.* New York: Garland.

Lipstadt, Deborah. (March 6, 1995). "Not Facing the History." *The New Republic,* pp. 26–27, 29.

Parsons, William S., and Totten, Samuel. (1993). *Guidelines for Teaching About the Holocaust.* Washington, DC: United States Holocaust Memorial Museum.

Pran, Dith. (1997). *Children of Cambodia's Killing Fields: Memoirs by Survivors.* New Haven, CT: Yale University Press.

Sabol, Marcia. (1995). "The Status of Holocaust Education in the United States." Unpublished paper. Washington, DC: United States Holocaust Memorial Museum.

Schwartz, Donald. (February 1990). "Who Will Tell Them After We're Gone?: Reflections on Teaching the Holocaust." *The History Teacher,* 23(2):95–110.

Smith, Roger. (1987). "Human Destructiveness and Politics: The Twentieth Century as an Age of Genocide," pp. 21–39. In Isidor Walliman and Michael Dubkowski (Eds.), *Genocide and the Modern Age: Etiology and Case Studies of Mass Death.* Westport, CT: Greenwood Press.

Strom, Margot Stern, and Parsons, William S. (1982). *Facing History and Ourselves: Holocaust and Human Behavior.* Watertown, MA: Intentional Educations.

Totten, Samuel. (1987). "The Personal Face of Genocide: Words of Witnesses in the Class-room." Special Issue of the *Social Science Record* ("Genocide: Issues, Approaches, Resources"), edited by Samuel Totten, 24(2):63–67.

Totten, Samuel. (1999). "The Scourge of Genocide: Issues Facing Humanity Today and Tomorrow." *Social Education*, 63(2):116–121.

Totten, Samuel, Parsons, William S., and Charny, Israel W. (Eds.). (1997). *Century of Genocide: Eyewitness Accounts and Critical Views.* New York: Garland.

Holocaust Education
for K–4 Students?
The Answer Is No!

The Holocaust is one of the most tortuously complex—not to mention horrific—subjects an educator can tackle. Over the span of twelve years, it is estimated that six million Jews—including one and a half million children—and at least five million other victims (Gypsies, Poles, other Slavs, Russian prisoners of war, and other groups) were gassed, shot, starved, worked, or brutally beaten to death. To even begin to comprehend the why behind the what, how, where, and when of the history, one needs to examine—at a minimum—German history (at least that related to the nineteenth century and early twentieth centuries) and the interconnecting skeins of traditional Christian antisemitism, political antisemitisim, racial antisemitism, social Darwinism, extreme nationalism, and industrialism. And that's not even to mention the impact of modernity and the concept of totalitarianism, to name but a few other key issues.

As one wrestles with the aforementioned topics and issues, there are still the people (perpetrators, collaborators, victims, bystanders, and rescuers) and their actions, the events (e.g., Kristallnacht, the Wannsee Conference, the St. Louis Affair), the legislation passed and implemented by the leaders of the Third Reich (some four hundred separate laws, including the infamous Nuremberg Laws), the incremental nature of the stranglehold that the Nazis slowly but surely applied to the Jews and others, the decisions made by the Nazis, and the abject brutality and horror perpetrated across Europe for twelve dark years to piece together and try to comprehend.

To even attempt to teach one aspect of the above in a way that is understandable to a five-, six-, seven- or eight-year-old would be folly. To do so by telling the "real story" with all of its hatred, abuse, ugliness, and murderousness would constitute miseducation. And yet, some educators advocate teaching such history—or something that approximates it, which is frequently referred to as "Holocaust education"—to young children. Further, a growing number of states are ostensibly committed to incorporating Holocaust education into the elementary curriculum. Indeed, in an article published in 1999, "Incorporating Holocaust Education into K–4 Curriculum and Teaching in the United States," Harriet Sepinwall, the codirector of the College of Saint Elizabeth's Holocaust Education Resource Center in New Jersey, touted Holocaust education for young children. Is this wise? Is this right? Is this pedagogically sound?

In trying to answer such questions, at least four additional questions come to the fore: What is the express purpose of teaching the Holocaust to young children? Can the Holocaust be taught to such young children? Should the Holocaust be taught to such young children? Is what is being advocated as Holocaust education truly Holocaust education, or is it misnamed?

What Is the Express Purpose of Teaching the Holocaust to Young Children?

While acknowledging that many "recognize that the study of the Holocaust may not seem an appropriate topic for our youngest students," the author of the afore-mentioned article reports that "they [certain states, school districts, and individual teachers] believe that there are some lessons of the Holocaust that can and should be taught at this level" (Sepinwall, 1999, p. P5). Continuing, she suggests, in part, that among the major purposes of teaching about the Holocaust to young children are: "learning the importance of tolerance and respect for others who are different, and to acquire and practice skills for resolving conflicts peacefully and for living together in a spirit of mutual cooperation and appreciation for the contribution of others" (p. P5). The author supports her call for what she deems "Holocaust edu-cation" (e.g., that which focuses on the latter components and certain elements of the history itself) by noting the fact that "American history is filled with examples of nativism, prejudice, racism, antisemitism, anti-Catholicism, and anti-immigrant actions and movements" (p. P5). This is incontestable, but does it call for a so-called Holocaust education program (or more aptly, a quasi-Holocaust education program) that focuses on the components she mentions for students so young?

A primary purpose of Holocaust education should be teaching students *the history* of the Holocaust. This means a focus on what happened and why it hap-pened; the key individuals and groups who were engulfed in the history and the myriad ways in which they were affected and/or impacted by key decisions and events; and when, where, why, and how key decisions and events played out, and the ramifications of the latter. If it neglects to focus on the history, then what is the purpose of Holocaust education? That is not to say, of course, that there are not lessons to be learned. But shouldn't the lessons bubble up and out of the history as the students wrestle with it and come to understand why and how the Holocaust evolved out of numerous and complex historical antecedents and was driven by an ideology and those wedded to it? At the same time, shouldn't students learn of the motivations of the perpetrators, collaborators, and the bystanders—*and*, the impact on the victims?

Can the Holocaust Be Taught to Such Young Children?

Can something as complex as the Holocaust be taught to young children? Granted, scholar Jerome Bruner (1968) asserted that "there is an appropriate version of any skill or knowledge that may be imparted at whatever age one wishes to begin teaching—however preparatory the version may be" (p. 35). Ostensibly, those who advocate Holocaust education at the K–4 level are likely to assert that they are implementing something that approximates Bruner's position. Possibly they are. But why call it "Holocaust education"? Why not "civil education"? Or "prejudice reduction education"? Or "conflict resolution"?

Some primary and upper elementary teachers, though, seem to be going a bit beyond preparatory work and are actually including fragments of the history into their lessons and/or bringing in Holocaust survivors to speak to the students. Can Holocaust history be taught in this way? Should it be taught in this way? Certainly, it could be. If it is watered down enough, if the major concepts such as the intertwining nature of traditional Christian antisemitisim, political antisemitism, and racial antisemitism, social Darwinism, and extreme nationalism, to mention a few, are totally passed over, ignored, or simplified to the nth degree, then, yes, it can be taught. *If* the differences between fascist, communist, and democratic states are passed over or simplified, then yes, it can be taught. *If* the complexities of the results of World War I and Germany's reaction to the Versailles Treaty, the Nazis' false notion of the "stab in the back" by the Jews, and the ensuing economic downturn in Germany are ignored or simplified beyond recognition, then yes, it can be taught. *If* the complexities of how people acted—depending on the time period, various events, personal and societal pressures—are more or less ignored or grossly simplified, then yes, it can be taught. *If* the abusive actions of the Nazis— including beating old men and women, many to death; slamming babies' heads against walls; lining up entire communities of thousands aside ditches and mowing them down, row after row, to the point that they piled up on one another, some still gasping for breath; gassing innocent men, women, and children; starving people to the point where they were walking skeletons; brutally playing with people's emotions, hopes, and lives and then quashing all of those with a flick of the wrist—are totally passed over or simplified beyond recognition, then yes, it can be taught.

Has a straw man been set up here and knocked down? That is, have I focused on aspects of the history that would probably not be taught to kindergarten through fourth graders and overlooked that history which is more "appropriate" for this age group? I think not. To be fair, however, one must consider those aspects of Holocaust history which some, if not many, think should be taught to K–4 students.

To support her position for incorporating "Holocaust education" at the K–4 level, the author of the aforementioned article cites a 1994 New Jersey law that reads as follows:

The instruction shall enable pupils to identify and analyze applicable theories concerning human nature and behavior; to understand that genocide is a consequence of prejudice and discrimination; and to understand that issues of moral dilemma and conscience have a profound impact on life. The instruction shall further emphasize the personal responsibility that each citizen bears to fight racism and hatred wherever that happens.*

The author goes on to note that the New Jersey law "points to studies reporting that many students do not know about the Holocaust; [and that, as a result,] New Jersey's governor and legislators resolved that *all children* in the state must so that the lessons of the Holocaust could be learned" (italics added) (p. P6).

The first half of the law (dealing with theories and what causes genocide) is certainly not germane to the education of K–4 students, whereas the second half (dealing with moral dilemmas, conscience, and personal responsibility) is certainly applicable to the life and education of any school-age child. Still, the question arises, "Is the term *Holocaust education* really the correct term to apply to the latter components, especially if the history of the Holocaust is not taught in conjunction with such goals?" Is that really Holocaust education? If so, how? And if it is basically preparatory in nature, then why—in light of the topics addressed—is it preparatory solely for Holocaust education and not something broader and more inclusive?

Discussing the plethora of books on the Holocaust available now for use in classrooms, Sepinwall (1999) states that: "Books recommended for use with K–4 *generally* do not provide graphic details of the horrors the Holocaust" (italics added) (p. P7). Generally? Why isn't it *never*? Indeed, what is the point of *ever* subjecting such young and tender minds and hearts to such atrocities? Not only are they unable to place such horrors in context, but learning such information *may* result in nightmares and other psychological distress.

Sepinwall further notes that although many books "may substitute metaphors or allegories" (p. P7) for the actual horrors of the Holocaust, "some books for young children do include stories relating to what happened to children during the Holocaust (p. P7). More specifically, she states that:

> They may tell stories of strained and lost friendships, or of hidden children and their rescuers, or they may deal more specifically with the Holocaust by describing the lives of those forced into concentration camps, of families separated and then reunited, or of children facing life as survivors after the Holocaust. Still other books encourage children to see the Holocaust in the context of historic antisemitism and to remember the victims of the Holocaust. (Sepinwall, 1999, p. P7)

*For a discussion over the sagacity of even mandating Holocaust education, readers should consult Karen Shawn's thought-provoking article, "Current Issues in Holocaust Education." *Dimensions: A Journal of Holocaust Studies*, 9(2):15–18, 1995.

Again, are these appropriate topics for K–4 students? I think not! Without contextualization, how will such young students even begin to understand why the children were in hiding, in need of rescue, or separated from their families? Conversely, when such contextualization is provided, teachers are almost forced to enter the horrific chambers of the Holocaust, which, again, is inappropriate for children this age. As for teaching anything about what life was really like in the ghettos, concentration camps, and death camps, that is obscenely inappropriate. And as for teaching them about historic antisemitism, many high school students at the junior and senior levels have great difficulty understanding that torturous history, so how can anyone expect a K–4 student to do so?

At another point Sepinwall asserts: "Increased use of the Internet links students in classrooms with Holocaust survivors and with other students who are studying this topic, and allows them to use Holocaust-related documents" (1999, p. P7). But, should such young children really be engaging in a discussion with Holocaust survivors? It is a simple but profound fact that many junior high school students, not to mention high school students, are often overwhelmed by the stories of Holocaust survivors.

And what about Holocaust documents? Although no specifics are supplied about what is meant by "Holocaust-related documents," one surmises that it pertains either to material that deals with the history in some fashion or another and/or the use of primary documents. Neither seems appropriate for use with K–4 students, and that is due to the simple fact that they are not likely to understand much if anything they read—if, in fact, they are even able to read such material.

The author goes on to mention that a third-grade teacher in Lyndhurst, New Jersey, "invites Holocaust survivors to speak to her students, and discusses newspaper articles concerning the lives of survivors today" (Sepinwall, 1999, p. P7). One has to wonder, What do the survivors speak about? If they speak solely about life before or after the Holocaust, does that have any real meaning for the students? Again, such information would be decontextualized if the facts of the Holocaust were not discussed. On the other hand, if the survivors talk about the prejudice and discrimination they faced in the early years of the Nazis' rise to power, does it make any sense if the students cannot figure out why the Jews were targeted? *Hopefully,* the survivors do not talk about the horrors of the deportations, slave labor, or life and death in the concentration and death camps.

Mention is also made of a fourth-grade teacher in Delaware who teaches her students "about the Nazi plans and actions, [and has them] wear a Star of David, and . . . meet and ask questions of a Holocaust survivor" (Sepinwall, 1999, p. P7). This teacher concludes the study by taking her students to the United States Holocaust Memorial Museum where she encourages "them to discuss what they are seeing and feeling" (Sepinwall, 1999, p. P7). The same question arises as above: Are fourth-graders—eight- and nine-year-old children—capable of understanding this history and handling the concomitant horror? And, if teachers believe they are not and thus teach this history without focusing on key but difficult concepts, as well as on the horrific nature of what really happened, are they really teaching the Holocaust at all? And yet again, if the teachers are focusing on the horror, should they be doing so with young children?

As for having students wear the star, what is the point? It sounds like little more than fun and games. Certainly, the students are not going to learn of the abysmal degradation and humiliation many, if not most, Jews felt by being forced to wear such an emblem that resulted in even more isolation and opprobrium. As the authors of the United States Holocaust Memorial Museum's *Guidelines for Teaching about the Holocaust* note, gimmicky activities "trivialize the importance of studying this history. When the effects of a particular activity run counter to the rationale for studying the history, then that activity should not be used" (Parsons and Totten, 1993, p. 7). (For real insight into what it meant for German Jews to be forced to wear such markings, see Victor Klemperer, *I Will Bear Witness: A Diary of the Nazi Years 1933–1941*. New York: Random House, 1998. See, in particular, pp. 429, 433–436, 438–439, 441–442, 444–445, 456.)

So, should Holocaust history even be taught to K–4 students? It seems as if a resounding "no" is in order. This is so for three main reasons. First, the history is far too complex for young children to understand. As previously mentioned, it comprises a host of extremely complex concepts. Second, without a fairly solid understanding of the aforementioned concepts, it is truly difficult for anyone to understand why and how the Holocaust unfolded. Third, it is simply and profoundly inappropriate to introduce, let alone immerse, such young children to the various horrors of the Holocaust.

Is What Is Being Touted As Holocaust Education Really Holocaust Education, or Is It Misnamed?

Among the many goals and objectives for K–4 Holocaust education that some tout are the need to "learn the importance of tolerance and respect for others who are different" (Sepinwall, 1999, p. P5); "acquire and practice skills for resolving conflicts peacefully and for living together in a spirit of mutual cooperation and appreciation for the contributions of others" (p. P5); "develop self-esteem" (p. P6); learn how "prejudice hurts everyone and ways we all (individually as a community, as a nation, and as a world) suffer because of it" (p. P6); "accept that each person is responsible for his/her actions" (p. P6); "think of ways in which [one] can stand up for what [one] believes is right and good" (p. P6); be "more kind and respectful toward others" (p. P7); and "reduce prejudice" (p. P7).

The upshot is, with certain key exceptions (e.g., inviting Holocaust survivors into the classroom, reading Holocaust-related documents, and visiting the United States Holocaust Memorial Museum), what is being described and advocated is not so much Holocaust education as prejudice reduction, bias reduction, or con-flict resolution. All of the latter are worthy goals for grades K–4. Indeed, when young people are forming their opinions, attitudes, beliefs, and ways of interrelat-ing with other individuals and groups, the early years seem to be an opportune time to instill in students respect and appreciation for other people.

What is the rationale, however, for referring to such educative efforts as "Holocaust education"? For the most part, the K–4 teachers are actually not teach-ing much of anything about the history of the Holocaust. From my perspective, that is an intelligent decision. As for those who are attempting to teach this history to such young students, their pedagogical actions are, at best, problematic.

On another note, the naming of something (an idea, concept, or situation) provides an imprimatur of sorts. Thus, referring to "conflict resolution" or "preju-dice reduction" as "Holocaust education" may lead some to think that it is proper to incorporate actual Holocaust topics and issues into such pedagogical practices. Indeed, it may lead to a situation in which the latter becomes the rule rather than the exception.

That said, if certain educators are so wedded to calling what they do in the way of multicultural education or conflict resolution "Holocaust education," then it may be better to refer to their curricular and instructional programs as "Pre-Holocaust Education" or "Preparatory Holocaust Education," signaling their understanding that the teaching of Holocaust history is not appropriate at the K–4 level but that it is to come later in the students' educational careers (e.g., at the junior high or high school levels).

When all is said and done, why not call the pedagogical efforts to teach for tolerance, respect, and a reduction in prejudice for what they are? What is it that drives the educators of the latter to deem their efforts "Holocaust education"?

At a recent Holocaust conference a rabbi, who also happens to be a Holocaust educator, referred to the extreme popularity and misuse of the Holocaust as "Shoah business." Is that what is at work in referring to prejudice reduction, bias reduction, and conflict reduction as "Holocaust education"? If so, it should not be.

What Does the Future Hold
for Holocaust Education
in the K–4 Grades?

So what does the future hold for *authentic* Holocaust education at the K–4 levels? Hopefully, nothing! That said, some wishing to carve out their own niche or unique place in Holocaust education are bound to forge ahead with their attempt to implement Holocaust K–4 education. Others, truly believing that young chil-dren "need to know" this history, will undoubtedly continue to bring aspects of this history into their classrooms. This may include the use of guest speakers such as Holocaust survivors or the second generation (the children of Holocaust survivors). It may include showing some of the more innocuous films, films that are inane and/or historically inaccurate and watered-down. It may include bits and pieces of the history—such as the actions of the rescuers—but in a way that decontexualizes the Holocaust to a state of pointlessness. It may include posters that make some but not entire sense. It may include story books or simple allegories that deal with some issues, such as prejudice, discrimination, and the bystander syndrome, but not with the history of the Holocaust itself. The latter, of course, would be fine; only, it is not Holocaust education, per se.

Eventually, *unless many voices are raised in concern about this issue,* teaching aspects of the Holocaust may actually trickle down to at least the fourth-grade level—indeed, to the point where many fourth-grade teachers may feel compelled to teach this history to their young charges. This could come about as a direct result of a collaborative effort—by individuals like the author of the aforementioned article and the teachers she mentions—to press state departments of education to recommend strongly or even mandate such teachings. That would be more than a shame; it would constitute a misuse, if not abuse, of the educational process.

Conclusion

So, where does this leave us? Especially those of us who care deeply about children learning to respect, appreciate, and interact with one another in a decent and civil manner? First, there is a critical need in this society to introduce and assist young people in appreciating the beauty of diversity (including the differences and similarities in individuals, themselves, and groups of people), honor the humanity in each individual, and avoid hurtful and harmful stereotyping, prejudice, bias, and discrimination against those who are different from oneself. Second, assisting students to differentiate between appreciation and looking askance at difference, honoring versus denigrating those in different groups from our own, and accepting versus rejecting "the other" have a rightful place in the primary curriculum. There is also a need to assist students in understanding the differences between and among prejudice, bias, stereotyping, and discrimination, and in understanding how and what the individual, families, and the larger society can do to avoid such hurtful and harmful behavior. All of the aforementioned goals and objectives can be accomplished by not mentioning, let alone focusing on, something as complex and horrific as the Holocaust. Third, school is a place where children should be safe and not a place where they are barraged and overwhelmed by something that is conceptually and developmentally inappropriate and/or simply beyond their ken. In essence, it is imperative that teachers and schools meet the children at their developmental level, challenge them, and not abuse them. It is as simple and profound as that.

REFERENCES

Bruner, Jerome (1968). *Toward a Theory of Instruction*. New York: W.W. Norton.

Parsons, William S., and Totten, Samuel (1993). *Guidelines for Teaching About the Holocaust*. Washington, DC: United States Holocaust Memorial Museum.

Sepinwall, Harriet (January/February 1999). "Incorporating Holocaust Education into K–4 Curriculum and Teaching in the United States." *Social Studies & The Young Learner*, pp. P5–P8.

Teaching about the Holocaust: A Select Annotated Bibliography

JOURNALS

Dimensions: A Journal of Holocaust Studies (published by the Anti-Defamation League's Braun Center for Holocaust Studies, New York City). An outstanding journal that regularly includes historical and, occasionally, pedagogical essays on various aspects of the Holocaust. The historical essays are often relatively short, highly readable, and ideal for use in the classroom.

Holocaust and Genocide Studies (published three times a year by Oxford University Press in association with the United States Holocaust Memorial Museum). An outstanding scholarly journal that regularly includes essays and book reviews on a wide variety of issues related to the Holocaust and other genocidal events.

Journal of Holocaust Education (formerly the *British Journal of Holocaust Education*, this journal is published Frank Cass and Company, Limited, Ilford, Essex, England). This journal generally includes a mixture of historical and pedagogical pieces on various aspects of the Holocaust.

Journal of Genocide Research (published four times a year by Carfax Publishing, Taylor & Francis Ltd.). This is the major journal that focuses on genocide theory and research as well as the full spectrum of genocidal acts.

NEWSLETTERS

Martyrdom and Resistance (published by the International Society for Yad Vashem, 500 Fifth Avenue, Suite 1600, New York, NY 10110–1699). This newsletter (which is printed in a newspaper format) generally covers news about the work of the International Society for Yad Vashem, and includes book reviews on various aspects of the Holocaust, information about survivor groups, general pieces on diverse aspects of the history and related issues, and an overview of campus and classroom activities related to Holocaust education.

GENERAL REFERENCE TOOLS: ATLASES, DICTIONARIES, ENCYCLOPEDIAS, GUIDES, AND HANDBOOKS

Edelheit, Abraham J., and Edelheit, Hershel (Eds.). (1994). *History of the Holocaust: A Handbook and Dictionary.* Boulder, CO: Westview Press. 524 pp. An extremely useful tool for educators and students, this volume is comprised of the following: Part I. History of the Holocaust (1. Antecedents; 2. World War I and Its Aftermath; 3. The Nazi Totalitarian State; 4. The Shoa; 5. The Geography of the Holocaust; 6. Jewish Responses to Persecution; 7. Jewish-Gentile Relations in Extremis; 8. International Responses; 9. Aftermath and Recovery); and Part II. Dictionary of Holocaust Terms. Both the history (pp. 3–157) and the definitions of the terms (pp. 161–460) are highly informative.

Edelheit, Hershel, and Edelheit, Abraham (1991). *World in Turmoil: An Integrated Chronology of the Holocaust and World War II.* Westport, CT: Greenwood. 450 pp. Spanning sixteen years, this extensive chronology includes events related to the Third Reich, the Holocaust, and World War II.

Epstein, Eric Joseph, and Rosen, Philip (1997). *Dictionary of the Holocaust: Biography, Geography, and Terminology.* Westport, CT: Greenwood Press. 416 pp. This volume is comprised of two thousand entries on major personalities, concentration and death camps, cities and countries, and significant events. It includes important terms translated from German, French, Polish, Yiddish, and twelve other languages. Biographical entries provide a brief overview of the individual and his or her place and/or significance vis-à-vis the period.

Friedman, Saul S. (Ed.). (1993). *Holocaust Literature: A Handbook of Critical, Historical, and Literary Writings.* Westport, CT: Greenwood Press. 677 pp. This text is divided into three sections: "Conceptual Approaches to the Holocaust," "Holocaust Area Studies," and "The Holocaust in Education and the Arts." The collection includes reflective essays by such individuals as Nora Levin ("The Relationship of Genocide to Holocaust Studies"), Shmuel Krakowski ("Relations Between Jews and Poles During the Holocaust"), and Henry James Cargas ("The Holocaust in Fiction").

Gilbert, Martin (1991). *Atlas of the Holocaust.* New York: Pergamon Press. 256 pp. Included in this volume are 316 maps drawn by the noted historian Martin Gilbert. The atlas traces each phase of the Holocaust, starting with the antisemitic violence of prewar Germany, the ever-increasing discrimination against the Jews, and finally, the genocide carried out in the death camps and elsewhere. More specifically, Gilbert states that "set out here is the spread of the early random killings, the systematic mass expulsion from thousands of towns and villages, the establishment of ghettos, the deliberate starvation of Jews trapped in these ghettos, the setting up of the death camps, the distant deportation to those camps, the slave-labour camp system, the death marches and the executions from the time of Germany's military domination to the very last days of the Allied liberation." Each map is fully annotated and based on documentary evidence from a wide range of sources. An excellent resource for use in the classroom.

Gutman, Israel (Ed.). (1995). *Encyclopedia of the Holocaust.* New York: Macmillan. Four volumes. 1905 pp. A massive and major work, this four-part set (which is divided into two large volumes) contains entries on a wide array of critical issues by some of the most noted scholars of the Holocaust. Highly recommended for the serious student of Holocaust history.

Laqueur, Walter (2001). *The Holocaust Encyclopedia.* New Haven, CT: Yale University Press. 765 pp. This massive work provides both a reflective overview of the Holocaust and numerous detail concerning major events, policy decisions, locations, and individuals. It includes essays by scholars from eleven countries who draw on a rich body of sources—including recently uncovered evidence from the former Soviet Union—to provide in-depth pieces on political, social, religious and moral issues. Among the noted scholars who contributed to this volume are Michael Berenbaum, Richard Breitman, Christopher Browning, Michael Burleigh, David Cesarani, Henry Feingold, Henry Friedlander, Saul Friedländer, Israel Gutman, Raul Hilberg, Michael Marrus, Sybil Milton, Livia Rothkirchen, Nechama Tec, and James Young.

Niewyk, Donald, and Nicosia, Francis (2000). *The Columbia Guide to the Holocaust*. New York: Columbia University Press, 473 pp. This book is comprised of the following five parts and sections: Part I. Historical Overview; Part II. Problems and Interpretations (Defining the Holocaust; Roots of the Holocaust; How the "Final Solution" Came About, The Perpetrators and Their Motivations, The Victims' Reactions to Persecution, The Behavior of Bystanders, The Questions of Rescue, and the Lasting Effect of the Holocaust); Part III. Chronology; Part IV. Encyclopedia (People, Places, Terms, Organizations); and Part V. Resources.

Overy, Richard (1996). *The Penguin Atlas of the Third Reich*. New York: Penguin. 143 pp. Making use of both maps and charts, this atlas delineates the rise and fall of Nazi Germany. In doing so, it addresses a wide range of issues germane to the political, cultural, and social history of the Third Reich.

United States Holocaust Memorial Museum (1996). *Historical Atlas of the Holocaust*. Washington, DC. 252 pp. An essential tools for teachers, this atlas presents the story of the Holocaust in more than 230 full color maps in all its specific geographical details. Maps and text explain the physical facts of the deportations, concentration camps, and the extermination of the victims of the Nazi state.

Wistrich, Robert (1995). *Who's Who in Nazi Germany*. New York: Routledge. 312 pp. A readable and useful compilation of brief biographies of individuals who influenced wide-ranging aspects of life in Nazi German.

Wyman, David S. (1996). *The World Reacts to the Holocaust*. Baltimore, MD: Johns Hopkins University Press. 981 pp. A major work that chronicles the impact of the Holocaust in the post-World War II world. It includes information on twenty-two countries and explores the difficulties and controversies involved in the efforts of various nations to come to terms with the Holocaust.

KEY HISTORICAL WORKS

Bankier, David (Ed.). (2000). *Probing the Depths of German Antisemitism: German Society and the Persecution of the Jews, 1931–1944*. Jerusalem: Yad Vashem (with Berghahn Books, New York). 585 pp. Comprised of over twenty-five essays, this impressive volume includes pieces by such noted Holocaust scholars as Yehuda Bauer, Leni Yahil, Otto D. Kulka, Marion Kaplan, and Richard Breitman. The headings of the various sections of the book provide one with a sense of the breadth of the volume: "Party and State Antisemitic Policy," "Nazi Antisemitic Policy on the Regional Level," "The Policy of Extermination," "Popular Attitudes to Nazi Antisemitism in Wartime," "Jewish Society Under the Nazi System," "Responses of the Churches," "Responses of German Resistance," and "Responses of the Bystanders."

Bartov, Omer (1992). *Hitler's Army: Soldiers, Nazis, and War in the Third Reich*. New York: Oxford University Press. 238 pp. A provocative book that challenges the view that the

Wehrmacht was an apolitical professional fighting force, having little to do with the Nazi party and the fulfillment of Nazi racial policy.

Berenbaum, Michael, and Peck, Abraham J. (Eds.). (1998). *The Holocaust and History: The Known, the Unknown, the Disputed, and the Reexamined.* Bloomington and Indianapolis: Indiana University Press. 836 pp. This is an outstanding collection of fifty-four essays by such noted scholars as Raul Hilberg, Yehuda Bauer, Michael R. Marrus, Hans Mommsen, Christopher R. Browning, Henry Friedlander, Sybil Milton, Randolph L. Brahm, Susan S. Zuccotti, and Nechama Tec. The book is comprised of eleven parts, each of which includes a series of essays: Probing the Holocaust: Where We Are, Where We Need to Go; Antisemitism and Racism in Nazi Ideology; The Politics of Racial Health and Science; The Nazi State: Leadership and Bureaucracy; "Ordinary Men": The Sociopolitical Background; Multiple Voices: Ideology, Exclusion and Coercion; Concentration Camps: Their Task and Environment; The Axis, the Allies, and the Neutrals; Jewish Leadership, Jewish Resistance; The Rescuers; and The Survivor Experience.

Berenbaum, Michael (Ed.). (1990). *A Mosaic of Victims: Non-Jews Persecuted and Murdered by the Nazis.* New York: New York University Press. 244 pp. This book includes a series of highly readable and informative essays on non-Jewish victims of the Nazis, including Gypsies, Poles, other Slavs, Soviet prisoners of war, non-Jewish children, Jehovah's Witnesses, pacifists, and homosexuals. A particularly outstanding essay for use in a high school classroom is "Non-Jewish Victims in the Concentration Camps," by Konnilyn Feig.

Bratton, Fred Gladstone (1994). *The Crime of Christendom: The Theological Sources of Christian Anti-Semitism.* Santa Barbara, CA: Fithian Press. 241 pp. A very accessible and easy-to-read account of the theological foundations and the growth of Christian antisemitism.

Breitman, Richard (1991). *The Architect of Genocide: Himmler and the Final Solution.* Hanover, NH: Brandeis University Press and the University Press of New England. 335 pp. Based on a wide array of sources—many of them used in a historical study for the first time—Breitman "conclusively counters efforts to portray the Holocaust as unpremeditated, the result of bureaucratic improvisations under wartime constraints. . . . He finds Himmler and Hitler to be complementary figures: Hitler envisioned the Nazi policy toward the Jews, and Himmler, the master organizer who controlled the SS and security forces, turned it into horrific reality." Noted Holocaust scholar Yehuda Bauer asserts that it is "a truly path-breaking book, one of the few that will have a lasting impact on historical research of the period. It shows both the primacy of Hitler as the motivating force in the mass murder, and the way in which his initiatives were accepted and internalized by the SS, on the basis of ideology."

Breitman, Richard (1998). *Official Secrets: What the Nazis Planned, What the British and Americans Knew.* New York: Hill and Wang. 325 pp. Using newly acquired evidence, Breitman examines how Germany's leaders initiated and implemented the Holocaust and when they did so. At one and the same time, he assesses the British and American suppression of information about the Nazi killings and the tensions between the two powers over how to respond. Much of the information used in this study was culled from previously marked "top-secret" files in British archives.

Browning, Christopher R. (2000). *Nazi Policy, Jewish Workers, German Killers.* New York: Cambridge University Press. 185 pp. This book "focuses on controversial issues in current Holocaust scholarship: How did Nazi Jewish policy evolve during the first years of the war? When did the Nazi regime cross the historic watershed from population expulsion and decimation ('ethnic cleansing') to total and systematic extermination? How did Nazi authorities attempt to reconcile policies of expulsion and extermination with the wartime urge to exploit Jewish labor? How were Jewish workers impacted? What role did local authorities play in shaping Nazi policy?" The six chapters of the book are as follows: 1. From 'Ethnic Cleansing' to Genocide to the 'Final Solution': The Evolution of Nazi Jewish Policy, 1939–1941; 2. Nazi Policy: Decisions for the Final Solution; 3. Jewish Workers and Survivor Memories: The Case of the Starachowice Labor Camp; 5. German Killers: Orders from Above, Initiative from Below, and the Scope of Local Autonomy—The Case of Brest-Litovsk; and 6. German Killers: Behavior and Motivation in the Light of New Evidence.

Browning, Christopher R. (1992). *Ordinary Men: Reserve Police Battalion 101 and the Final Solution in Poland*. New York: HarperCollins. 231 pp. Deemed a "truly pioneering study" by Holocaust scholar George Mosse, this book examines in minute and graphic detail the sequence of events and individual actions and reactions that made it possible for ordinary men to become mass murderers—men who, in cold blood and up close, shot and killed thousands of men, women, and children.

Browning, Christopher R. (1995). *The Path to Genocide: Essays on Launching the Final Solution*. New York: Cambridge University Press. 191 pp. In this book, Holocaust scholar Christopher Browning provides "an authoritative account of the evolution of Nazi Jewish policy; and in doing so, he seeks to answer some of the fundamental questions about what actually happened and why, between the outbreak of war and the emergence of the Final Solution. Browning assesses [various] historians' interpretations and offers his own insights, based on detailed case studies."

Bukey, Evan Burr (2000). *Hitler's Austria: Popular Sentiment in the Nazi Era, 1938–1945*. Chapel Hill: University of North Carolina Press. 320 pp. Although Austrians comprised only 8 percent of the population of Hitler's Reich, they made up 14 percent of SS members and 40 percent of those involved in the Nazis' killing operations. . . . Exploring the convictions behind these phenomena, Evan Bukey, professor of history at the University of Arkansas, Fayetteville, offers a detailed examination of popular opinion in Hitler's native country after the Anschluss (Nazi Germany's annexation of Austria) of 1938. He uses evidence gathered in Europe and the United States to dissect the reactions, views, and conduct of disparate political and social groups, most notably the Austrian Nazi Party, the industrial working class, the Catholic Church, and the farming community.

Burleigh, Michael (1997). *Ethics and Extermination: Reflections on Nazi Genocide*. New York: Cambridge University Press. 261 pp. A series of essays concerned with three central subjects: German relations with the "East," so-called Nazi euthanasia, and extermination.

Burleigh, Michael, and Wipperman, Wolfgang (1991). *The Racial State: Germany 1933–1945*. New York: Cambridge University Press. 386 pp. This book deals with the ideas and institutions that underpinned the Nazis' attempt to restructure a "class" society along racial lines.

Dawidowicz, Lucy S. (1986). *The War Against the Jews, 1933–1945*. New York: Bantam Books. 466 pp. This book presents an account as to why and how the Nazis carried out a genocide of the Jews, *and* how the Jews responded to the assaults against their rights, their livelihood, and their very lives.

Feig, Konnilyn (1981). *Hitler's Death Camps: The Sanity of Madness*. New York: Holmes & Meier. 547 pp. Partially based on Feig's visit to nineteen camps, this historical study of the world of Nazi concentration and extermination camps focuses on the major camps, including Auschwitz, Dachau, Buchenwald, and Majdanek.

Feingold, Henry L. (1995). *Bearing Witness: How America and Its Jews Responded to the Holocaust*. Syracuse: Syracuse University Press. 322 pp. In this major study, Feingold examines why the efforts of the U.S. government and Jewish leaders were ineffective in halting or mitigating Germany's genocidal policy during the Holocaust period.

Friedlander, Henry (1995). *The Origins of Nazi Genocide: From Euthanasia to the Final Solution*. Chapel Hill: University of North Carolina Press. 421 pp. Based on extensive research in United States, German, and Austrian archives as well as Allied and German court records, Friedlander, a survivor of the Holocaust and a noted historian, "traces the rise of racist and eugenic ideologies in Germany, describing how the so-called euthanasia of the handicapped provided a practical model for mass murder, thereby initiating the Holocaust. In doing so, he analyzes the involvement of the German bureaucracy and judiciary, the participation of physicians and scientists, and the motives of the killers."

Friedländer, Saul (1997). *Nazi Germany and the Jews: The Years of Persecution, 1933–1939. Volume I*. New York: HarperCollins. 436 pp. Examining both the latest published material and a wealth of new archival findings, Friedländer describes and interprets the steadily increasing anti-Jewish persecution in Germany following the Nazis' ascent to power in 1933. In doing so, "he demonstrates the interaction between intentions and contingencies, between discernible causes and changing circumstances. He also shows how Nazi ideological objectives and tactical policy decisions enhanced one another and always left an opening for ever more radical moves." Volume II will be entitled *The Years of Extermination*.

Glass, James M. (1997). *"Life Unworthy of Life": Racial Phobia and Mass Murder in Hitler's Germany*. New York: Basic Books. 252 pp. Glass, a scholar of political psychology and political theory, argues that "the rise of a particular ethos of public health and sanitation emerged from the German medical establishment and filtered down to the common people. Building his argument on a trove of documentary evidence, including the records of the German medical community and of other professional groups, he traces the development, in the years following World War I, of theories of 'racial hygiene' that singled out the Jews as an infectious disease that had to be eradicated if the Aryan race were to survive."

Hayes, Peter (Ed.). (1991). *Lessons and Legacies: The Meaning of the Holocaust in a Changing World*. Evanston, IL: Northwestern University Press. 373 pp. Among the many thought-provoking and informative essays in this book are the following: "The Use and Misuse of the Holocaust" by Michael R. Marrus; "The Reaction of the German Population to the Anti-Jewish Persecution and the Holocaust" by Hans Mommsen; "Genocide and Eugenics: The Language of Power" by Claudia Koonz; "'A Monstrous Uneasiness': Citizen Participation and Persecution of the Jews in Nazi Germany" by Robert Gellately; "One Day in Jozefow: Initiation to Mass Murder" by Christopher R. Browning; "Redefining Heroic Behavior: The Impromptu Self and the Holocaust Experience" by Lawrence Langer; and "Popularization and Memory: The Case of Anne Frank" by Alvin H. Rosenfeld.

Hilberg, Raul (1985). *The Destruction of the European Jews*. New York: Holmes & Meier. Three Volumes. 1274 pp. A major and landmark history of the Holocaust, this three-volume set provides a detailed description of the bureaucratic machinery of destruction. Extremely well documented, this is an essential work for those involved in Holocaust studies. Commenting on this work, Holocaust scholar Michael R. Marrus has stated: "The lasting achievement of Hilberg's volumes is his portrayal of the perpetrators, acting both individually and as part of a horrifyingly effective destructive apparatus. No other work gives such a complete and awesome sense of the Nazis' Final Solution, link-ing the most banal administrative tasks to mass murder. . . . In its originality, scope and seriousness of theme, this is one of the great historical works of our time."

Hilberg, Raul (1992). *Perpetrators, Victims, Bystanders: The Jewish Catastrophe 1933–1945*. New York: HarperCollins. 340 pp. As the title suggests, this fascinating, highly informative and important study focuses on the lives, motivations, and actions (and, in certain cases, inaction) of the perpetrators, victims, and bystanders during the Holocaust period.

Kaplan, Marion A. (1998). *Between Dignity and Despair: Jewish Life in Nazi Germany*. New York: Oxford University Press. 290 pp. This book vividly details the ever-increasing tension and constricted lives faced by German Jews as the Nazis implemented—from 1933 onward—one policy after another aimed at isolating, disenfranchising and, ultimately, exterminating the Jewish populace. Based on memoirs, diaries, interviews, and letters of Jewish women and men, this book provides a highly readable and intimate portrait of Jewish life in Nazi Germany. *It is a must read for anyone wishing to begin to understand the early years of Nazi rule and how the Nazi regime slowly strangled the life out of German Jewry.*

Laqueur, Walter (1983). *The Terrible Secret: Suppression of the Truth About Hitler's "Final Solution."* New York: Penguin. 262 pp. Laqueur examines when and how information about the genocide of the Jews became known to millions of Germans, international Jewish organizations, leaders of Jewish communities throughout Europe, and top government officials in neutral and Allied countries.

Leitz, Christian (Ed.). (1999). *The Third Reich: The Essential Readings*. Malden, MA: Blackwell. 307 pp. This book is comprised of eleven essays by such noted scholars as Omer Bartov, Robert Gellately, Hans Mommsen, and Christopher Browning. The essays are entitled as follows: "Rise of the NSDAP"; "Seizure and Consolidation of Power Towards Dictatorship: Germany 1930–1934"; "Foreign Policy: The Structure of Nazi Foreign Policy 1933–1935"; "Economy: Germany, 'Domestic Crisis' and War in 1939"; "Working Class and Volksgemeinschaft: The Appeal of Exterminating 'Others': German Workers and the Limits of Resistance"; "Police State: Surveillance and Disobedience: Aspects of the Political Policing of Nazi Germany"; "Women: Victims or Perpetrators? Controversies about the Role of Women in the Nazi State"; "Hitler as Dictator: 'Working Towards the Führer.' Reflections on the Nature of the Hitler Dictatorship"; "Resistance: German Society and the Resistance Against Hitler, 1933–1945"; and "Holocaust/'Final Solution': Nazi Resettlement Policy and the Search for a Solution to the Jewish Question, 1939–1941."

Lipstadt, Deborah E. (1986). *Beyond Belief: The American Press and the Coming of the Holocaust, 1933–1945*. New York: Free Press. 370 pp. This acclaimed work presents an examination of the American press and how it covered (and "covered up") the ever-increasing discrimination and annihilation of the Jews in Nazi-dominated Europe.

Marrus, Michael R. (1987). *The Holocaust in History*. New York: Meridian. 267 pp. This volume constitutes the first comprehensive assessment of the vast literature on the Holocaust. Drawing on the entire range of historical literature on the Holocaust and applying the tools of historical, sociological, and political analysis, Marrus examines many of the thorniest questions that have concerned scholars over the years.

Michalczyk, John (Ed.). (1994). *Medicine, Ethics, and the Third Reich: Historical and Contemporary Issues*. Kansas City, MO: Sheed and Ward. 258 pp. Prominent voices in the field of bioethics reflect on the medical experiments on human subjects during the Third Reich.

Ofer, Dalia, and Weitzman, Lenore J. (1998). *Women in the Holocaust*. New Haven: Yale University Press. 402 pp. Chapters by eminent historians, sociologists, and literary experts examine Jewish women's lives in the ghettos, the Jewish resistance movement, and the concentrations camps. The volume also includes valuable testimonies of Holocaust survivors. "By examining women's unique responses, their incredible resourcefulness, their courage, and their suffering, the book enhances our understanding of the experiences of all Jews during the Nazi era."

Ritter, Carol, and Roth, John (Eds.). (1993). *Different Voices: Women and the Holocaust*. New York: Paragon House. 435 pp. This major anthology includes the powerful testimony of women survivors ("Voices of Experience"), insights of key scholars ("Voices of Interpretation), and reflections of theologians, philosophers, and others ("Voices of Reflection") regarding women's experiences during the Holocaust. Among the contributors to this pioneering volume are: Ida Fink, Etty Hillesum, Charlotte Delbo, Olga Lengyel, Sybil Milton, Vera Laska, Gitta Sereny, Magda Trocmé, and Deborah Lipstadt.

Sofsky, Wolfang (1997). *The Order of Terror: The Concentration Camp*. Princeton, NJ: Princeton University Press. 356pp. In this book, a renowned German sociologist examines the Nazi concentration camp system from the "inside"—"as a laboratory of cruelty and a system of absolute power built on extreme violence, starvation, 'terror labor,' and the businesslike extermination of human beings." Using historical documents and the reports of survivors, he delineates in great detail how "arbitrary terror and routine violence destroyed personal identity and social solidarity, disrupted the very ideas of time and space, perverted human work into torture, and unleashed innumerable atrocities."

Trunk, Isaiah (1972). *Judenrat: The Jewish Councils in Eastern Europe Under Nazi Occupation*. Lincoln: University of Nebraska Press. 663 pp. This is the first-full length account of the Judenrat (the Nazi-assigned Jewish leadership councils of the ghettos). Exhaustive in its examination, Trunk describes the establishment of the ghettos, life and death in the ghettos, the role of the Judenrat in carrying out Nazi directives, and the many and often deadly ramifications of the latter.

Weiss, John (1996). *Ideology of Death: Why The Holocaust Happened in Germany*. Chicago: Ivan R. Dee. 427 pp. In this book, Weiss, a professor of history at Lehman College and the Graduate Center of the City of University of New York, "rejects the notion that the Holocaust was a product of Nazi fanaticism. He shows instead how racist ideas ingrained in German culture led to [the mass murder of millions]. Weiss argues that Christian antisemitism took a special form among German Protestants and Austrian Catholics and achieved greater intensity. Luther's Germany had rejected the liberal ideas of the Enlightenment, which in other countries created a counterforce to racism. In Germany and Austria racism flourished. Tracing the culture of racism and antisemitism among powerful elites and ordinary Germans, Weiss shows how it grew rapidly during the Napoleonic era, became a forceful popular ideology in the 1870s, and in the 1890s gained the dedicated support of the generation that eventually brought Hitler to power. Without this historical base, antisemitism would not have exploded with such fury after 1918, producing hundreds of thousands of followers whose ideas were not different from those of the Nazis." (Jacket copy)

Wyman, David S. (1984). *The Abandonment of the Jews: America and the Holocaust, 1941–1945*. New York: Pantheon. 444 pp. This is a major and disturbing study of the United States government's totally inadequate response to the Nazi assault on the European Jews. Thoroughly documented, this book provides answers as to why the United States miserably failed to carry out the kind of rescue effort it could have. In essence, it constitutes an indictment showing why and how the United States basically became what Wyman calls passive accomplices to the annihilation of the Jews.

Yahil, Leni (1990). *The Holocaust: The Fate of European Jewry, 1932–1945*. New York: Oxford University Press. 808 pp. This prize-winning history provides a "sweeping look at the Final Solution, covering not only Nazi policies, but also how Jews and foreign governments perceived and responded to the unfolding nightmare." Yahil presents a systematic examination of the evolution of the Holocaust in German-occupied Europe, probing its politics, planning, goals, and key figures.

REFERENCE AND HISTORICAL WORKS SPECIFICALLY FOR SECONDARY-LEVEL STUDENTS

Altshuler, David (1978). *Hitler's War Against the Jews—the Holocaust: A Young Reader's Version of the War Against the Jews 1933–1945 by Lucy Dawidowicz*. West Orange, NJ: Behrman House. 190 pp. While this is a truncated and simplified version of Dawidowicz's text, it remains true to the original work. For young people (middle level and junior high school students), it provides a good overview of the history of the Holocaust.

Bachrach, Susan D. (1994). *Tell Them We Remember: The Story of the Holocaust*. Boston: Little, Brown. 109 pp. A well-written and accurate history of the Holocaust appropriate for a younger audience (upper elementary, middle level, and junior high school students). It is highly readable and packed with photos that complement the text.

Bauer, Yehuda, with Nili Keren (1982). *A History of the Holocaust*. Danbury, CT: Franklin Watts. 398 pp. Coauthored by a highly respected Israeli historian and an Israeli teacher educator, this volume is comprised of fourteen chapters: 1. Who Are the Jews?; 2. Liberalism, Emancipation and Antisemitism; 3. World War I and Its Aftermath; 4. The Weimar Republic; 5. The Evolution of Nazi Jewish Policy, 1933–1938; 6. German Jewry in the Prewar Era, 1933–1938; 7. Poland—The Siege Begins; 8. Life in the Ghettos; 9. The "Final Solution"; 10. West European Jewry, 1940–1944; 11. Resistance; 12. Rescue; 13. The Last Years of the Holocaust, 1943–1945; and 14. Aftermath and Revival.

Berenbaum, Michael (1993). *The World Must Know: The History of the Holocaust as Told in the United States Holocaust Memorial Museum*. Boston: Little, Brown. 240 pp. Written by the former director of research at the United States Holocaust Memorial Museum, this is a thorough, engaging, and highly readable historical work that is thoroughly accessible to secondary level students. Colored and black-and-white photographs complement the text. *Highly recommended as a class text for a high school course on the Holocaust.*

Friedman, Ina R. (1990). *The Other Victims: First-Person Stories of Non-Jews Persecuted by the Nazis*. Boston: Houghton Mifflin. 214 pp. Specifically written for students in grades 5 through 9, this volume includes first-person accounts about the following individuals impacted by the Holocaust: a Gypsy, a Jehovah's Witness, a deaf person, a Czech schoolboy, a Christian and Jewish couple, a dissenter, and a young boy who was forced into slave labor.

Gilbert, Martin (1987). *The Holocaust: A History of the Jews of Europe During the Second World War*. New York: Henry Holt. 959 pp. A powerful and highly readable book in which Gilbert interweaves first-person testimony throughout the text in order to illustrate the impact that the Nazis' policy had on individuals and communities.

Hilberg, Raul (1985). *The Destruction of the European Jews.* Student Edition. New York: Holmes & Meier. 360 pp. This is the student edition of Hilberg's highly acclaimed three-volume set, *The Destruction of the European Jews.* Commenting on the three-volume set, Holocaust scholar David Wyman asserted that it constitutes "the standard text in the field."

Kirk, Tim (1994). *The Longman Companion to Nazi Germany.* Reading, MA: Addison-Wesley. 277 pp. A compilation of facts and commentary about German society, culture, and economy during the Nazi period. It includes a useful glossary, concise biographies, and an annotated bibliography.

Books Containing Primary Documents

Aly, Gotz (1999). *Final Solution: Nazi Population Policy and the Murder of the European Jews.* New York: Arnold Publishers and Oxford University Press. 301 pp. Using extensive primary source documents, many of the latter recently released, Aly shows the close connection between the Nazis' view of the "new order" in Europe and the extermination of the Jews.

Arad, Yitzhak, Gutman, Yisrael, and Margaliot, Abraham (Eds.). (1981). *Documents on the Holocaust.* Jerusalem: Yad Vashem. 504 pp. An impressive and extensive collection of primary source documents on the destruction of the Jews of Germany, Austria, Poland, and the Soviet Union. It includes documents issued by both the perpetrators and the victims (e.g., resistance organizations, leaders of the Judenrat, and excerpts from diaries). This book is a must for those educators who wish to include primary documents into their curriculum on the Holocaust.

Berenbaum, Michael (Ed.). (1997). *Witness to the Holocaust: An Illustrated Documentary History of the Holocaust in the Words of Its Victims, Perpetrators and Bystanders.* New York: HarperCollins. 364 pp. Highly useful for classroom use, this volume includes documents related to the topics listed in the chapter titles: 1. The Boycott; 2. The First Regulatory Assault Against the Jews; 3. Early Efforts at Spiritual Resistance; 4. The Nuremberg Laws; 5. The Conference at Evian; 6. The November Pogroms—Kristallnacht and Its Aftermath; 7. The Beginning of Ghettoization; 8. The Judenrat; 9. A Mosaic of Victims: Non-Jewish Victims of Nazism; 10. The Einsatzgruppen; 11. Babi Yar; 12. The Call to Arms; 13. Hitler's Plan to Exterminate the Jews; 14. The Killers: A Speech, A Memoir, and an Interview; 15. Choiceless Choices; 16. The End of a Ghetto: Deportation from Warsaw; 17. The Warsaw Ghetto Uprising; 18. What Was Known in the West; 19. Why Auschwitz Was Not Bombed; 20. Liberation and Its Aftermath; and 21. The Nuremberg Trials.

Dawidowicz, Lucy (Ed.). (1976). *A Holocaust Reader.* West Orange, NJ: Behrman House. 397 pp. A collection of documents about various facets of the Holocaust, this book is comprised of the following parts and chapters: Part I. The Final Solution (1. Preconditions: Conventional Anti-Semitism and Adolf Hitler; 2. The First Stage: Anti-Jewish Legislation; 3. The Interim Stage: "All Necessary Preparations"; 4. The Final Stage: Mass Killings, "Resettlement," Death Camps); Part II. The Holocaust (5. The First Ordeal: The Jews in Germany 1933–1938; 6. The Ordeals of the Ghettos in Eastern Europe; 7. The Ordeals of the Judenräte; 8. Confronting Death: The Ordeals of Deportation; 9. Resistance: The Ordeal of Desperation).

Housden, Martyn (1997). *Resistance & Conformity in the Third Reich.* London and New York: Routledge. 199 pp. This book, which was designed for use with students, examines the complex relationship between ordinary Germans and the Nazi government. It includes key primary sources, including but not limited to first-person accounts by survivors, former *kapos,* former Hitler Youth members, a member of the Luftwaffe, a Nazi bureaucrat; leaflets by resistance members; statements and speeches by various Nazis; sections of a report by Reinhard Heydrich; police reports and summaries of interrogation sessions; declarations by opponents of the Nazis; and copies of school curricula designed and implemented by the National Socialists. In the preface it is stated that: "A distinctive feature of [this series] is the manner in which the content, style and significance of documents is analyzed. The commentary and the source are not discrete, but rather merge to become part of a continuous and integrated narrative."

Marrus, Michael R. (1997). *The Nuremberg War Crimes Trial 1945-46: A Documentary History.* Boston: Bedford Books. 276 pp. A superb collection of over seventy primary documents about various facets of the Nuremberg Trials. The book is divided into nine chapters and a set of appendices: 1. Historical Precedents; 2. Background; 3. Preparations; 4. The Court; 5. Crimes Against Peace; 6. War Crimes; 7. Crimes Against Humanity; 8. Last Words; and 9. Assessment. The appendices are entitled: Chronology of Events Related to the Nuremberg Trial (1919–1946); The Defendants and Their Fate; Charges, Verdicts, and Sentences; and Selected Bibliography. Among the documents are such pieces as "Winston S. Churchill, Franklin D. Roosevelt, and Joseph Stalin, Moscow Declaration, November 1, 1943"; "Robert H. Jackson, Opening Address for the United States, November 21, 1945"; "Robert Jackson, Cross-Examination of Hermann Göring, March 18, 1946"; "Marie Claude Vaillant-Couturier, Testimony on the Gassing at Auschwitz, January 28, 1946"; "Robert H. Jackson, Cross-Examination of Albert Speer, June 21, 1946"; and "Rudolf Höss, Testimony on Auschwitz, April 15, 1946."

Milton, Sybil (Trans. and Annotator) (1979). *The Stroop Report.* New York: Pantheon. n.p. *The Stroop Report* is SS leader Juergen Stroop's actual record of the battle against the Jews during the Warsaw Ghetto Uprising. It includes his summary record and daily reports of German actions, as well as over fifty photographs taken by the German forces at the time.

Mosse, George (1981). *Nazi Culture: A Documentary History.* New York: Schocken. 386 pp. This anthology of original source material includes pieces taken from contemporary literature, diaries, newspapers, and speeches. Mosse, a noted scholar of the Holocaust, provides useful introductions to each section and each selection.

Noakes, J., and Pridham, G. (1984). *Nazism 1919–1945: A Documentary Reader.* Three Volumes. Exeter, England: University of Exeter. The three volumes of this set (Volume 1, *The Rise to Power, 1919–1934*; Volume 2, *State, Economy and Society, 1933–39,* and Volume 3, *Foreign Policy, War and Racial Extermination*) are comprised of a collection of documents on Nazism. All of the volumes "contain material from a wide range of sources both published and unpublished: State and Party Documents, newspapers, speeches, memoirs, letters, and diaries."

Remak, Joachim (Ed.). (1990). *The Nazi Years: A Documentary History.* Prospect Heights, IL: Waveland Press. 178 pp. The editor reports that in this book the ideology and practices of National Socialism "are described by way of documents nearly all of which were written by the actors, victims, or simple witnesses of the time and at the time." Continuing, Remak asserts that the purpose of the book is "to tell, the whole essential story of National Socialism, from its obscure ideological beginnings to its seizure of power; to show the uses to which the power was put, at home and abroad, until the bitter end of the Third Reich" (p. vii). The eleven chapters in the book are as follows: The Roots, The

Soil, The Program, Power, The Attractions, Propaganda, The Churches, War, Eugenics, The Jews, and Resistance.

Wolfe, Robert (1993). *Holocaust: The Documentary Evidence*. Washington, DC: National Archives and Records Administration. 37 pp. This pamphlet includes an introduction that highlights key aspects of the Nazis' ideology and exterminatory policies as well as a set of "facsimiles" of key Nazi documents dealing with various aspects of the Holocaust years. The documents included herein are a report by Reinhard Heydrich, Chief of Security Police, to Hermann Göring about the destruction that took place during Kristallnacht; a telegram from Reinhard Heydrich to chiefs of all operation commands of the security police regarding the "concentration of Jews from the countryside into the larger cities"; an invoice regarding the shipment of 390 canisters of Zyklon B cyanide gas to be used for "disinfection and extermination" at Auschwitz; a "Statistical Report Regarding the Final Solution of the Jewish Question in Europe"; and a speech by Heinrich Himmler on October 4, 1943. In the latter, Himmler asserted that: "The question arose for us: what about women and children?—I decided here, too, to find a clear-cut solution. I did not believe myself justified to root out the men—say also, to kill them, or to have them killed—and to allow avengers in the form of their children to grow up for our sons and grandsons [to confront]. The hard decision had to be made for this people to disappear from the earth." Unfortunately, none of the documents are translated in their entirety. Further, most of the documents have deteriorated and are now difficult to read. Still, this is a highly valuable booklet for teachers and students, for it includes key documents that illuminate important aspects of the history.

PAMPHLETS ON HISTORICAL ISSUES FOR USE IN THE CLASSROOM

United States Holocaust Memorial Museum (n.d.). *Handicapped*. Washington, DC: Author. 20 pp. This pamphlet provides a highly readable and informative overview of the plight of the mentally and physically handicapped at the hands of the Nazis. It focuses on both the forced sterilizations and "euthanasia" killings suffered by the victims. It also includes primary documents and photographs.

United States Holocaust Memorial Museum (n.d.). *Homosexuals*. Washington, DC: Author. 16 pp. This pamphlet provides an overview of the treatment of homosexuals by the Nazis from 1933 through 1945. It includes an excerpt from a first-person account and numerous photographs.

United States Holocaust Memorial Museum (n.d.). *Jehovah's Witnesses*. Washington, DC: Author. 15 pp. An informative piece on the beliefs of the Jehovah's Witnesses, why the Nazis persecuted Jehovah's Witnesses, and the treatment the Witnesses faced at the hands of the Nazis. It includes a facsimile of a Nazi-issued document, other primary documents, and photographs.

United States Holocaust Memorial Museum (n.d.). *Poles*. Washington, DC: Author. 27 pp. This pamphlet provides an overview of the plight of the Polish people at the hands of the Nazis. Among the many topics addressed are: The invasion and occupation of Poland, Nazi terror against the intelligentsia and clergy, expulsions and the kidnapping of children, forced labor and the terror of the camps, and Polish resistance. It includes a facsimile of a Nazi-issued document, two first-person accounts, a map, and photographs.

United States Holocaust Memorial Museum (n.d.). *Sinti & Roma*. Washington, DC: Author. 21 pp. A highly informative piece about the plight of the Gypsies at the hands of the Nazis. Viewed as "asocials" (that is, as being outside "normal" society and being racial "inferiors") by the Nazis and their collaborators, the Sinti and Roma were targeted for extermination. Between 220,000 to 500,000 Sinti and Roma were killed during the Holocaust period. It includes primary documents and photographs.

United States Holocaust Memorial Museum (1999). *Voyage of the St. Louis: Refuge Denied*. Washington, DC: Author. 26 pp. This magnificent booklet for use in the classroom thoroughly and cogently addresses the fate of the nine hundred Jewish passengers on the St. Louis, a transatlantic ocean liner, who were fleeing Nazi persecution and were turned away by both Cuba and the United States. Particularly powerful is the inclusion of the personal stories of individual families.

BOOKS ON FILM

Avisar, Ilan (1988). *Screening the Holocaust: Cinema's Images of the Unimaginable*. Bloomington: Indiana University Press. 212 pp. Disagreeing with those theorists who believe that art cannot deal with the Holocaust in a meaningful way, Avisar examines how filmmakers have struggled with the task of depicting the atrocities of the Holocaust on film.

Doneson, Judith (1987). *The Holocaust in American Film*. Philadelphia: Jewish Publication Society. 262 pp. An investigation into the ways in which specific films influenced and reflected the Americanization of the Holocaust and how film has helped to highlight the event in the popular culture.

Grobman, Alex, Landes, Daniel, and Milton, Sybil (Eds.). (1983). *Genocide: Critical Issues of the Holocaust: A Companion to the Film "Genocide."* Los Angeles: The Simon Wiesenthal Center, and Chappaqua, NY: Rossel Books. 501 pp. In addition to serving as a companion volume to the film *Genocide* (which is ideal for use in the classroom, as it provides a succinct but powerful overview of the Nazis' polices and actions), this text also includes a discussion as to how the Holocaust is portrayed through film, an examination of aspects of modern antisemitism, and implications of the Holocaust for today's world.

Insdorf, Annette (1990). *Indelible Shadows: Film and the Holocaust*. New York: Cambridge University Press. 293 pp. Richly illustrated, this book is a valuable introduction to the ways in which filmmakers have dealt with the subject of the Holocaust. It critically examines seventy-five fictional and documentary films, and includes a list of over one hundred films and their distributors.

Lanzmann, Claude (1985). *Shoah: An Oral History of the Holocaust. The Text of the Film*. New York: Pantheon. 200 pp. This is the complete text of Lanzmann's nine-and-a-half-hour documentary in which witnesses, survivors, former SS officers, and Polish villagers speak about their experiences vis-à-vis the Holocaust.

Leiser, Erwin (1974). *Nazi Cinema*. New York: Macmillan. 179 pp. Through his analysis of films created by the Nazis, Leiser reveals how the use of film served as a medium for indoctrination.

Loshitzky, Yosefa (1997). *Spielberg's Holocaust: Critical Perspectives on* Schindler's List. Bloomington and Indianapolis: Indiana University Press. 250 pp. This volume is comprised of a compilation of essays that assess the strengths and limitations of *Schindler's List*. In doing so, the various authors examine the film from different perspectives and contexts, including the aesthetic, religious, historical, and social.

PEDAGOGICAL RESOURCES

Books

Facing History and Ourselves. (1994). *Facing History and Ourselves: Elements of Time*. Brookline, MA: Author. 402 pp. An outstanding volume and major resource that provides a detailed and intelligent discussion regarding why and how video testimony by Holocaust survivors can and should be incorporated into the classroom.

Schilling, David (Ed.). (1998). *Lessons and Legacies: Teaching the Holocaust in a Changing World*. Evanston: Northwestern University Press. 233 pp. Conveniently divided into three sections ("Issues," "Resources," and "Applications"), this collection includes essays by Michael Marrus ("Good History and Teaching the Holocaust"), Gerhard Weinberg ("The Holocaust and World War II: A Dilemma in Teaching"), Christopher Browning ("Ordinary Germans or Ordinary Men? Another Look at the Perpetrators"), and Judith Doneson ("Why Film?").

Totten, Samuel (Ed.). (2001). *Teaching Holocaust Literature*. Boston: Allyn & Bacon. This volume is comprised of rich narratives by secondary level teachers (grades 7–12) on the process they used to teach a specific piece of Holocaust literature (a poem, novel, short story, play, or memoir) to their students. Among the contributors are such noted Holocaust educators as Rebecca Aupperle, Elaine Culbertson, Carol Danks, Peggy Drew, William Fernekes, Karen Shawn, and Samuel Totten.

Totten, Samuel, and Feinberg, Steven (Eds.). (2001). *Teaching and Studying the Holocaust*. Boston: Allyn & Bacon. In addition to chapters on the historiography of the Holocaust, the development and use of rationales for teaching this history, and key instructional issues, it includes individual chapters on incorporating primary documents, first-person accounts, literature, films, art, and music into Holocaust lessons and units.

United States Holocaust Memorial Museum (1994). *Teaching About the Holocaust: A Resource Book for Educators*. Washington, DC: Author. 115 pp. This volume includes a host of valuable resources, including the USHMM's *Guidelines for Teaching About the Holocaust*, an annotated bibliography, an annotated videography, a section of frequently asked questions, a piece entitled "Children and the Holocaust," a historical summary of the Holocaust, and a detailed chronology.

Teaching Guidelines

Parsons, William S., and Totten, Samuel (1993). *Guidelines for Teaching About the Holocaust*. Washington, DC: United States Holocaust Memorial Museum. 16 pp. This set of guidelines addresses key issues that educators ought to consider when preparing to teach about the Holocaust. Noted Holocaust educators Stephen Feinberg, William Fernekes, and Grace Caporino were major contributors to the development of this publication, as was Holocaust historian Sybil Milton.

Essays/Articles About Pedagogical Strategies, Lessons, Units, and Resources

Danks, Carol (October 1995). "Using Holocaust Stories and Poetry in the Social Studies Classroom." *Social Education*, 59(6): 358–361. In this article Danks succinctly discusses certain caveats and guidelines to be taken into consideration when using short stories and poetry in a study of the Holocaust. She also explores ways to teach Ozick's "The Shawl," the short stories in Borowski's *This Way for the Gas, Ladies and Gentlemen*, and various pieces of poetry.

Darsa, Jan (1991). "Educating About the Holocaust: A Case Study in the Teaching of Genocide," pp. 175–193. In Israel W. Charny (Ed.). *Genocide: A Critical Bibliographic Review.* Volume 2. New York: Facts On File. While not actually a case study, this is a thought-provoking essay that raises and examines numerous key issues vis-à-vis Holocaust education. It includes an extensive and useful annotated bibliography that highlights key Holocaust curricula, adjunct resources, and essays on Holocaust pedagogy.

Drew, Margaret A. (October 1995). "Incorporating Literature into a Study of the Holocaust." *Social Education,* 59(6): 354–356. Among the issues Drew discusses in this piece are criteria teachers ought to use in selecting literature for use in the upper elementary and secondary classrooms, key issues that should be addressed in the study of the Holocaust, and various first-person accounts and novels that can be incorporated into such a study.

Drew, Peg (Fall 1989). "Holocaust Literature and Young People: Another Look," *Facing History and Ourselves News.* pp. 20–21. Drew argues that in addition to reading literature, students need a solid grounding in the history of the Holocaust. Only in that way, she argues, will they be able to make sense of the events that led up to and resulted in the Holocaust.

Farnham, James (April 1983). "Ethical Ambiguity and the Teaching of the Holocaust." *English Journal,* 72(4):63–68. A thought-provoking piece that discusses the clash between the value systems of students and actions of victims in the camps, the complexities of ethical behavior, and "ethical problems from the [Holocaust] literature."

Fernekes, William (2000). "Education for Social Responsibility: The Holocaust, Human Rights, and Classroom Practice," pp. 496–512. In Ted DeCoste and Bernard Schwartz (Eds.), *The Holocaust: Art, Politics, Law, Education.* Alberta, Edmonton, Canada: University of Alberta Press. This is an extremely interesting and thought-provoking essay by a noted Holocaust educator that discusses the rationale for bridging the gap between the study of the Holocaust and contemporary human rights infractions. Included is the description of a unit of study that sets out to accomplish the latter. In his introduction, Fernekes states that in his essay he aims to answer the following questions: "1. What can young people learn from studying the Holocaust that can aid in the realization of human rights guarantees articulated in the post-World War II period? 2. What aspects of curriculum design and classroom practice should be emphasized to realize the ideals embodied in major international human rights documents? 3. What should young people know about the relationships between thought and action which inspired humans to author international human rights documents in response to the Holocaust and other atrocities of the World War II era? and 4. How can young people be educated to engage in socially responsible behaviors to defend humans rights while applying lessons from study of the Holocaust?" (p. 496).

Greeley, Kathy (1997). "Making Plays, Making Meaning, Making Change," pp. 80–103. In Samuel Totten and Jon E. Pedersen (Eds.), *Social Issues and Service at the Middle Level.* Boston: Allyn & Bacon. In this fascinating essay, Greeley discusses and explains how she involved her students in the writing and production of a play that dealt, in part, with issues germane to the Holocaust.

Kalfus, Richard (February 1990). "Euphemisms of Death: Interpreting a Primary Source Document on the Holocaust." *The History Teacher,* 23(2): 87–93. Kalfus describes a powerful learning activity in which he uses a primary document that he asserts "illustrates the all-pervasive, destructive force that was National Socialism" (p. 87). Continuing, he states: "[T]he insidious, administrative language used here is a concrete, dramatic example of how an entire caste of civil servants could become active participants in the extermination process" (p. 87). Part of the activity includes having the students replace the euphemisms with their intended meaning, e.g., "*merchandise, pieces* and *load* become Jews; *operating time* becomes annihilation; *operation* becoming gassing," and so forth (p. 88).

Kettel, Raymond P. (Fall 1996). "Reflections on *The Devil's Arithmetic* by a Holocaust Survivor: An Interview with Jack Wayne—B 8568." *The New Advocate,* 9(4):287–295. This is a fascinating article/interview in which a survivor comments on how moved he was by Jane Yolen's novel, *The Devil's Arithmetic.* He notes that he especially appreciates the work because the protagonist's experiences are so much like his own. Information in the interview can be used by teachers to highlight and illuminate, for their students, various aspects of *The Devil's Arithmetic.*

Kimmel, E. A. (February 1977). "Confronting the Ovens: The Holocaust and Juvenile Fiction." *The Horn Book Magazine,* pp. 84–91. In his examination of juvenile fiction about the Holocaust, Kimmel notes that as of the late 1970s no Holocaust fiction written for children had been written about the death camps. After predicting that a novel about the death camps would eventually be written, he raises the issue as to "whether or not that novel [would] come any closer to the question at the core of all this blood and pain" (p. 91).

Meisel, Esther (September 1982). "'I Don't Want to be a Bystander': Literature and the Holocaust." *English Journal,* 71(5):40–44. This succinctly discusses the use of two poems: Nelly Sach's "The Chorus of the Rescued," and Ka-Tzetnik's "Wiedergutmahung."

National Council for the Social Studies (October 1995). Special Issue of *Social Education,* "Teaching About the Holocaust. Samuel Totten and Stephen Feinberg (Eds.). 59(6). Recipient of the EdPress Award for special topics, this issue includes, among others, the following pieces: "Teaching About the Holocaust: Issues of Rationale, Content, Methodology, and Resources," "Anti-Semitism: Antecedents of the Holocaust," "The Other Victims of the Nazis," "Altruism and the Holocaust," "Incorporating Literature into a Study of the Holocaust: Some Advice, Some Cautions," "Using Holocaust Short Stories and Poetry in the Social Studies Classroom," "The American Press and the Holocaust—A Unit of Study," Anti-Semitism: A Warrant for Genocide—A Unit of Study," and "Hitler's Death Camps—A Unit of Study."

Rudman, Masha Kabakow, and Rosenberg, Susan P. (Summer 1991). "Confronting History: Holocaust Books for Children." *The New Advocate,* 4(3):163–176. This article presents and discusses numerous rationales for including literature in a study of the Holocaust, issues several caveats in regard to selecting and using Holocaust literature in the classroom, and provides a critique of different types of Holocaust literature on a variety of subject matter.

Rushforth, Peter (1994). "'I Even Did a Theme Once on That Anne Frank Who Kept the Diary, And Got an A Plus on It': Reflections on Some Holocaust Books for Young People." *Dimensions: A Journal of Holocaust Studies,* 8(2):23–35. In this bibliographical essay, Rushforth, author of the novel *Kindergarten,* provides a thorough and intelligent critique of ten popular books used by many teachers at the upper elementary, middle, and junior high levels of schooling to teach about various facets of the Holocaust. The books he critiques are: *Anton the Dove Fancier, and Other Tales of the Holocaust; Gentlehands; Journey to America; Alan and Naomi; Number the Stars; Daniel's Story; The Island on Bird Street; Friedrich; A Pocket Full of Seeds;* and *The Devil's Arithmetic.* This is a valuable article that should be consulted by any teacher who is considering the use of Holocaust fiction in his or her classroom.

Schwartz, Donald (February 1993). "'Who Will Tell Them After We're Gone?' Reflections on Teaching the Holocaust." *The History Teacher,* 23(2):95–110. A thought-provoking and well-written essay that addresses, among other issues, the place of the Holocaust in current school curricula, textbook coverage of the Holocaust, and various rationales for teaching the Holocaust to school-age students.

Shawn, Karen (1993). "The Warsaw Ghetto: A Documentary Discussion Guide to Jewish Resistance in Occupied Warsaw 1939–1943." *Dimensions: A Journal of Holocaust Studies*, 7(2): G1–G15. This discussion guide, which includes a succinct historical overview of Jewish resistance in occupied Warsaw, is packed with fascinating primary documents and photographs from the period.

Shawn, Karen (1995). "Liberation: A Documentary Guide to the Liberation of Europe and the Concentration and Death Camps." *Dimensions*, 9(1):G1–G23. This excellent study guide is packed with key information about the liberation of the Nazis' concentration and death camps. In addition to both questions for discussion and questions for further research, it includes a solid historical overview of liberation, photographs from the period, excerpts from eyewitness testimony, and a short bibliography and videography on liberation.

Totten, Samuel (1998). "Examining the Holocaust Through the Lives and Literary Works of Victims and Survivors: An Ideal Unit of Study for the English Classroom," pp. 165–188. In Robert Hauptman and Susan Hubbs Motin (Eds.), *The Holocaust: Memories, Research, Reference*. New York: Haworth Press. (Note: This article was copublished simultaneously in *The Reference Librarian*, Numbers 61/62, 1988.) This essay includes a detailed discussion as to how Totten assisted his students to begin to understand how a writer's life experiences often influence not only the stories he or she tells, but also the allusions, symbols, and motifs he or she uses in his or her works.

Totten, Samuel (1998). "Incorporating Contemporaneous Newspaper Articles About the Holocaust into a Study of the Holocaust," pp. 59–81. In Robert Hauptman and Susan Hubbs Motin (Eds.), *The Holocaust: Memories, Research, Reference*. New York: Haworth Press. (Note: This article was copublished simultaneously in *The Reference Librarian*, Numbers 61/62, 1988.) The author suggests ways in which teachers can use newspaper articles from the 1933–1945 period to assist students in grappling with key aspects of Holocaust history.

Totten, Samuel (2000). "The Critical Need to Establish an Accurate and Thorough Historical Foundation When Teaching the Holocaust." In Ted DeCoste and Bernard Schwartz (Eds.), *The Holocaust: Art, Politics, Law, Education*. Alberta, Edmonton, Canada: University of Alberta Press. The author discusses the dangers in not providing students with a historically accurate foundation of the Holocaust. He concludes with a discussion of effective ways to establish an accurate and thorough historical foundation when teaching the Holocaust.

Totten, Samuel (in press). "How They Taught the Holocaust to High School Students: A Semester-Long Course Co-Taught by a University Professor and a High School English Teacher." *Journal of Holocaust Education*. A discussion of the trials, tribulations, frustrations, compromises, methods, limitations, and successes of a team-taught course on the Holocaust.

Wieser, Paul (October 1995). "The American Press and the Holocaust." *Social Education*, 59(6):C1–C2. The purpose of this lesson by a high school social studies teacher is to engage students in a study about the fact that while news of mass killings of millions of Jews reached the United States in the early 1940s, the press gave the subject little prominence.

Wieser, Paul (October 1995). "Anti-Semitism: A Warrant for Genocide." *Social Education*, 59(6):C4–C6. The purpose of this lesson is to engage students in an examination of the

impact of the relentless build-up of Hitler's antisemitic policies and anti-Jewish legislation.

Wieser, Paul (October 1995). "Hitler's Death Camps." *Social Education,* 59(6):374–376. The
purpose of this lesson, which features a top-secret Nazi document on the shipment of
used clothing and possessions taken from Jewish deportees to the Majdanek and
Auschwitz camps, is to engage students in a study of the existence and function of the
Nazi extermination camp system.

Yolen, Jane (March 1989). "An Experiential Act." *Language Arts,* 66(3):246–251. Yolen discusses the value of the literary device of "time travel," especially as it relates to her
Holocaust novel, *The Devil's Arithmetic.*

Zack, Vicki (January 1991). "'It Was the Worst of Times': Learning About the Holocaust
Through Literature." *Language Arts,* 68:42–48. Zack, a fifth-grade teacher in Canada,
discusses a study of the Holocaust that she and several of her students conducted using
Jane Yolen's *The Devil's Arithmetic.*

Educational Research, Criticism, and Philosophical/Pedagogical Essays

Braham, Randolph L. (Ed.). (1987). *The Treatment of the Holocaust in Textbooks: The Federal
Republic of Germany, Israel and the United States.* Boulder, CO, and New York: Social Sci-
ence Monographs and the Institute for Holocaust Studies of the City University of New
York. 332 pp. While dated, this detailed study is still valuable.

Carrington, Bruce, and Short, Geoffrey (1997). "Holocaust Education, Anti-Racism, and
Citizenship." *Educational Review,* 49(3):271–282. In this article the authors report the
findings of a case study the purpose of which was to "assess the potential of Holocaust
education as a medium for developing; 'maximalist' notions of citizenship among
students of secondary school age. . . . The sample, comprising both males and females
from a variety of ethnic backgrounds, was drawn from six secondary schools in south-
east England. The discussion focuses upon: (1) the impact of Holocaust education in
the students' understanding of racism (and, in particular, their ability to recognize and
deconstruct stereotypes); and (2) the students' opinions on the value of Holocaust education in preparing young people for active citizenship in a participatory pluralist
democracy" (p. 271). It concludes with a discussion of the pedagogical implications of
the study.

Dawidowicz, Lucy (1992). "How They Teach the Holocaust," pp. 65–83. In Lucy Dawidowicz (Ed.), *What Is the Use of Jewish History?* New York: Schocken. A highly critical essay
on the inaccuracies, gaps, and general inadequacy of much Holocaust curricula developed in the United States. *This is a key essay that every educator should read and ponder prior to developing and/or teaching a curriculum, unit, or even a single lesson on the
Holocaust.*

Friedlander, Henry (1979). "Toward a Methodology of Teaching About the Holocaust."
Teacher's College Record, 81(3):519–542. An early and outstanding essay on teaching
about the Holocaust. Friedlander, a noted scholar and Holocaust survivor, discusses
various difficulties in studying and teaching about the Holocaust, issues key caveats to
educators, and suggests and discusses major points/concerns that should be considered when teaching this history. *This is a key essay that every educator should read and ponder prior to developing and/or teaching a curriculum, unit, or even a single lesson on the
Holocaust.*

Lipstadt, Deborah E. (March 6, 1995). "Not Facing History." *The New Republic,* pp. 26–27, 29. While basically a critique of the Facing History and Ourselves program, the focus of this article is germane to all educational programs that focus on Holocaust history. Lipstadt basically argues that teachers and curriculum developers must avoid eliding "the differences between the Holocaust and all manner of inhumanities and injustices" (p. 27); for if they don't, instead of "making history relevant, [they] will] distort [its meaning]" (p. 27).

Shawn, Karen (Spring 1991). "Goals for Helping Young Adolescents Learn About the Shoah." *Ten Da'at,* 5(2):7–11. [To obtain a copy of this article, contact the Ten Da'at office at 212–960–5261.] In this well-thought-out and thought-provoking article, Shawn discusses the importance of using solid rationales when teaching about the Holocaust. She also addresses such issues as affective and cognitive goals, and the selection of controlling ideas or themes.

Shawn, Karen (1994). " 'What Should They Read and When Should They Read It?': A Selective Review of Holocaust Literature for Students in Grades Two Through Twelve." *Dimensions: A Journal of Holocaust Studies,* 8(2):G1–G16. Shawn provides an excellent critique of forty-seven literary works. The article also includes a short but thought-provoking introduction that suggests possible criteria to use when selecting Holocaust literature for classroom study. The article concludes with a section entitled "Second Thoughts," at the outset of which Shawn notes: "The following books, while frequently recommended by critics, teachers, publications, et al., raise, for me, anyway, troubling questions. These might involve historical content or 'message,' or tone." *This is a must read for educators.*

Shawn, Karen (1995). "Current Issues in Holocaust Education." *Dimensions: A Journal of Holocaust Studies,* 9(2):15–18. Shawn cogently argues that the negative side of the proliferation of educational activity and development of resources to teach about the Holocaust is that "such rapid, broad-based popularization could conceivably dilute and diminish the impact of the Holocaust" (p. 16). In her discussion, Shawn examines the problematic nature of statewide directives for Holocaust education, current staff development programs in place purportedly for the purpose of preparing teachers to teach this history, and "the recent alarming proliferation of poorly conceived and executed textbooks, teaching aids, and lesson plans flooding our schools" (p. 18). Shawn also offers suggestions for ameliorating many of the aforementioned problems.

Short, Geoffrey (1994). "Teaching the Holocaust: The Relevance of Children's Perceptions of Jewish Culture and Identity." *British Educational Research Journal,* 20(4):393–405. In this study, seventy-two children between the ages of twelve and fourteen "were interviewed in order to explore their knowledge of Judaism, the nature of any misconceptions they have about the faith, the extent to which they appreciate the commonalties between Judaism and Christianity, and their awareness of anti-Semitism." Ultimately, Short argues that "for the Holocaust to be taught effectively, teachers will need some idea of how children . . . perceive Jewish culture and identity" (p. 393).

Short, Geoffrey (Winter 1995). "The Holocaust in the National Curriculum: A Survey of Teachers' Attitudes and Practices." *The Journal of Holocaust Education,* 4(2):167–188. In this study, Short, a senior lecturer in education at the University of Hertfordshire, Great Britain, interviewed thirty-four secondary-level history teachers in order to ascertain their attitudes and practices in regard to Holocaust education. Among the questions Short asked his respondents were: What do you see as the main advantage and disadvantages of teaching the subject? Do you relate the Holocaust to contemporary developments—that is, the resurgence of nationalism and racism across much of Europe? Do you and should you draw parallels between the Holocaust and other atrocities committed against ethnic groups in the past? How do you contextualize the teaching of the Holocaust? Do you do anything to explore and undermine students' misconceptions and stereotypes about Jews and Judaism prior to teaching about the Holocaust?

A key finding of the study is that "The vast majority of teachers are committed to Holocaust education, but see its value in terms of combating racism rather than anti-Semitism. In fact, the nature and history of anti-Semitism was the area most often omitted as a result of the shortage of time" (p. 186).

Short, Geoffrey (1997). "Learning Through Literature: Historical Fiction, Autobiography, and the Holocaust. *Children's Literature in Education*, 28(4):179–190. In this piece, Short argues "against the common-sense view that children's literature dealing with the Jews in Nazi Germany is necessarily useful as an aid to studying the Holocaust" (p. 180). Concerned about how the history of the Holocaust is taught in British schools, Short asserts that: "Ostensibly relevant literature cannot be relied upon to remedy these defects. . . . Some of the literature may not, in fact, be at all informative about the attempted annihilation of European Jewry" (p. 180). Following a discussion of his research findings, Short discusses the shortcomings in using two popular books—*Friedrich* and *Mischling Second Degree*—for teaching students about this history.

Totten, Samuel (Winter 1998). "A Holocaust Curriculum Evaluation Instrument: Admirable Aim, Poor Result." *Journal of Curriculum & Supervision*, 13(2):148–166. This essay constitutes a critical analysis of the Association of Holocaust Organization's (AHO) *Evaluating Holocaust Curricula: Guidelines and Suggestions*.

Totten, Samuel, and Riley, Karen (n.d.). "State Department of Education Sponsored Holocaust and/or Genocide Curricula and Teaching Guides: A Critique." Unpublished paper. In this essay, Totten and Riley critique the historical accuracy of eleven state-department-sponsored and/or -developed curricula for use in secondary level schools. The key finding is that many of the curricula are rife with errors and/or address key concepts in a sorely inadequate manner.

Wegner, Gregory (Winter 1998). "What Lessons Are There From the Holocaust For My Generation Today?" Perspectives on Civic Virtue from Middle School Youth." *Journal of Curriculum and Supervision*, 13(2):167–183. An interesting study that examined 200 essays by eighth graders that addressed the following question: What lessons from the Holocaust are there for my generation today?

Adjunct Resources

Littell, Franklin H. (Ed.) (1997). *Hyping the Holocaust: Scholars Answer Goldhagen*. Merion Station, PA: Merion Westfield Press International. 177 pp. This volume includes a collection of often scathing critiques of Daniel Goldhagen's *Hitler's Willing Executioners*. Among the contributing essayists are Franklin H. Littell, Hubert G. Locke, Hans Mommsen, Jacob Neusner, Didier Pollefeyt, and Roger W. Smith.

Totten, Samuel (Ed.). (forthcoming). *Examining the Past to Protect the Future: The Personal Stories of Holocaust Educators on the Genesis and Evolution of Their Pedagogical Endeavors* (working title). Westport, CT: Bergin & Garvey. This book is comprised of the personal stories of noted Holocaust educators around the world in which they discuss their pedagogical efforts vis-à-vis the Holocaust. Among the many noted educators included in the volume are Sid Bolkosky (United States), Franklin Bialstyok (Canada), Steve Cohen

(United States), Carol Danks (United States), Stephen Feinberg (United States), Daniel Gaede (Germany), Harold Lass (Canada), Ephraim Kaye (Israel), Nili Keren (Israel), Leatrice Rabinsky (United States), Stephen Smith (England), Karen Shawn (United States), Geoff Short (England), Margo Stern-Strom (United States), and Paul Wieser (United States).

Bibliographies

Cargas, Harry James (Ed.). (1985). *The Holocaust: An Annotated Bibliography.* Chicago: American Library Association. 196 pp. This bibliography addresses a wide array of topics and issues germane to the Holocaust. Though it is now dated, it is still a useful resource.

Darsa, Jan (1991). "Educating About the Holocaust," pp. 175–193. In Israel Charny (Ed.), *Genocide: A Critical Bibliographic Review. Vol. 2.* London and New York: Mansell Publishers and Facts On File, respectively. Includes a thought-provoking essay and an annotated bibliography of key works on the subject of teaching about the Holocaust.

Drew, Margaret (1988). *Facing History and Ourselves Holocaust and Human Behavior: Annotated Bibliography.* New York: Walker. 124 pp. Though dated, this bibliography, designed specifically for use by educators, is still a useful reference. The bibliography includes and "describes those books, from the profusion of Holocaust materials, that best explore the wide range of human responses to the Holocaust, on the part of victims, victimizers, and rescuers." It is divided into five key parts, including children's books and adult books. It also includes useful appendices, including: A. Basic Readings List; B. Literature as History; C. Legacy of the Holocaust: A Supplementary Reading List; and D. Human Behavior: A Supplementary Reading List.

Edelheit, Abraham, and Edelheit, Hershel (1986). *Bibliography on Holocaust Literature.* Boulder, CO: Westview Press. 842 pp. A massive bibliography that includes sections on life in prewar Europe, antisemitism, fascism, Nazism, the extermination of the Jews, and the aftermath of the Holocaust.

Edelheit, Abraham, and Edelheit, Hershel (Eds.). (1990). *Bibliography on Holocaust Literature: Supplement.* Boulder, CO: Westview Press. 684 pp. A valuable and updated addition to the original bibliography.

Roskies, Diane K. (1975). *Teaching the Holocaust to Children: A Review and Bibliography.* New York: KTAV Publishing House Inc. 65 pp. An early and interesting bibliography that includes information on the following: methodology, pedagogical issues, school curricula, and children's literature. In her conclusion, Roskies addresses issues that she thinks curriculum developers and teachers need to consider when developing units of study on the Holocaust: antisemitism, life and death in the ghettos, eastern European Jewry, death and historical time, and physical resistance. The booklet concludes with a lengthy bibliography of pedagogical articles, curricula for children at the elementary and secondary levels, children's literature, and analytical pieces about various Holocaust curricula. While over twenty-five years old, this short bibliography still includes much that is useful.

Shulman, William L. (Ed.). (1998). *Holocaust: Resource Guide—A Comprehensive Listing of Media for Further Study.* Volume 8 in *Holocaust.* Woodbridge, CT: Blackbirch Press. 80 pp. This annotated bibliography is divided into four main parts: (1) Bibliography (General Reference Works; European Jewry Before the Holocaust; The Holocaust: A General Overview; Country/Cultural Studies; Germany, Hitler, and the Rise of Nazism; Ghettos; Concentration and Extermination Camps; Resistance; Rescue; Perpetrators,

Bystanders, and Collaborators; Other Victims of Nazi Persecution; Liberation and Judgment; Memoirs and Diaries; Survivors and the Generation After; Antisemitism; Specialized Studies); (2) Illustrated Books (including books on art about the Holocaust) and Videos; (3) Web Sites and CD-Roms; and (4) Museums and Resource Centers.

Szonyi, David. M. (1985). *The Holocaust: An Annotated Bibliography and Resource Guide*. New York: KTAV. 396 pp. Though extremely dated, teachers are likely to find this bibliography to be of some use. Among the sections in the book are: Scholarship, Memoirs, and Other Nonfiction of the Holocaust; Literature of the Holocaust; Bibliographies on the Holocaust for Young People; Audio-Visual Materials on the Holocaust; An Introduction to High School Holocaust Curricula; Teacher Development; and Oral History with Holocaust Survivors.

Totten, Samuel (1991). "First Person Accounts of the Holocaust," pp. 91–273. In Samuel Totten (Ed.), *First-Person Accounts of Genocidal Acts Committed in the Twentieth Century: An Annotated Bibliography*. Westport, CT: Greenwood Press. Contains hundreds of annotations of diaries, letters, memoirs, autobiographies, oral histories, and video accounts.

Totten, Samuel, and Feinberg, Stephen (2001). *Teaching and Studying the Holocaust*. Boston: Allyn & Bacon. In addition to the extensive annotated bibliography at the end of the book (which includes annotations of major historical works, pertinent journals, and key pedagogical essays on the Holocaust), various chapters in the book include separate bibliographies on Holocaust literature, first-person accounts, primary accounts, Holocaust art, Holocaust music, and Holocaust films.

Trynauer, Gabrielle (Ed.). (1989). *Gypsies and the Holocaust: A Bibliography and Introductory Essay*. Montreal: Interuniversity Centre for European Studies & Montreal Institute for Genocide Studies. 51 pp. Though dated, this landmark bibliography is comprised of annotations on a wide range of significant works related to the genocide of the Gypsies by the Nazis.

United States Holocaust Memorial Museum (1993). *Annotated Bibliography*. Washington, DC: Author. 31 pp. Contains three distinct sections (middle level, high school, and adult) on general history, specialized history, biographies, fiction, memoirs, art, and general history pertaining to the Holocaust.

United States Holocaust Memorial Museum (1993). *Annotated Videography*. Washington, DC: Author. 13 pp. Includes annotations on films that address a wide range of issues (e.g., overviews of the Holocaust, life before the Holocaust, propaganda, racism and antisemitism, "enemies of the state," ghettos, genocide in camps, rescue, resistance, responses, perpetrators, liberation, post-Holocaust, Anne Frank, and Janusz Korczak).

INDEX